D1810374

Aventura
Alaska
Brasil

Aventura Alaska Brasil

William Carroll

Coda Publications Raton New Mexico 87740 U.S.A.

Aventura Alaska Brasil

by

William Carroll

First Edition

Copyright 2003 by William Carroll

All rights reserved, which includes the rights to reproduce this book in any form whatsoever except as provided under copyright laws of the United States of America

Printed in the United States of America
ISBN 0-910390-10-X
Library of Congress Control Number 2002095207

Coda Publications
P.O.Box 71
Raton, New Mexico 87740, U.S.A.

Contents

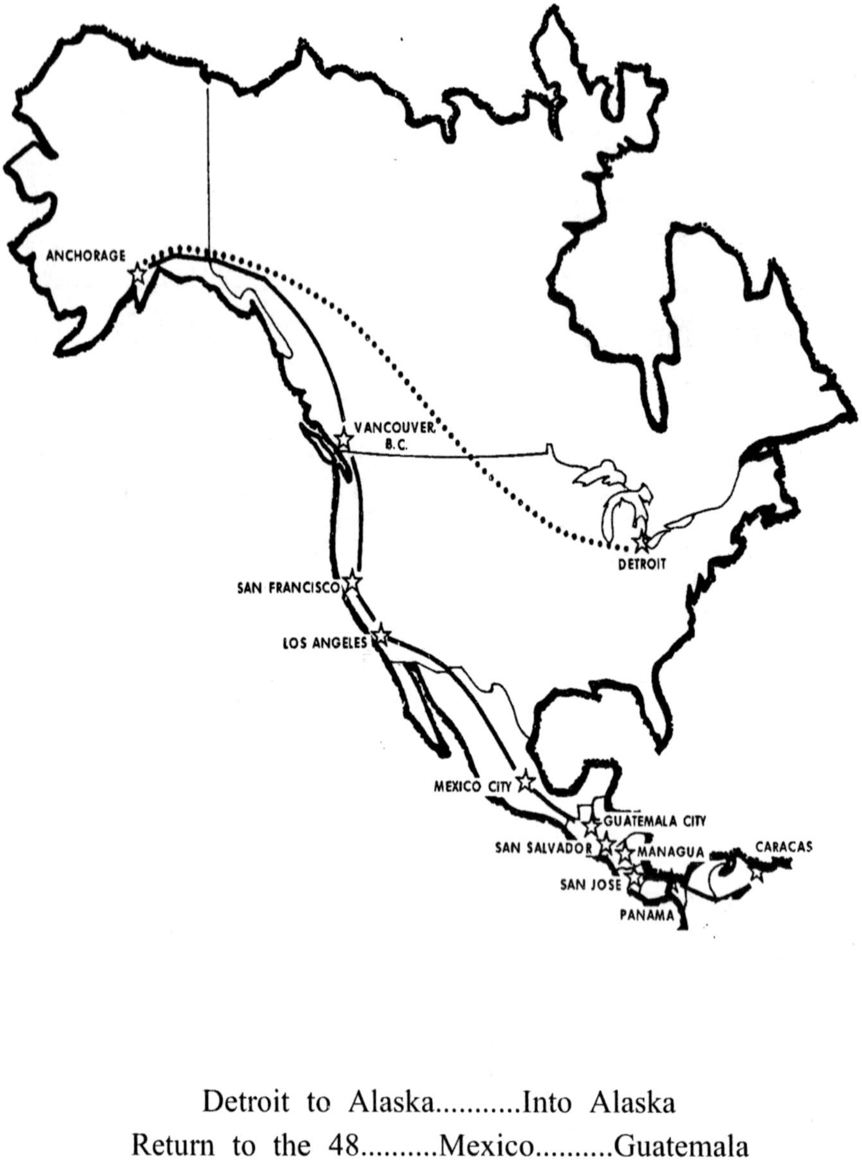

Detroit to Alaska...........Into Alaska

Return to the 48..........Mexico..........Guatemala

El Salvador.........Honduras.........Nicaragua

Costa Rica.........Panama..........The *Santa Flavia*

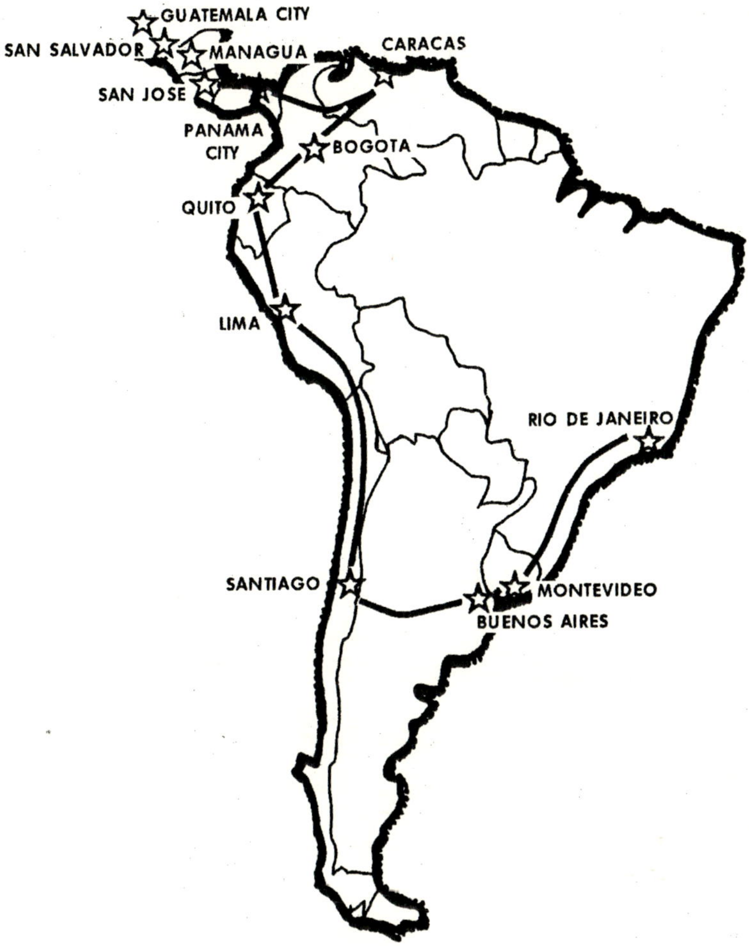

Venezuela.........Colombia..........Ecuador

Peru.........Chile..........Argentina

Uruguay........Brasil

PREFACE

Readers are more than likely to wonder why *Aventura Alaska Brasil* uses so little space to describe historic sites or cities. The reason is simple. This is a report of adventurous travel with enough details for serious consideration of doing the same thing. Explorations of any area are so much a matter of personal taste that for some a museum is delightful, others are indifferent. For the young, swinging festivities are the best, while for us more conservative souls a delightful restaurant, quiet dinner, good wine and beautiful women are much more desirable. Accordingly, *Aventura* is primarily concerned with expanding your travel opportunities while leaving it open for you to find your way about the destination.

On this trip it was heartwarming to enjoy so many nations which are proud of their heritage and even prouder of their potential for growth. You too will be rewarded often while enjoying differences of concept, differences of goals and even more physical differences of the countries. In some, wine was a luxury. In others, as common as butter. Lands rich with cattle featured meat to the point where we couldn't look another steak in the face. Next door was a nation with neither meat nor fish but an excess of fowl. A third country, by virtue of its seacoast and highly developed fishing industry, stuffed us so full with varieties of seafood that we never wanted to go near the water. Our best behavior was to never discuss politics. We tried to abstain from any concern with local situations and limited discussions to scenic and tour values. Besides there was so much to see and do that our current activities were the most important thing possible. So read on to enjoy the adventures and misadventures of driving from Alaska to Rio de Janerio, in a standard Mercury passenger car, while operating the engine day and night for the equivalent of more than eleven years use during the trip of a lifetime..

1

DETROIT TO ALASKA

This wild and wonderful *Aventura* of driving the Pan American Highway from Alaska to Brasil began in Lorain, Ohio where the Lincoln-Mercury division of The Ford Motor Company had built a lovely Mercury Coupe: Serial number 137. Ten days later, the car was in Anchorage. After attaching Alaskan license plate number 48, it was given a rather frantic TV interview send-off for its road run toward Brasil via Vancouver, San Francisco, Los Angeles, Mexico City and all of Central America into Panama. There we loaded the Mercury aboard a Grace Line freighter, the *Santa Flavia*, which carried it around Panama's nonexistent portion of the Inter-American Highway to La Guaira, the major seaport of Venezuela. After a layover in Caracas, for photography and modest rest, we bumped and bumbled across the upper part of South America, through Ecuador and south into Peru and Chile. From Chile we climbed the Andes (over one of the highest roads in the world) and rolled down into Argentina. From there the Mercury was ferried across the Rio de la Plata to Urugauy and driven into Brasil which concluded *Aventura* in Rio de Janeiro. We flew home in 14 hours. The Mercury arrived eight weeks later, by sea.

This was *Aventura, Alaska Brasil.* All I had to do was be driver, mechanic, public relations specialist, photographer, journalist, author and engineering observer. And daily explain to questioners and media how the car was performing over one of the longest and most entertaining trips man can make on the continents of North and South America. Renee, my wife, had the most difficult task: keeping her husband happy for over 100 days while both of us were cooped in the coupe for hours on end.

You could say, "It is not possible."

But it was. With more unusual and interesting situations connected with this effort than seemed imaginable. It all began with serious preplanning while the Lincoln Mercury Division of the Ford Motor Company took care of building our car. At least that was one "do-it-yourself" project we didn't have. A few telephone calls and several letters determined the minimum vehicle equipment it should have and when it would be ready for us to accept delivery at the factory. While this program was underway, I contacted Morton International, the makers of Simoniz polish, STP Corporation and the Firestone Tire and Rubber Company for sponsorship support. They joined with Ford in approving the project and supported it from beginning to end.

We visited our Automobile Club of Southern California and learned, much to our amazement, that traveling southward to Panama was relatively simple. Documents would be easily and almost instantly issued. Talk of going further, into South America, floated a ponderous gray cloud onto the horizon. Its silver lining was in our eyes: To wit, the trip. The gray cloud was composed of equal parts of lack of information, Latin Government regulations that were not clearly understood and a delightful little bit about a $6,000 to $8,000 deposit for the Carnet de Passage which would be required before our car could enter a few of the nations further south. It seemed, our AAA representative said, that a few South American governments had been seriously disturbed by tourists driving a late model American car into their republic where new cars were hard to obtain. The day before the tourist flew home he would sell the car for two or three times the number of dollars it was worth in the United States. The South American buyer attached his old license plates and drove merrily. Meanwhile his government had lost import duty, excise tax and sales tax on the vehicle. The American tourist had gone home carrying badly needed foreign exchange. Accordingly, before driving your car into their country, a whopping deposit must be made. The amount being from one-half to two times the value of the car you're using. In the case of Brasil, you can't bring any car into the nation, so the Brasilian Consul told us, if it costs more than $3,500.

Somewhere amidst this commotion we'd written for all the free books we could find on the area and bought a set of pamphlets from the

Pan American Union, located in Washington, D.C. AAA sent us a set of extremely valuable (at no cost to Auto Club members) books on the Pan American (Inter-American) Highway in Alaska, Central and South America. These books were used in basic planning as we found them an invaluable source of reasonably current information. In addition to data from the Auto Club, we obtained travel maps from petroleum companies marketing in Latin America. In some instances, I found highways on oil company maps that were not listed on maps obtained from the local AAA. In other cases the AAA showed routes not on oil company maps. Apparently local inquiry should be an important part of our plan.

With the help of a Spanish-speaking bank staffer I had text created for two small signs which were to be hung inside the Mercury's windows. Both would explain that the engine was supposed to be operating, the purpose was to test its durability and please do not worry about it. Though in Spanish, we often had to point noses toward the information to quiet objectors to the ever-running Mercury engine.

Jim Scares of the Southern California Club's Travel Service gave us an imposing bundle of documents to be filled in at home. On survey, they proved to be rather simple; calling only for such personal information as might normally be found on a credit statement; plus basic data on the car, license and serial number, color, interior trim, accessories and, in that day of transistors and chips, number of "tubes" in the radio. Soon the papers were mailed back to him, with enough background photographs for the applications, a $100 deposit, $55 for costs and a few hundred dollars for personal, accident, and health insurance while enroute. The document requirements indicated there could be further requests for photographs: Such as other-nation customs documents, drivers license, tourist cards, police inspections, visa applications and of course, passport privileges. One Sunday we loaded the family camera, moved a bar stool into the backyard and banged happily away. As you can imagine, neither Renee's picture nor mine turned out very well. But we accepted such backyard efforts as far less expensive than going to a passport photographer and ordered 24 prints for each of us. Hopefully, this was going to be enough. It was, although we carried individual negatives with us for additional copies if necessary. Using maps and books from everywhere, we began laying out a simple schedule. Our estimate was an average of about 35 miles an hour in nations where most of the roads were paved which proved to be about half of the trip. For Columbia and Ecuador, with their mountain passes and generally reputed-to-be poorer roads, we lowered the planning average to 25 miles an hour. On the basis that we would be on the road about ten hours a day, including lunch and gasoline stops. This suggested an average of 250 to 350 miles of traveling daily. The next planning job was to find cities approximately those distances apart. We wanted AAA listed hotels, or others large enough in a capital city, to indicate they offered reasonably good accommodations. Several evenings later we had a very rough schedule listing some days of 200 to 225 miles, and a very few days of traveling as many as 400 miles. This was our program of reasonable objectives for the trip in Latinland below the Mexican border. In the United States we planned driving from 450 to 500 miles a day on the Interstates with little stopping and few photographs. Now we had a reasonable idea of how many days our trip was going to require. The exceptions proved to be unexpected construction areas and an unwise side trip we attempted to fit into an already full day. The next thing was estimating cost. We began by calculating gasoline requirements at the low rate of 15 miles per gallon and estimating what each gallon of gas would cost us. One quart of oil for every thousand miles added another dollar per thousand miles to transportation costs. On top of which we added a half-cent a mile to make the cents-per-mile figure come out even and pay for bridge fees, tolls and incidental costs.

Personal expenses were estimated on the basis of AAA guidebook suggestions of dollars per day for food and accommodations for the two of us. Now we had our route, and our budget, with only a vague idea of the fun involved. About this time our belief in the ease of Latin touring was shaken by a letter from Scares covering another set of impressive documents. It seemed that he/we had forgotten to apply for driving documentation required in the Central American republics which do not recognize paperwork acceptable in South America. More papers to be filled in. More pictures to be forwarded. With Jim assuring us these would be the last necessary They were.

From the local phone book we made a list of consulates in Los Angeles and Renee charged off to obtain visas. In some it was delightfully easy. As she reported, "It was like walking up and asking for a glass of water. They gave it to you on request, plus all sorts of paperwork detailing attractions of their nation. With others it was less than simple." She learned that a few nations would only issue documents to automobile tourists entering from a bordering nation. Officials told her that before approaching the frontier of such nations we must stop at their consular offices in the city nearest the border of the adjacent country. There, in a foreign land, from their local consul, we could obtain travel documents which would permit entry into the next country. For this there would be a fee and, of course, "Be sure to have the necessary pictures." Other consuls told us they only issued traveler's permits valid for a specified length of time. Reviewing our schedule showed that for one nation our permit would expire before we reached their frontier. Accordingly, we could not enter until we obtained visas and tourist permits in the adjacent nation. There's little connection between Renee's mention that "The consulate for Brasil is one of the most beautiful visited" and the fact that Brasil was the most difficult Latin American nation into which to take an automobile. According to the AAA, Brasil required a deposit into a Brasilian bank of $6,500 American dollars before they would allow the *Aventura* Mercury to enter. In hopes we could ease the financial strain, we asked the Ford Motor Company to certify, to the Brasilian government, that the car would be exported. They agreed to try and try they did: But their effort was not fully accepted by Brasil. Which may be a good time to point out that comments about difficulties while entering Latin American nations do not apply if you are flying or sea voyaging. It appears that such public carriers have special dispensation to issue or arrange documentation for you. Accordingly, no need to visit consulates.

It appeared that only vehicular traffic, which could create valuable tourism in Central and South America, was burdened with archaic procedures and what turned out to be unnecessarily irritating regulations. Nevertheless, border controls are founded in good intent and only in few instances did we find rudeness or face unusual personal difficulty. For us it was more a matter of living with regulations which were unfamiliar. In most instances, (unless you resort to bribery and we'd recommend you never) no border official has authority to amend, alter, change, evade or discuss the effect of regulations. If the big book says "No green automobiles may pass on Sunday", rest assured, your green Essex will not pass that frontier on Sunday. And, believe it or not, there was one border across which the Mercury could not pass on Sunday. A border officer's job is so precious that he or she is not about to jeopardize it by allowing you to pass sight unseen. On the other hand there are legitimate fees for Special or Extraordinary services which frontier offices may assess the tourist, such as working during the lunch hour when the border is closed.

A situation we had a great time with, and our friends suffered through on a secondhand basis, was the matter of "anti-anti" shots. To be absolutely certain we received those required, and did not take any we needed not, Renee had called the U.S. Public Health Service. A kindly gentleman at the other end of the line read off the list of necessary inoculations. "Under Typhus" he reported, "it says that if you are going to South America for more than 30 days you should have a typhus shot. But, I don't understand that one. It only takes 3 seconds to get typhus. So if you're going to South America, you should get a shot!"

Renee laughed and replied, "We will."

And we did!

I'm not too much of a sissy and Renee goes along quite well with shots but the second typhoid shot reacted with me. I began to sweat with a fever and shiver with chills at the same time. Recognizing symptoms of extreme "upset" I downed two aspirin and crawled under a bundle of blankets, with teeth and knees chattering like castanets at a voodoo dance. About 24 hours later everything cooled off and my dysentery-ish intestinal system restored itself to normal. At least the bed rest hurt me not.

Another facet of a trip like this is the attitude of one's friends and business acquaintances. They all managed to fall into two categories. Those warmly and genuinely happy souls who saw us venturing something they would love to do themselves. And dullards who considered us are completely out of our skulls: "Number one, to leave home. Number two, to leave the United States. And Number three; Good gosh, drive a car from Alaska to Brasil? "Why?" asked they with a glaze of wonderment.

Because, replied we, "Traveling is one of the great experiences of a lifetime which enhances understanding and appreciation of that which you have." With modern automobiles comfortable, reliable, and fast, there is every reason anyone with time and a modest bank account could duplicate *Aventura* for themselves. The rewards are so great that to ignore the travel potential of North and South America is to ignore major cultural riches of this world. Sure, Europe is great. We've driven most of it. But for adventurous touristing, the Latin American continent has Europe beat a mile. There's so much that has been untouched by commercial interests that traveling south is visiting an entirely new world. These were the lands that *Aventura* enjoyed most, while driving a standard passenger car from Alaska to Brasil, in one reasonably troublefree grand tour of the best of North and South America. As we noted earlier, this is a book about adventure travel and what you might expect while enjoying the same trip. For information on historic and unusual sites along the way, or in a city of passage, you'll need a sizeable collection of guides and community tourist information pointing you toward places of interest.

It's interesting that all the women that I'd talked with about the *Aventura* run had built a fire in their eyes and said, in effect, "Let's go. I'll either shoot my husband or quit my job." On the other hand, most men, except a young reporter, have said, "Oh boy, you're nuts. How far is it? That's too far. I've never driven that far," or some such rather negative comment. I wonder if this indicates that it's the women of today who are true adventurers and man has become so domesticated that he can neither see his way clear to vacation a job, or move into any area of excitement.

Because the Mercury had to be picked up at the factory, with the subsequent rather dull drive from there to Anchorage, I left my wife home, much to her disgust. Nevertheless, good girl that she was, Renee upped early one morning and tilted me toward the airport to begin what proved to be a somewhat catastrophic day of transportation. We were running late and accordingly arrived at the airport only minutes before the gate was closed. A quick kiss, a tug at our hearts and she waved me down the walkway. At this late hour my "reserved" seat was already filled by a charming brunette with two soldiers for company. She's not about to move because soldiers are more important to her than sitting where she belongs. Realizing the situation, a stewardess says, "Mr. Carroll, you may take any seat in the plane that you wish," I leaped for a seat on the emergency aisle, which has extra space for my long legs, and relaxed for a fast run down the field and that throat-tightening leap into the air. All fine and dandy except that American Airlines, Flight 192, scheduled to leave at 8:15 is, at 8:15, sitting on the ground like a great big tired bird. At 8:16 the unctuous voice of the captain oozes from the speakers with all the uneasiness of a small boy telling mother that he's dirtied his drawers. "There will be a slight delay. Our transmitter is not functioning properly," says he. The pilot, not the small boy. We passengers groaned audibly and thought of other things. My ploy was to lean back and begin to impress no one by reading the Wall Street Journal, which I only purchase for the sake of impressing people during air trips. A few minutes later, the captain returned to his microphone. "We have found the trouble," he said, "and it will be about 15 minutes." No one pays attention this time.The plane's passengers have resigned themselves to being trapped in the aluminum monster from which there is no escape. I finished the Wall Street Journal, tilted my seat further back and went sound asleep. An hour later, I woke to find my head propped sideways on the arm rest and my sleep-filled eyes blinking at a pair of knobby "A-cup" knees. By the time I unwind my frame, the stewardess with the knees stops laughing and asks, "Mr. Carroll, would you like a cocktail?" My watch reminds me that I always have a martini about 9:20 in the morning and it's an hour after the captain said it was only going to be 15 minutes. Anyhow, I order the martini. She takes my money, smiles sweetly and says, "We're going to start serving after we're in flight," which, of course, effectively killed dreams of sitting on the ground and enjoying a cool martini. So I sat. And I sat, and I sat some more.

Hours later (really only 15 minutes) the captain is on the horn with a new announcement, "It is only going to be five minutes more." Lo and behold he was right. I heard engines roaring before he comes on again. "We're about ready to take off. Please buckle your seat belt." As if this wasn't enough good news, there is now a commotion in the back of the plane. I turned my head to watch two blue-suited American Airlines mechanics, walking at a funeral pace with an appearance of solemn concentration and patience, lock-stepping one behind the other up the aisle. Between them, hanging somewhat corpse-like, is a rather ancient assembly of "things" in a metal framework. What the "things" were I hadn't the slightest idea. But I'm firmly convinced they were a standard airline presentation designed to pacify delayed passengers by introducing a dummy assembly that could be paraded along the aisle to assure us something has been done. Now we had nothing further to worry about. Except arriving where we're going. I considered singing a hymn, except that I don't sing, as the funeral duet disappeared out the front of our aircraft. The door was shut, engines whirred and in a few minutes we were airborne. Twenty minutes later my stewardess arrives with a tray-full of drinking things. She looks at a note, realizes I am the one who ordered the martini, and decorates my tray with a glass, ice cubes and a tiny bottle marked "11-1 Martini." I'm living at last. Very promptly the martini is poured over three ice cubes. Unfortunately, I hadn't gotten the message. These were tired ice cubes which, at the touch of the martini, melted into nothingness. Now 11-1 meant 11 parts of water and one part of martini. However, it must have worked. Soon I was asleep again and didn't wake until we touched ground in Chicago.

Touching the ground usually implies landing the airplane. However, in this case, our pilot was attempting to demonstrate his dancing skills. First one wheel came down, then another, and another, before he'd bounce back on the first wheel. In fact we danced all over the airport before he decided to plant the Boeing, fully firm and packed with passengers, into Chicago for the unscheduled late-late arrival. Being late wasn't so bad. We were only an hour and 15 minutes behind. But it seems that no one in Chicago ever heard of our flight or those passengers with onward reservations. A young American Airlines passenger agent said he thought maybe he could do something about getting me on a flight for Detroit if I'd stand at a distant desk for a few minutes. I stood. But when I turned my back, he disappeared. This was no help. I lugged my bags to the main American ticket buying area and proceeded to wait in that line.

A rather pleasant agent came over and asked if anyone had talked to me yet. I said, "No," and gave him my ticket, explaining that the flight had been about an hour and 15 minutes late, and would he please get me to Detroit. His stories were: Number one: American Airlines did not have enough airplanes for their Chicago-Detroit flight, and accordingly could not accommodate me for three or four hours. Number Two: all competing airlines were booked solid and he knew this for sure. I listened to this tale of woe, while swallowing four letter words, before expressing myself to the point, "I hear you but I won't accept a word you're saying." He then repeated his stories while emphasizing his many years of American Airlines experience at the Chicago passenger desk and the fact that you just apparently can not walk up and buy a trip ticket from Chicago to Detroit. All the while he's writing out something known as a standby ticket which is good for nothing but standing. I accepted the ticket and said, "That's fine. Now let's see if you can confirm a seat for me on the next flight to Detroit. You advertise as an airline for professional travelers, but I'm of the opinion it is operated by children: None of whom had the wisdom to radio ahead to arrange transportation for those with onward destination tickets."

This must have cut him to the quick. My apologetic agent now dashed behind the counter and hammered away at a tiny piece of nonautomatic machinery for several seconds before returning to announce, with a big broad smile, that I was very lucky. I had only then gotten the last seat on the flight leaving in 40 minutes for Detroit. Whether I had or not was really of no consequence I acknowledged that he was really lucky, thanked him for being lucky, thanked myself for being lucky, he thanked me again for being so lucky and away I trudged to wait in a new line for the flight to Detroit to be called. I tried to be as early as possible for boarding, so that if there was an "oversold" problem at least I would have a seat from which it would be hard to eject me. And I was right, they were oversold. The cabin filled like a can of sardines. About ten minutes before we were ready to depart, a very pleasant appearing gentleman and his attractive wife appeared with tickets in their hot little hands. The stewardess, not the person who sold their tickets, had to tell them there were no seats. The couple were more polite about it than I would have been and, after a small amount of discussion, left. I flew to Detroit, with a feeling of shame for using what may have been one of their two seats.

That evening my friends in Detroit tried to arrange for the motel operator to nudge me awake at 6 AM the following morning. She thought that Renee would object and I agreed. Accordingly my telephone didn't go off until 7 o'clock, with the announcement that it was time to get up. Now 7 o'clock in the morning doesn't seem bad. And it isn't really bad in Detroit. But my body was running on California time which, at four in the morning, is fairly sleepy no matter how you slice it. After a rather salty breakfast and lukewarm coffee, I waited in my room for expected Lincoln-Mercury staff people to pick me up. They arrived about 9 o'clock and off we charged, Carroll driving, in the general direction of Cleveland. Of the three of us, none of us knew exactly where Cleveland was until the rear seat passenger produced a road map and proceeded to navigate. Three hours later we passed through Cleveland to finally arrive at the Lorain, Ohio, assembly plant for Mercury coupes. I was all eyeballs, trying to find a coral-colored hardtop but unfortunately we were directed into a rather staid reception room. Because it was lunch time, my Mercury hosts suggested we eat in the executive dining room. But we didn't look like executives so no matter how many times we asked the receptionist, we always received instructions as to how to find the cafeteria. This would have been fine with me, but my hosts were not to be put off. After wandering around the plant's general offices for ten minutes, we found a beautiful vanished wooden door amid a row of painted doors. On opening, it led to a comfortable dining room. Though on a diet, I ended my executive lunch with strawberry short cake.

Another search found the man who had our car and he led us to the garage. Looking at a number of ordinary brand new cars was not half so much fun as the excitement of hearing the squeal of our tires approaching when the gorgeous coral-colored hardtop pushed its nose through a narrow driveway entrance. Though almost everyone nearby was a hard-bitten automotive man, it was worth noting they stopped work to turn and admire our sparkling coupe. Arrangements were made to take pictures at the end of an assembly line. This caused a lot of backing and filing as the car was shifted over to a nonworking line and photography completed by the Ford photo team. Then to the parking lot where we attached transportation license plates, to the plant gate where a blue-uniformed officer checked serial number, tires, tools, and me before letting us out the gate with the first Mercury the public could see, almost a month before its official factory introduction date.

It was slow driving back to Detroit because the Mercury had only 14 miles on the odometer and we needed time to "break in" the engine properly. Then to complicate matters, I missed a turnoff and we drove 90 miles too far. The blasted expressway had turnoffs every umpteen miles, and when you missed one there was no way to return unless you bumped across the median strip: which highway law enforcers frown upon.

Did anything go wrong?

Of course. I've never had a new car in my life without a problem or two. And for sure my Mercury hosts were rather put out when we came to a very quiet, smooth and engineless halt in the center of the tollbooth driveway at the expressway exit. Cars racked up behind us, horns blew, and the toll booth attendant became red and redder in the face. When I asked him to help push the car out, he turned his back and began to studiously count pennies he had on the register. Repeated attempts to start the Mercury failed. Need I say...failed miserably. Finally we outed and pushed, luckily downhill, off to the side of the pavement. While my hosts went for a telephone I dove under the hood where an important little coil wire was lying happily on its disconnected side, on top of the engine. I frantically called my friends back to observe replacement of the wire so we could buzz off for Detroit. In the passenger seat there was gnashing of teeth and muttered complaints of "What a hell of a place for our new model to break down in public." Once away from the expressway, we couldn't find reliable directions. No one seemed to quite know the way to Detroit though it was only about 40 miles distant. A problem apparently compounded by our asking the wrong people who didn't care to visit Detroit and had never been there.

Near collisions on the highway ranged from big trucks slowing or pulling over while drivers and swampers eyeballed our car, to little old ladies in fat Cadillacs, charmed with petite grace of the Mercury coupe. As we were coming into Detroit my knees began to weaken when I noticed a Michigan state police car looming larger and larger in the rear view mirror. Though I'm sure I really couldn't detect the officer's expression, it seemed there was a concentrated look of dedicated chase in his eyes. No question about it. He pulled behind us, then to on one side and to the other before slowing down to run near my left door while eyeballing the Mercury. Finally, with a flip of his hand, the patrolman put a foot in his Ford and zoomed away from our staid 60 miles an hour. With a deep sigh of relief we watched him charge madly off after, we hoped, no hapless out-of-state speedster.

The next day Ken Kelley of *Automotive News* came over to talk about his recent book on pickup trucks, which I had published the week before. After four hours of mulling around his ideas we hopped into the Mercury and took off along back-country Michigan roads to learn about the car's handling and stability. Tests included driving as rapidly as reasonable on gravel roads before braking to lock all wheels and determine how the Mercury balanced out when subjected to emergency treatment. We roared over small bridges to make the car leap free of the roadway to determine handling stability when it thudded back to the ground. And charged along a plowed farm road to determine suspension capabilities under the roughest imaginable conditions. The only time Ken became slightly unhappy was while I sampled the car's cornering stability by turning sharply and sliding sideways on gravel roads for 20 to 35 feet to make sure that the Mercury was controllable, should such a situation become necessary on roads of Latin America. (P.S. The Mercury proved to provide superior handling during our entire journey.)

One of my projects the following day was going over the car with a fine-tooth comb to arrange for minor modifications suiting my personal taste. For example: The front seat was raised an inch to make it more comfortable for my long legs. Mechanics figured out a method by which we could lock the transmission out of gear. Two five-gallon fuel cans were ordered, for the trunk area, so that we would have an emergency fuel supply. It was noticed, and fixed, that one of the windows whistled at road speed and an air vent control wasn't opening fully. These fixes, and adjusting the carpet, covered every item necessary to bring the car up to delivery specifications. We ordered spare parts to be on the safe side, as any traveler would. They included a fan belt, spark plugs, fuel pump, radiator hoses, etc. The next day involved installation of our spare gas cans in the trunk, a sealed meter inside the right rear window to totalize numbers of hours use on the engine, the lock on the transmission and a means of immobilizing the ignition key. It would seem that these projects were simple but unfortunately they proved rather difficult for mechanics assigned to the job because a sign painter was involved. While he was doing maps of North and South America on the car the mechanics couldn't work. When mechanics were working the sign painters couldn't. As a result, the day was a time-consuming "After you, my dear Alphonse," situation. The night before we left, I'm sure I had a dozen heart attacks and three fainting spells, because the beautiful Mercury wasn't delivered to my motel until the following morning, about 15 minutes before I was ready to breakfast. The telephone advised me that my car was in the parking lot where a red-eyed mechanic apologized profusely for the delay. At last the *Aventura* coupe was ready to travel.

So was I: Ready for 25,000 miles of reshaping my backside to fit a Mercury bucket seat. Meanwhile, I answered a call from the factory's public relations office. Someone had decided that pictures would be in order. Said they, "Perhaps local newspapers will be interested in anyone funny enough to buy a car and drive it to Alaska for no better reason than it's a good place to begin a trip to Brasil."

Shortly after breakfast we...the Mercury and Carroll...were shifting about in front of a Ford Motor Company building while carefully attended to by motion picture and still cameramen. We had finished when the Firestone Tire and Rubber people thought this was an excellent idea for them to emulate. Hurried telephone calls assembled a number of their executives for a photo session at their offices some miles from Ford. With a Firestone representative leading, we proceeded to get lost three times on the way. I then took over the lead position and not only lost the Firestone man but lost myself as well. Soon a friendly service station attendant was pointing me in the right direction. Separately, by unknown and devious routes, the Firestone man and Carroll arrived at their district offices about the same time. Here a group of executives presented a charming ash blonde. "We need some glamour," said a tire executive when he appeared on the scene, as did rain. Nevertheless, we shifted car, blonde, Carroll and people about to photograph the Mercury in front of a Firestone sign.

While I am inviting the glamour department to participate in my trip and she is nodding her head eagerly, "Yes, yes, yes, yes," my friendly Firestone representative is gleefully telling her that my wife is going along. A nice guy who completely kills any possibility of enjoying travel company from Detroit to a point two miles outside of San Francisco; where I plan to meet Renee in about 30 days. Twelve pictures, 14 hand shakes and a flip of the hand to my friendly female put the affair completely in order. Now I was free and clear. Except that somewhere in the recesses of my memory the Mercury people had planted a message. "Call us before you leave town, we may think of something else." Like a good guy I called. It was pleasant news as the secretary said, "Sorry Mr. Carroll, we have no messages for you at this time."

A few minutes later Carroll was on his way out of Detroit. A service station attendant supplied gas and instructions on how to reach Brasil by way of Toledo and we were off down the expressway. What a tremendous relief this was. Finally I was on my own, with a car, road map, tank of gas and enough Travelers Checks to do the job. My glee was short-lived. The logbook displayed a note: "Be sure to call Ford and Simoniz in Chicago. They may want to talk with you." Near South Bend, on the Indiana Turnpike, I tanked with hot vegetable soup and spent no money making a collect call to Ford in Chicago. "Yes," they said, "Stop here. One of the newspapers would like to interview you." An hour and a half later, in Chicago, I am following their detailed instructions and obviously quite confused between east and west because I'm traveling in the wrong direction. After cursing such miserable luck, and inability to read direction signs, I made a U-turn in the wrong place and found the right Chicago street. Then all I had to do was thread my way along a confusing maze called Wacker Drive: Construction on the right, police in the middle, a canal along the other side, busses trying to herd me off the road, and eager hot-rodders, eyeing the Mercury, tailgating my behind.

I drove while staring straight ahead and paying attention to none of them, when the building I was seeking appeared on the right. "It's only 24 stories high and brand new," someone had said. I hung a left down a dark alley and entered a maze of utter confusion. It was the building's garage, at 5:15 in the afternoon when everyone, all at once, wanted their 20-foot limousine available for a trip home. Griped the attendant, "And here's a guy coming in with another car and he not only wants to park, but he won't even let us drive it." After much complaining and fumbling he found a little slot for me to back the Mercury into. "Now leave it," he quaintly put it, "and we won't have to bother you anytime today."

After my 'phone call a Ford man appeared, we piled into the Mercury and started for the newspaper office. Now keep in mind that the Ford man lived in Chicago. "Turn right," says he, "down that dark tunnel." So down the dark tunnel we went. "This is Lower Wacker Drive." What it's "lower than" I never found out. I assure you, who've not been in Chicago, that it's a dungeon of posts, darkness, speeding automobiles and dank misery that no one could enjoy passing through. After a few devious rights and lefts, we came against a blank wall. Deadend! "Whoops," says my Ford man, "I goofed." A postal truck stopped. A bus stopped. And several nervous pedestrians glared as I made a U-turn right where I supposed I shouldn't. Luckily no policemen were at hand. A quick right, another left down a street of railroad tracks, right up an alley, and the Ford man leaned back to announce, "Look, we're on the right road." And believe it or not, there we were, out of upper-lower Wacker Drive and rolling along in the brightness of day. A few blocks ahead we parked on the wrong side of the street in a No Parking zone across from the *Chicago Tribune* newspaper offices.

At rush hour, this was rather an exciting experience. In the rear-view mirror I could see busses rushing at me, braking, flipping turn signals and headlights, then trying to hitch around me in bumper-busting traffic. Surprisingly enough, no one gave me the finger. Then I looked up and saw a grumpy policeman walking toward me, citation book in hand. Luckily, those people waiting included a newspaper photographer who convinced the officer he should not give me a citation but should pose as though he were. A few minutes later, a now friendly Chicago cop was grinning for the camera while pretending to give an unhappy appearing Carroll a citation for parking where no one in their right mind would possibly park. All this while traffic is streaming around us in a never-ending flow of homeward-bound Chicagoans. The reporter sent to interview me was a friendly young man who had the wanderlust as badly as Renee and I. After a few minutes of interviewing, during which he made notes, we shifted to talking about his trips and where he'd like to go. As he was leaving, "Don't be surprised if I meet you down there someday."

While we were parked, a Simoniz representative found us. He had an evil gleam in his eye which meant more things for Carroll to do. His proposition was simple. "Would I take time to drive to a nearby hotel and park in front of the lobby entrance so Simoniz executives could see the car they were sending off to test their polish in the jungles of Latin America?" This proved easy. Luckily, three busses tangled with each other while picking up passengers which slowed traffic to the point where I could flip around. My friendly policeman, a half block away, was looking the other way. I waved to him as we passed. He stuck out his hand to wish me good luck and Godspeed. At the front of the hotel, where Simoniz was holding a distributor's convention, Maurice the doorman came over, extended his hand, and said, "Welcome to Chicago. I hope you enjoy your trip." It seems that Maurice too had the wanderlust. His son, a bellman, soon showed up and the three of us quickly decided there would be nothing better than using the Mercury to leave their maze of frustration known as Big City. We hadn't dug far on this subject before a flood of executives pushed us out of the way. They "Oohed" and "Aahed" at the car, more pictures were taken, three vice-presidents shook my hand and said "Godspeed" before they all returned to the cocktail party.

By following instructions of their photographer, I managed a few more Chicago streets and actually found myself on the turnpike without becoming lost. Other detailed instructions included, "Down the road a piece, you turn left toward Rockford." Well, down the road a piece, I would have turned left toward Rockford except for being in the wrong lane which meant about 20 more miles before I could find an exit. Then I couldn't find a ramp to return in the other direction. Driving became a matter of wend and wiggle through back country roads until I found another Illinois tollway going in the general direction of Alaska. At the end of the money part, the collector told me, "Three miles further on, are motels." Three miles further on I didn't see any motels. I saw a sign but no motels. I kept right on going. Five miles further, a friendly motel bed and warm dinner eased me into the sack for a much-needed nine hours of solid, solid, solid, sleep. Bright and early the next morning, bright out side and much too early for Carroll, I was up, washed, shaved, and at the local service station checking tire pressures. This was one thing Firestone had asked me to do every morning. Now as everyone realizes, checking the air in tires is no problem at all. But lucky me. Then I learned that Mercury had installed special wheel covers. Wheel covers so special that I had to take them off to find the tire valve. For those of you who haven't enjoyed the experience of removing and replacing wheel covers, early in the morning, when all ten thumbs are nippy cold, it's not the most fun in the world. Anyhow, 37-24-28-28 (original tire pressures) was soon all carefully adjusted to the recommended 30 pounds of pressure all around.

An interesting sidelight to this business of obtaining maps, came to light the night I asked a station attendant in Illinois if he had a map of Illinois. "No, those are the ones we run out of first," he replied. From then on I asked for a map of an adjacent state or, in effect, collected maps one state ahead of time. It seems that Illinois stations had gobs of maps of Michigan, Indiana and Wisconsin, but not one of their own state.
The moment I reached Minnesota I asked for a map of North and South Dakota. In return, I was so lucky, I even received one for the balance of the United States covering my run all the way up to Calgary in Canada.

A fat breakfast and we were on the road, heading toward Minnesota and the Dakotas for another overnight stop. These north-country people build fabulous highways through beautiful countryside, that one could cruise at 75 mph without the slightest bit of danger. But everywhere the same smooth rolling Interstates were cluttered with fine new taxi cabs with big emblems on the door and flashing red lights on the roof. We did our best to make sure we didn't add to their judge-administered cash box. Somewhere near The Dells, in Wisconsin, another Mercury, with father, wife and mother-in-law in the front seat and kids in back, tagged me for five miles while everyone in the car eyeballed our door maps. The children had noses glued to windows while father paced alongside as they slowly read every word. After they dropped behind to follow, my rear view mirror showed mother-in-law in the front seat tracing our maps in the air while expounding on which part of the road she knew we were going to follow on our run from north to south.

I stopped in Eau Claire, Wisconsin and spent an hour and a half wandering around town for additional bits and pieces. It was easy to locate an automobile parts store to buy a swivel socket wrench for spark plugs and a screen to put across the radiator to keep bugs from clogging the cooling fins. Not so simple were my efforts to find flexible filler spouts for two "Jeep" cans the mechanics had installed as our spare gas tanks. Neither contained a flexible filler spout with which I could transfer fuel from the can to the Mercury's tank. A discount store, several service stations, another auto part store and a pleasant gentleman in a hardware store produced no spouts. The hardware store owner, suggested that in St. Paul, 83 miles up the road, there was a dandy surplus store that could have cans and spouts left over from World War II. Half an hour further my stomach began calling for food because it was now after 1 o'clock. The Wisconsin town of Menomonie offered the first exit ramp which appeared as though it might have food. It also had an Army surplus store offering brand new flexible filler spouts for a buck and a quarter each. Two were bought. We filled both five-gallon cans to their brim and buckled them inside the trunk. Rapid travel from Wisconsin to Minnesota ended where Interstate Highway 94 reached the outskirts of St. Paul. Here we entered "Turn-of-the-Century" roads which must give Twin City residents a great deal of historic pride. The roads varied from two lanes, to three lanes, to one lane and to no-lane. Most seemed to have been plotted by a drunken Pilgrim using a piece of wet string to keep pavement a consistent width. On the other hand, there was a nice touch in Big Lake, Minnesota. Every third telephone pole was decorated with a large and beautiful basket of red flowers. Whether they were real or artificial, I don't know. It was a lovely sight to drive through this mid-western town, with its red brick court house in the central square and kids peddling bicycles while eating popsicles, to find it freshened with flowers.

Sauk Center, Minnesota, lived up to its vaudevillian reputation as typical rural America. When asked if there was a good place to eat in town, the service station attendant "Lowed as how there ain't none around worth a darn, but there is a couple up the street you might try." Then he decided to send me to a third place. This one, close enough that he could point to it, was "Down that'a way and first one on the left." From the outside, Roses' Cafe was an unprepossessing stucco building with a typical storm-entrance doorway. Inside was even better: Linoleum floor, chrome dinette tables and chairs and a plastic-topped bar, behind which were all types of half-filled bottles. I took a dining room booth between two groups of college students more concerned with grades and methods of grading than food. The waitress took my order and disappeared into the kitchen. Soon she returned with a great pile of dough and busied herself making pizza. Unfortunately, she forgot to light the oven. When the pizzas were ready to be cooked, she had no heat. She tried to light the oven but something else was wrong. It would not function and the students received their orders one at a time from a "one-pizza" oven in the kitchen. About twenty minutes later she remembered me, rushed madly into the kitchen to return with a salad heaped with bleu cheese dressing, plus bread, butter and a cup of coffee. I had addressed myself to the salad, and buttered a piece of bread, when she reappeared with my steak, vegetables, a baked potato, and the comment, "Whoops, it seems to have all arrived at once, doesn't it?" As I left later, the students were still discussing grades and awaiting the next pizza. Bar-hangers were enjoying their beer and the bartender wished me a fond adieux with, "Come back again!" To Sauk Center?

After an overnight sleep in Valley Center, North Dakota, I was feeling much better about life. In fact, looking at my plate of scrambled eggs in Mac's Cafe caused me to become highly philosophical. During ten days of traveling, I'd eaten ten varieties of scrambled eggs ranging from fried eggs beaten to death with a sharp knife to something approaching a very good soufflé. For those of you who want all cooking to be similar, try ordering the identical simple meal for a week at a time. I warn you, be constantly amazed at the variety of food you receive under the same name. It strikes me these people of North Dakota are eminently practical. Not only did they have a completed Interstate highway bisecting the state from east to west, but it had a realistic speed limit of 75 miles an hour for cruising the flat lands. Now on the other hand, the only thing I can say about adjoining Montana is, there is a lot of Montana, it's up and down and there's certainly not very many people.

Crossing the border into Canada, at Sweetgrass, Montana, was a 45 second operation. "Where are you going?" resulted in raised eyebrows when I told the Canadian officer in Coutts, "Alaska then South to Brasil, take your pick of destinations?" "Do you have any guns, beer or liquor?"

"No," said I.

"Are you going to do any promotional work in Canada?"

"No."

"Okay, have a good trip," and off we went into the Province of Alberta. Then, did I ever goof on my first business transaction. I finished buying gas, and was paying for it, when it was brought to my attention these were Imperial gallons, which are the gallon measure in Canada. I turned to the attendant, also owner of the station, and asked, "Well, how many is that in standard gallons?"

You could see the hair on the back of his neck bristle as I implied that our gallon was standard and his was not. Realizing that my faux pas had done nothing to encourage international friendship, I apologized and rephrased the question; this time relating amount as United States gallons. He replied, "I am told that ours are 1/5 larger." I was quite chagrined at pulling such a boner.

Several things about driving in Northwestern Canada were interesting, including the use of "BUMP" signs which meant exactly what they say. Somewhere ahead of you the pavement has buckled during extremely cold weather. It's a spine-jarring bump well worth slowing for. In some instances, the highway department had installed tiny red flags to indicate the exact point of the dangerous road condition ahead. The next morning, while I was checking tire pressures, the service station attendant decided to examine our Firestone tires. He took a good look at them and said, "Hey, those are four-ply with an eight-ply rating. Where do you get them?" I explained that they were optional equipment on Mercury cars and standard on station wagons with a wide base rim. He took another good look before commenting, "Boy there is sure a lot of tread on these tires. They oughta last for at least 50,000 miles." I replied that as far as I was concerned they'd run south to Rio and have plenty of tread left over. Which they did.

While stopped for lunch between Calgary and my planned overnight at Dawson Creek, British Columbia, I couldn't help but notice effect of the unusual Mercury on passersby. Two boys on their way to a nearby river stopped to "Oh" and "Ah." One boy, standing ten feet away, used the tip of his fishing pole to point out, to the other lad, our exact route at the same time a highway patrolman did a "double-take" as he sailed past on his way out of town. That evening I was reminded that on any trip, particularly during summer time, you'll find restaurants staffed with high school boys and girls earning vacation money. Many are less than ideal servers and some are hilariously funny. In Dawson Creek, the student waitress was not too knowledgeable about food. When I asked what kind of cocktail came with the dinner, she replied, "I don't know, it must be something made with lettuce." Bravely I ordered the cocktail. She delivered three shrimp with a little ketchup on top, then asked me, "What kind of dressing would you like on your salad?"

"What do you have?"

"Oh, all kinds, anything that you want," she replied.

"Just bring me some of that."

She grinned, got the idea and went back to the kitchen. A minute later, my salad was on the table. I asked about what I had for dressing. "Thousand Island," she laughed. Certainly "a little of anything" answer.

My first taste of how rough the Alaskan highway was reputed to be came while buying gasoline after dinner. The young attendant, upon learning of my destination, offered to sell me a huge screen to cover the front of the car and protect it from flying stones that chip paint. He also suggested that I carry a couple of spare tires. When I indicated that I had fine tires and did not want the bug screen to show in planned photography, he said, "Well, be sure to take it easy. It's best if you drive about 40 miles an hour and pull off to the right when campers and trucks go by."

Here, also known as "Mile Zero," the Mercury was parked in the Travelodge parking lot. In previous cities people had pulled in off the street to admire the car, and boys in Calgary chased me across town so they could examine it. But people in Dawson Creek stormed the little coupe like it was honey dripping from solid gold buckets. One young man was brought over by an elder gentleman. The young man took pictures of the car while the elder explained what he knew about it: which must have been considerable as neither of us had talked. I had been warned that, while driving the Alaskan Highway, there is great value in telephoning ahead. Not only are you more likely to insure a place to sleep, but calling gives tremendous confidence because you won't have to hurry to arrive before other travelers when rooms are in short supply. Somewhat like the confidence gained from spare gasoline. About a half hour before retiring, I telephoned 250 miles ahead, to Fort Nelson, for accommodations the following night. The clerk asked me when I expected to arrive. I said that I had no idea, as I was calling from Dawson Creek and had been told that about 250 miles a day was about right. She replied that this could be a valid estimate, "Depending on how fast one traveled."

"I'm traveling pretty fast," I replied.

"Lots of luck," she laughed and hung up, leaving me to consider sleep while worrying about the coming day's 250 mile run. Nevertheless, the call resulted from making better use of the guidebooks. Onc of the best, the AAA Guidebook on "The Alaskan Highway", was free. Though extremely accurate in most respects, I strongly suggest you interpret the word "Accommodations" as meaning just that: Everything from fine motels to rude cabins, or a rustic hotel with small cells for sleeping, and common toilet facilities. I even found a breezy latrine installation appealing more to the nature lover than seeker of five-star comfort. Considering that the north country is reported to be cold, one of the strangest things was that only one blanket was on the bed and no spares were in the closet. Perhaps trappers and tourists brought their own. I didn't...and froze.

In major trading areas such as Dawson Creek, Fort Nelson, Watson Lake and Whitehorse there are one or more service stations open all night. So, if you plan to leave early, it's a good idea to find this always-open service station the night before to eliminate driving all over town in the chill dawn seeking a suitable refueling spot. Telephone service was prompt and efficient and my U.S. telephone credit card worked well. In fact, if anything, service was a little better as friendly operators made small talk while waiting for my stateside number to ring.

On Labor Day, September 4, I filled the tank with gas before starting from Milepost Zero on the run to Anchorage. The first few miles out of Dawson Creek were on high speed pavement with a 60 mile an hour limit. It passed up, down and around rolling hills, through an occasional forest and past farms with cleared fields or broad stretches of grain. An occasional service station, with exterior telephone booth and nearby school bus warming-hut, reminded me that civilization remained around at this early part of the day. At Mile Post 20 the Mercury and I had our first sample of a rough road with teeth jarring suddenness. The pavement gave out and we dropped onto a rutted half mile of gravel; apparently an area that had washed out during early rains. In a minute or so I was back on pavement. Later I was surprised to come around a bend and discover a helicopter parked by the side of the road. Two men, near a small camper, were by a campfire apparently discussing flight patterns for the day.

Then a big sign by the shoulder announced that we were entering that section of the highway maintained by the Department of Public Works in Whitehorse, British Columbia. It also marked the point at which paving ended and we begin to bump along hard packed clay and gravel of the 800 odd miles of the Canadian Alaskan Highway. Another sign told me to "Keep Headlights On At All Times." On the Alcan it's an early warning when someone is coming toward you. You can see their cloud of dust in the distant daylight long before you can see the dim glow of headlights through the haze. Later I noticed the sun casting a huge birdlike shadow of the helicopter. Its pilot, while pacing the Mercury, was reading inscriptions on the doors through his binoculars. I stopped for gasoline at Sikanni Chief River which was at Mile Post 62. A man with a Firebird registered in Alaska was also refueling. His only question was, "What ply tires are you using?"

"They're four-ply tires with an eight ply rating, as supplied on Mercury station wagons," I told him. His question was well founded, for I hadn't driven two miles further toward Anchorage before I passed a station wagon from California. Friend husband was diligently trying to erect a bumper jack so he could replace a broken tire.

Unfortunately my stop for gasoline also put me behind a huge transport truck. Now I had to peer through his dust and brave flying stones to pass. Which may well be a good time to note that the speed limit on the Alcan Highway was 50 miles an hour. And it was highly unwise to drive much faster because there were so many unexpected chuckholes and graveled corners. Faster than 45 or 50 miles an hour meant you couldn't evade the more spectacular holes and entering a graveled corner too fast can lead one to broadside around with fearless abandon. Nevertheless, at this stage of the game, I had the feeling that much commotion about the Alaskan Highway was based on comments by pioneer residents who enjoy overemphasizing difficulty of the road to adventurize their being there. We would soon see, because the first 300 miles were said to be the most heavily traveled and easiest. A passing station wagon, with Alaskan license plates, displayed no unusual preparations that I could see. There was no wire screen across the front nor stack of spare tires on the roof such as last night's service station attendant suggested I buy. I did notice that a number of cars and trucks coming toward me had only one headlight. This puzzled me for a few minutes until I decided such damage must be caused by flying stones or "floaters" as Alaskan drivers called them. It wasn't but a few minutes after making this momentous decision that a tiny Volkswagen, traveling in the opposite direction, tossed a floater at the Mercury. " Pop" went the left front headlight and I too joined the clan of one-eyed drivers. Hoping to save the other light, I decided that the further to the right each passing car drives, the less chance there is of being sprayed with paint-removing gravel and headlight or windshield busters. To encourage oncoming cars to swing to their right I began to switch on my right-turn signal lights. This apparently gave them the same idea and most moved over quite promptly to establish as much passing space as possible.

The Alcan will give most amateur photographers a hard time. After you stop to take what appears to be a unique and lovely picture, everything is fine and dandy. But around the next corner is another scenic vista that beats the one first all hollow and picture on top of picture continues for mile after mile. I'd certainly suggest taking every affordable roll of film in anticipation of shooting your head off to return with a whopping bundle of colorful memories to share with your friends.

One of the nice things about the little Mile Post markers is that you never seem lost. The little rascals, which turn up every 80 seconds or so, are a friendly reminder that you are only that specific distance from a known point on the highway as listed in the AAA book "The Alaskan Highway". They do much to eliminate the feeling of desolation and location concern that could predominate did they not exist.

At Mile Post 264, the Mercury almost became a dump truck. Road crews who were widening the road or some such strange thing, had misplaced their signs where the road forked. At the left fork was a sign "Road Closed." On the right fork was a sign "Dump Trucks Only." Obviously, if a dump truck could go through, the Mercury could. So up we drove along the narrow bumpy 'Only' trail. What seemed to be the end of the graded path included a steep drop-off at the bottom of which two backhoes were noisily loading a dump truck. I waited a few minutes for another truck in front to move out of the way. The look of surprise on the backhoe operator's face, when he saw that next in line was an automobile and not another truck, was worth the wait. I slithered around stationary machinery and curious operators, bounced back onto the main road and hurried out of there before they put me to work or sent me back to where I had come from. After I pulled into Fort Nelson, my overnight stop, the little Firebird that I had met earlier at Sikanni Chief Creek pulled in. Its driver, Bob Glen of Anchorage, Alaska noted that one of my headlights was broken and suggested purchasing plastic covers to protect the lights. While giving me other good advice about driving the road, Bob emphasized, "Take it easy and don't get in a hurry."

Then he asked if I minded publicity. Being in the book business, I assure you the answer was "Gosh no, go ahead. We'll take all that you can give." Bob pointed to a lengthy antenna on his car, saying that he was a member of an amateur radio group of 40 "hams" in Alaska. He had been telling some of his friends about meeting my car and the trip I was making. Now, with my permission, he was going to pass the word throughout the network that *Aventura* was on its way to Anchorage. He concluded our conversation with a thoughtful gesture. If, in Anchorage, I'd like to talk to my people at home, he would arrange to feed my call through the amateur network and eliminate the cost of making a telephone call.

Fort Nelson, which billed itself as "The Heart of the Gas Capital," (whatever that may be) is certainly my nominee for accepting the tube should the world ever need an enema. The Highway, which at this point changed from gravel and dirt to a mile of town pavement, goes through the center of Fort Nelson. About 100 feet back, on each side of the road, are twin rows of buildings, motels, stores and gas stations. Plus what appears to be the local cat house, masquerading as a modern motel, about 200 feet further into the boondocks behind other buildings.

Even my hotel, decorated as it was in early Sears Catalog (1947), boasted many refinements. The dining room had beautiful linen table cloths. Each was carefully covered with worn scratched plastic to keep the linen clean. Charming dining room furnishings were of brilliantly polished chrome with colorless plastic "leather" seats, which harmonized well with studded-nail wall covering of vinyl. In a corner, adding another touch of sophistication, was a single chrome-plated ice bucket undoubtedly used for occasions of great festivity. All I could think was "Thank goodness my wake up call is 5:30 in the morning." The theory of bright and early in Fort Nelson was for taking pictures while the rising sun was casting its most interesting shadows. In reality I was up early because there was not much sleep thanks to the hotel's bar patrons. I took a few shots of "Main Street" before breakfast, during which the Chinese cook spent time with me discussing the art of photography.

He displayed a set of very good pictures taken of Fort Nelson from a helicopter, while I was reloading my camera and stuffing the belt line with unbroken poached eggs. Though I was primed to take "beauty shots" along the road, success was not talking with art that morning. I hadn't driven ten miles before the area was under an overcast that was effectively blocking the sun and leaving nothing more than dull gray haze as far as the eye could see. A few miles further, the sun cut through the haze and glared across my windshield. It also demonstrated that my windshield was streaked. I pulled off to the side of the road and by following Mike McDivitt's suggestion, tried the impossible. I waxed my windshield. Eureka! The Simoniz Master Wax cleared the glass and restored its clarity to the point where there was almost no glass at all.

By the way, don't horse around with warning signs on the Alaskan Hiqhway. When they read "Bad Corner," what they're talking about is a corner that is really bad. It's slippery with gravel of unusual sharpness, or involves an unsuspected tilt to the roadway. Occasionally you'll read something about a "Steep Hill." Which meant steep like you can't see over the nose of the car when you reach the crest. But though all Alaskan tourists seem to complain of gravel, bumps and dust; there's one nice thing about the Highway. It doesn't go anywhere but Alaska. No matter what you do (other than returning your car by air freight or boat) you drive it twice. All of which greatly improves the quality of bragging on return to civilization. After my first couple hundred miles of the Highway's gravel, I finally figured out a better way to pass huge trucks which run a tight schedule carrying goods and mail to Alaska. Downhill, they can go as fast or faster than a passenger car. And clouds of dust make it impossible to see far enough beyond to pass safely. Their uphill journey is so much slower that by waiting for such a stretch, that's not too dusty, you can usually get up enough steam to pass uphill without endangering either yourself or trying to use the same width of road occupied by the truck. Which is a bit dicey on rough gravel.

With your eyes open, all manner of funny events seemed to happen on the Alcan. I was coasting down into a small valley, through which ran a stream, when I glanced to the right. There was a huge tank truck parked near a river bed, with a small gasoline pump busily shoveling river water into the tank. Apparently the driver had fallen asleep in the cab, or the tank filled faster than he expected, for water was running over the top of the tank, down the sides, and thoroughly soaking marshy ground on which the truck was resting. As I slowed to watch, the driver was slipping and sliding madly through thick new mud while trying to reach the gasoline pump and turn it off. Little doubt his mind was full of visions of the truck sinking hopelessly into the muddy bog, from which he could never retrieve it. Steamboat Mountain, at Mile Post 351 provided my first experience inside an unusual roofless restroom. Its fenced area, open to the sky, had a trough at one side for standing and a sawed off oil barrel, over a hole in the ground, on the other side for sitting. The plus value was that users could look upward toward the heavens while appreciating a flowing breeze arriving through the adjacent forest. Every once in a while during these early Highway miles I had the terrible feeling that I was missing something. After driving along at my usual 50 miles an hour, I would suddenly find a sign reading "End Of 30 Mile An Hour Zone." But at no time did I ever see the beginning of such zones. Nor, thank goodness, did I see any sign of highway patrolmen with their bothersome red lights and taxi-striped sedans.

In this same area it was "God Bless Hughie Peet", of the Yukon Territory. My experience with Hughie began about 15 miles south of Watson Lake when, after crashing down into a particularly fearsome chuck hole, I began to hear an equally fearsome "Clunk-Clunk-Clunk" from the front suspension. This sent what is known as "that sinking feeling" racing through my body like a lead brick dropping from a ten story window. While fueling in Watson Lake, inspection revealed that a bracket, normally holding the front sway bar to the frame, had failed for no better reason than someone on the assembly line had sneezed and not completed an important bit of welding. Luckily I was buying gas at Watson Motors Ltd., Hughie's operation which catered mostly to heavy trucks. After discovering my problem, I asked around for someone to weld it. The best information I could get was "Look for the man in the red shirt."

The first red shirt I tried said "No, I'm just a tourist."

The second red shirt "L'owed as how" he did a little welding. This was Hughie. After 20 minutes of wandering around his place while handling six or eight other jobs, including parts and gasoline sales, he came to the Mercury and buried his head under the hood. There was much fumbling, head scratching and quizzical peering before Hughie "L'owed as how" again, that he could fix it. But it would have to wait a while because he had a couple of trucks to take care of first.

Though I looked around, I couldn't figure out where the needy trucks were parked. Although there were dozens of trucks, none seemed to be in need of welding repair. At that moment a big Canadian freight liner pulled in as Huqhie sauntered in its direction to greet the driver. It seemed that this truck, like others of the same make, was suffering from a differential-case fracture at the upper link pad. Grease was running from the case in a torrent. In a thrice, the tractor was pulled to the left and jackknifed into a more open position. A minute or so later, Hughie was underneath, with his electric welding rod, laying one of the neatest beads I've seen for a long time. While Hughie was welding, one of the drivers came over, asked what I was doing and we began swapping lies about our trips. He told me it took six days to run one of the big rigs from Seattle to Anchorage. "The mail must go through, you know" he said. He added that wintertime was best for rapid running because the road was smoother. In summer the road's condition stemmed from ability of the area supervisor. He mentioned areas of the Highway which were in better condition than most only because the maintenance supervisor had a sincere interest in his work. About one man the truck driver quipped, “He’s gonna retire next year, thank goodness. He should ‘ave gone 20 years ago.” Welding completed, Hughie went over to fix another truck. After banging away for a few minutes, Hughie told the driver to forget it. The best thing to do would be to put new bolts into the broken part.

Now he came to the Mercury and directed me to drive into one of the garage stalls. Soon it was on a hoist with both of us peering at the loose bracket from underneath. The problem being: To lift the bracket into position so it could be tack-welded. We pried and pushed, banged and knocked, and nothing worked. Hughie needed a larger hammer to pound the bracket but couldn’t find one. He disappeared and in a couple of minutes came back with a brand new sledge which whacked the offending metal into position. When he finished with the sledge it was tossed toward a corner with piles of other and more expensive tools lying around his oddly competent shop. Next Hughie wandered about seeking a length of timber long enough to do more. It was slow to be found because Hughie’s garage was such a wonderful collection (for anyone who likes garages) of tired automobiles, disassembled engines, outboard motors, tool rooms, lathes and every conceivable type of equipment usable in the repair of automobiles. Finally Hughie returned with a length of two by four, which we pushed up against the broken part. While he held the timber in place, I pumped a greasy truck jack under the end of the two by four to force the bracket firmly into position. But this wasn’t enough. I was also instructed to simultaneously lever a crowbar to pull the bracket sideways to hold it in place while he began to weld.

With sparks flying in every direction, most of which were singeing hair off my arms, Hughie proceeded to tack weld the bracket to the frame. He tilted his welder’s helmet up and inspected the work quizzically. Then he commented, “Well that looks like it will hold, now we can finish.” With that bit of good news the gasoline engine powering his welding generator presumed it was finished and promptly ran out of gas. This didn’t shake Hughie a bit. He disappeared into the office, returned a few minutes later and asked me, “Gee, I wonder what happened to the gas can?” as though there really was a chance I’d know. We both looked for the gas can which he eventually produced as a galvanized watering can with a long spout for filling radiators. At the pump he filled it with gas and came back to fuel the generator engine. At this point someone came in with an equally serious problem and Hughie disappeared again.

Later, back on my job, the power generator was restarted and welding proceeded with more sparks flying and more hair singed off arms before we were ready to lower the car off the hoist. As I should have guessed, the hoist didn't function too well. Hughie had me hold the air pressure valve open with my foot to bring the hoist down. This would have been great except nothing came down because Hughie had forgotten to open a few other controls. I stood there rather foolishly waiting for something to happen before he grinned a bit. "Oh my, I forgot to open the valves."

After the Mercury reached the floor we moved it to another area where, as Hughie put it, "There's more light." He now proceeded to weld the bracket from the top. It was a most difficult position from which to weld as the electrode had to pass through a small gap about three inches wide. Yet Hughie laid another beautiful bead that should last forever.

As I paid Hughie in his office, he passed on the information that he hadn't done much welding in recent years because he had a crew of three people working in the shop. He was the owner and just happened to be filling in for the day. All his mechanics had gone hunting over the weekend and failed to show up for work.

That afternoon, when I was a short distance prior to entering Whitehorse, the road became vastly improved. Though the speed limit remained 50 miles an hour, as it had been all the way, long straight stretches of smooth gravel allowed 60 and 65. This did not appear unusual, for I didn't catch any cars, nor was I passed. Vehicles going in the other direction appeared to be going as fast as I was. Unfortunately such straight stretches seldom lasted more than three or four miles before another group of continuously winding corners would slow the most eager driver.

Whitehorse, transportation center of the Yukon Territory and headquarters for the territorial government; had television, daily air transport service, a railroad, taxis, sightseeing buses and historical monuments. Population, according to my hotel's manager, was between 6,000 and 7,000: According to a service station owner, between 3,000 and 4,000. Take your pick. New and modern homes were mixed with relics and remnants of gold rush days. The Yukon and White Pass Railroad was 110 miles of narrow gauge track wandering between Whitehorse to Skagway. Though primarily used for hauling freight and building materials for mines in the area, it also scheduled a modified passenger service. When I visited the railway office to ask when the train was due, the clerk gave me an approximate time and added "I hope." Accordingly I asked about the prayer toward maintaining a schedule. He gave me a story about the train frequently being delayed by wandering moose, deer or track washouts. On arrival this day the train unloaded six tourists, ten cameras and one camper truck. After leaving the railway station I was stopped by a young man driving a truck marked "Television Channel 4." He wanted to look at the Mercury. On inquiry, he told me that television tapes were flown from Edmonton to Whitehouse every day and broadcast one day late over the cable TV station. Residential charges were $34.00 for a connection and $15.00 to $20.00 a month for entertainment.

All types of wheeled equipment were seen using the Alaskan Highway. Trailers, campers, pickup trucks, four wheel drives, house cars, and the ever-present cargo-carrying cross-country trucks. For most travelers it appeared that a conventional passenger car equipped with heavy-duty tires and suspension would be desirable, as there were plenty of accommodations along the way for food and lodging. For hunters, the best routine would appear to be a pickup truck with camper body mounted in back. There were so many stopping places along the road for picnicking or overnight sleeping, that such camper-bodied pickups could be the ideal way to travel. Pulling a trailer up and down the Highway, although I saw people doing it, did not appear to be the greatest of fun. Occasional areas of strong wind caused small trailers to swing back and forth while the continually bumpy road would be total harassment to the driver. An Alaskan resident told me that trailers were extremely cheap in Anchorage. He said that was because visitors would tow one way and dump them rather than tow back to the United States over Canada's "1000 mile detour."

Leaving Canada to enter Alaska, through Canadian customs, at Beaver Lake, was more a matter of discussion of the Mercury, and where it was going, than of any great interest in paperwork or birth certificates. Inasmuch as we were merely passing through Canada, it had not been necessary to obtain temporary registration or any form of special permit.

2

INTO ALASKA

Moments after the Mercury crossed the line into Alaska, we were on asphalt paving. For a mile or so I thought something was wrong with the steering the coupe handled so well on the relatively smooth surface. Formal entrance into the United States at Tok was as little complicated as leaving Canada. Our Customs and Immigration officer wanted to see my driver's license and asked where the front license plate was. He accepted my word that there was a plate at the rear for he didn't bother to go back and look. Then this had to be the time that I couldn't find my driver's license. After fumbling a bit I found the paperwork for his review. He returned it with, "If you'd like a fresh cup of coffee, they have some in the information building." He was pointing toward a small building past the customs station. A sign on the outside offered guidance to Alaska entry tourists. We departed Tok on paved roads of good quality which meant the 326 miles to Anchorage could be driven in six or seven hours. Adventure began again a few miles before entering Anchorage at dusk while I'm driving with only parking lights on because of the one broken headlight. There's heavy homeward traffic and control signals hint of civilization near at hand. Suddenly I had to slam on the brakes because there was an animal in the road. A cow moose, largest representative of the area's animal family, was ambling across the street like a stray puppy while slowing humanity's vehicular progress to a walk. There's little room for argument because a moose, meese or mooses may be six or seven feet tall.

Civilization in Anchorage included a Travelodge (they had the longest beds) and bright lights of a modern bustling metropolis. My first day consisted of wandering around town, finding a haircut, having the car washed and buying two city maps that weren't much better than a free map from a visitor's center next to the municipal building. Though it was September, the weather was mild. A slight wind did little more than refresh, rather than chill. However, I was told that within a matter of weeks cold weather could set in and Anchorage would bed down for the winter. Here was my first experience with this modern madhouse known as a Laundromat where I washed driving clothes and managed to partially dry them. Women in curlers and women without, women with girdles and women that should have, and women mixed with dozens of temporarily homeless children biding time while waiting for machinery to turn itself off. Keeping the Mercury clean, which my agreement with Simoniz had me accomplishing twice weekly, proved to be something less than a pastime. The local wash rack had a supersize charge which slowed my running there every 15 minutes to have mud or dirt scrubbed off.

In seeking a change of routine, one bright and early Saturday morning I upped at 6 o'clock, and headed for the Portage Glacier about an hour's drive south of Anchorage. Not only was it foggy that morning, but it was mighty sleepy inside the Mercury. For the first few miles, I chugged along at 30 miles an hour before the fog lifted and Carroll woke up. Then the world became a much better place in which to live. At the glacier, which is accessible by paved road, I planned to wash the car. A plastic wastebasket "borrowed" from the motel was filled with glacier water from a roadside ditch. With a bristle brush purchased in Wisconsin a few weeks before, I diligently scrubbed tires and sponged sides of the body while even more diligently batting the world's most aggressive insects. It seemed that Alaska was plagued with flying warriors of all sizes, shapes and interest. Some liked to light and irritate. Others would light and bite. I'm not sure which I had the most of because it seemed I was doing more swatting than washing. Eventually, the Mercury was clean and the bright blue of my frozen fingers matched the sky above. I wanted to photograph the results of all this effort in front of the glacier but 15 minutes of sun proved to be all that was available. It ducked behind clouds and left me in the car, holding a camera, while waiting for sunshine to reappear. After a reasonable time I gave up and headed back to Anchorage. As those of you who are photographers have already guessed, I hadn't driven more than a mile from the glacier before I was under brilliant sunlight with gorgeous blue skies and fluffy clouds parked on top of craggy mountains: Wonderful pictorial possibilities. But no glacier.

Shopping for Eskimo goodies that Saturday afternoon included surveying hotel gift shops and downtown stores. Although their offerings seemed to be of extremely good quality, they were rather high priced. I found fur caps from Argentina, stoles from Norway, as well as parkas, mukluks and pelts from Alaska. Luck was with me a little later when I wandered into a small Eskimo specialty shop about six blocks out of town. The Indian woman clerk had flown in from New York the week before. She was helping a sick relative by keeping the store open. It had its proportion of questionables including brass "temple" bells from India and plastic toys in the likeness of Eskimos. But there was a wonderful selection of beautiful Eskimo carvings in both stone and ivory. For my daughter Kim, I found an "impossible to operate" Eskimo yoyo made of fur and hide. For my wife, the symbol of her Aries personality: A hand-carved Eskimo snow goose mounted on a fish bone pedestal.

This was an unusual store made more so by the woman's willingness to provide hot coffee while I shopped. She explained that genuine Alaskan carvings by individual Indians or Eskimos were becoming more and more difficult to obtain because only older men and women continued their hand arts. Young people were going to college or working as truck drivers, clerks, or secretaries. One result was that most carvings were factory made instead of being produced by native artisans. She suggested that in years to come handmade art and crafts would become even more rare and valuable as the true artists pass on. "One of the area's problems," she said, "is that many Eskimos come to town over the weekend and run out of money from buying too many good things or enjoying an excess of fire water. So, on Monday morning there are usually three or four of them outside our door, offering to sell handmade articles or family trinkets at extremely low prices to obtain money to get back home again."

From her I also learned about the term "sourdough." It was applied to early pioneers in Alaska who, as prospectors, miners or other entrepreneurs, carried with them a yeasty type of cooking mixture from which they could make hot cakes or bread. The resulting baked product tasted somewhat sour, like French bread. Accordingly the pioneers were called sourdoughs, on the presumption that if they spent a winter in Alaska the distinction and title were well earned.

Aventura Alaska Brasil

Sunday in Anchorage was like any other city its size in the southern 48. Everything came to a screeching halt except for the few tourists walking the streets in search of something to photograph. My Sunday included touring the town, visiting the International Airport and shopping at a widely advertised "Flea Circus" market in the civic auditorium. Unfortunately, my admission ticket bought little more than an opportunity to browse a wondrous collection of useless junk, discarded car parts, paperback books and secondhand clothing. Entrepreneurs were on hand with fogless eyeglass cleaner, miraculous household chemicals and the ever-present encyclopedia salesman with his "Register now and win a free set" pitch. While returning from the flea market, I made contact with one of Anchorage's leading citizens. He turned and I turned. Unfortunately I didn't turn quickly enough. The right front fender of the Mercury gently nudged the good doctor's Oldsmobile. Surprisingly enough, we were both very polite and detached about it. What damage there was, was more to our egos than to anything else. Later, a little elbow grease and modest amounts of Simoniz repaired the bruised Mercury's fender.

Being a firm believer in not hiding one's self under a bushel basket, I wrote a short press release and carried it around to local newspapers. They were interested in the trip and both papers had pictures taken of the Mercury. One girl reporter read the release and spent half an hour interviewing me to turn out a three-inch story with four typographical errors and two incomplete sentences. On the more vocal side of publicity, the major television station learned of *Aventura* and I was invited to appear on "A Morning Show" with its host Roger Latham. As a result, at 7 o'clock Thursday morning, instead of leaving Anchorage directly, I drove to the TV station. There I was seated on an oversoft couch to answer questions about the trip, explain to Roger that much of the fun lay in casual enjoyment rather than making "safari" preparations and pretending to be a heroic adventurer. Studio personnel were so tickled with the project that I had the feeling that Latham and half the staff would have left then and now to participate in the run to Brasil. To top this, when I left the recording studio, a charming woman (who was to appear next and talk about flower arranging), grinned and said "You wouldn't like to have a passenger, would you?"

Outside I sat quietly in the Mercury while making notes of speedometer and engine hour readings. Then I locked the engine "On" at ten minutes of eight for what was planned to be a continuous-operation test all the way. This would be a period of over four months. So off I charged to leave spectacular Alaska with its trees changing color in front of snow-capped peaks touched with clouds wandering in a brilliant blue sky. For pictures I stopped on the far side of a river where two moose stood idly chewing their cud while watching me. A few minutes later I stopped to picture the Matanuska Glacier, near the Glen Highway between Anchorage and Tok. As I was ready to trip the shutter a great big fat bird lit on the corner of a nearby bench, peeped at me over his shoulder, waited while I snapped a picture then zipped off in pursuit of lunch.

Living became curiouser and curiouser during that first night at Tok junction where three main highways merged. My bed for the night was at Hopps' Motel where I had requested reservations. On arrival I couldn't find any of the motel rooms, only the "Office" sign by the restaurant door. Into the cafe I went for information. There I found a women taking care of the souvenir counter, registering motel guests, waiting on tables, doing the cooking, cleaning up dishes and trying valiantly to answer the telephone. I ordered dinner from her and seated myself. Next to me was a young couple, then three elderly retired school teachers and, further down the table row, a young man trying to hitch a ride. Some were eating, some were souping, and some were patiently waiting to be found. The hitchhiker gave up. He dropped a coin into the soft-drink machine and began nursing a can of soda so he could lay claim to his table long enough for someone to invite him on a ride to the next town.

By the time I received my soup a gentleman who appeared to be the owner wandered in, surveyed the confusion and decided it was not for him. He eased behind the counter, realized the box of free matches was empty and proceeded to fill it, then straightened souvenirs and disappeared. Three or four minutes later he returned; this time to accept money from the young couple who had finished. He consulted with the waitress, came over and told me that things were pretty bad because his cook and another waitress were sick which slowed things up quite a bit. "Yes, it is rather slow." I agreed. "I understand you've just run out of coffee. May I please have some milk?" A few minutes later the waitress brought dinner and a glass of milk to go with it. Meanwhile, as an encore, someone left the door to the service station open. Now we could be sure the attendant was busy repairing a tire, which was the first time I ever knew that air leaks could be patched with a hammer. I was ready to leave but couldn't find the waitress. The owner examined the menu, decided how much my dinner was worth, collected money and ushered me out the door. As I walked toward my room I saw the waitress answering the telephone.

My second day south began by leaving Tok much too early in the morning; like 5:30. Nocturnal restaurants and cafes along the highway were not open when I passed which meant it was close to 8 o'clock before I could find scrambled eggs. These were in a tiny cafe a few feet ahead of the Canadian border office through which I had passed from Canada some days before. After eating I drove into the exit lane. The first question the Canadian officer asked was, "Where are you going?"

"Brasil," I replied.

His jaw dropped about three degrees as he inspected me closely while apparently wondering if I was trying to be funny. "Where, did you say?" he asked again.

"Brasil," I said.

This time he believed me and only wanted identification that would explain who I was and where I was from. A driver's license did the job. The final question was, "What is your occupation?"

When I told him, "A journalist" he responded with a quiet nod of the head, as though this explained everything; including a tall American blandly saying that he's on a drive to Brasil, some 20,000 miles due south.

At Mile Post 1047 on the Alcan I stopped for fuel and interesting conversation. Here, Charley Beason, his wife, son and two dogs (one small, one large) were working their way toward a planned future. Eleven months before they had arrived in the area where forest land was not cleared and only puddles rimmed the side of the highway. Now they had their service station and garage built. One cabin for tourists was finished, another almost so, a third cabin framed and the entire forecourt area had been cleared for parking. "Though it's mud now, it's ready to be hard surfaced for future traffic," Charley told me. "We looked over the area pretty good and when they pave the Highway we should be in fine shape."

His wife added, "We don't want to get too big. We just wanna be big enough so we can handle it. Besides, there's moose in the mountains and any time we want to pick berries, there's plenty of them."

I filled the Mercury's gas tank and, while I took pictures, Charley's wife poured a can of STP into the crankcase because I had 5,000 miles on the odometer. It should be pointed out that on the *Aventura* run we did not plan to change crankcase oil because we wanted to give the engine the maximum amount of abuse. We only added oil as required.

Near Mile 1016, which designated a rather modest motel with cafe and service facilities, two men were busily hammering a signpost into the center of the roadway. The sign read "Highway blocked ahead. Stop." I pulled up to read the sign while one of the workmen came over, opened the car door and said, "It's okay. You can go on as long as you stay ahead of me."

At Mile 997 we finally got the message about the blockage. Here, straddling the highway from side to side, was a large four-bedroom bunk-house for use by a highway construction crew. It was mounted on rollers towed by a big truck. Luckily they had stopped in an area that allowed drivers to easily turn off the roadway into a dry ditch and, in so doing, pass around the impressive blockade with little trouble.

During my overnight in Whitehorse, sometime around 3 clock in the morning, one of the motel guests became enormously irritated by the Mercury's nonstop engine. When I woke up he was stomping along the hallway shouting, "Carroll, Carroll, Carroll!" The last time he shouted I sat up in bed with a sleepy subconscious memory of his previous shouts. By this time, he had retired to his room. Nevertheless, under snug warm covers, I could hear the operating engine becoming louder and louder as my overactive imagination enhanced the minor noise it was making. I couldn't go back to sleep. So, at 3:30 on that rainy, black-pitch morning, the Mercury rolled out of Whitehorse for Watson Lake. It was so dark I soon learned that driving at night on a gravel road in the rain could be exciting. There were few reflections to tell where the road was and no white line to define one side from the other. The best indicators appeared to be a line of snow and telephone poles along sides of the Highway.

Sunlight and scenery soon reminded me of the one terrible problem for those of us interested in photography. It's the ever-present danger of running off the road. With one's head swiveling right to left, while looking at each picturesque scene for its photographic potential, there's little excess time for driving. This can be harrowing when an unexpected curve is found on the opposite side of a hill. The opposite situation was my 30-minute wait for a truck to pass and demonstrate traffic flow. It began when I found a particularly picturesque area that was ideal to photograph one of the Alcan's famous postal trucks running at top speed. I parked and (by my watch) waited a full 30 minutes. No truck. Only one Volkswagen and two campers. Two minutes after leaving the site a most attractively painted truck roared past in a cloud of flying gravel.

Because I'd made such an early start from Whitehorse, thanks to my "friend" stomping the hallway, I arrived in Watson Lake about 1:00 in the afternoon for my next overnight stop. With plenty of time for pictures, I wandered around town shooting what seemed to be a typical Yukon Territory community. It was also the home of a detachment of the Royal Canadian Mounted Police. Because I wanted to film these young men and show that they did not wear red coats all the time, I went to the detachment offices. A court case was in session so I waited quietly while two young men defended charges of illegal possession of liquor. It seemed that in the Yukon it was against the law to have an open bottle of liquor anywhere except in a public place where liquor was sold for consumption or in the privacy of a home. These men had been arrested with open beer bottles in and near their car. With the arresting officer acting as prosecutor, the two men were advised of their violation of the law. Each agreed to speak in his own defense. They spoke. The judge, in civilian clothes sitting behind a desk, said they had no defense; then inquired as to their employment and residence. With these facts in hand he sentenced them to identical penalties: Ten dollars plus five dollars costs. When asked if they needed time to make the payment, one man said he had only four dollars and would need some time. He was given 15 days to come up with 15 bucks. The other gentleman elected to pay his fine immediately. After court was adjourned I discussed my mission with one of the "Mounties."

I told him I was making a travelogue and would like to shoot a short length of film of an officer in his car without his red coat. He looked at me rather oddly, blinked, and said he didn't know that he could. After thinking about this reply for a moment, he disappeared into an interior office to return with a loose-leaf folder about eight inches thick. This was the "Policy" manual for the post. Ruffling through he found nothing under Public Relations. He could find nothing under photography. Nor anything under acts of kindness for tourists. After the policy manual failed to reveal a satisfactory answer, the young officer asked about the direction I was traveling. I explained that I was going south. He responded with, "Wish you were going north to Whitehorse, where headquarters is. Then I could push you off on them to make a decision."

After more soul searching and head scratching, we agreed that he couldn't do anything for me. Following which he told me a terrible tale of the "Mounty" who was asked to dress in his red coat and pose for a picture amid a violent snowstorm. It seems that said "Mounty" was given what doesn't come naturally when the picture appeared in a national magazine published in the States. I acknowledged no desire to get anyone into trouble and, accordingly, would he please tell me where he was going next. I could just stand on a street corner and photograph him as he drove past. He grinned and didn't answer.

I needled a bit with, "As you well realize, you can't throw me in jail for taking pictures of you on the street."

He laughed, "No, I guess I can't."

Thanking all present for their courtesy, I drove my car a half block away and parked, door open, camera ready. Luck was with me. In five minutes another RCMP officer drove past. I photographed him getting out of his car, talking with people outside the detachment building and walking into the office. No sooner in than out. The office literally erupted Royal Canadian Mounted policemen (three) and a judge (one) who lined up about a hundred yards away while obviously discussing my photographic actions. I tipped my hand in thanks and drove peacefully away.

Breakfast the next morning in the Lower Post Hotel was almost the height of informality. The waitress, cook and counter girl (all the same person) was pleasantly busy taking care of a local road crew and several Indian school employees. I noticed that each of them went behind the counter and served themselves coffee. So, I did the same thing. She caught me with, "Oh, that's fine, what will you have?" I gave an order of French toast and bacon. "That'll be a couple of minutes. In the meantime I'll get your hardware," she replied in a well clipped British accent. I watched three other people go through the same routine with the addition of circulating through the spotlessly clean kitchen to place their order. Only one man reviewed a menu pasted to the wall with sticky ends of flesh-colored Band-Aids. If you've ever wondered what people who live in frontier areas talk about, the road crew breakfasting in Lower Post were sitting so close I could not help but overhear answers amid their conversation. It concerned "The fella who shot a moose the night before...the fella who stayed out all night...the fella who got tired of putting quarters in the slot machines for Indian girls...the fella who was sick with flu for three days...so what were you gonna do today, like go fishing, because I gotta fix my car?" Otherwise, the men knew each other as well as they knew the lunch counter menu, about which one quipped, "I know it by heart," when I passed it to him.

Later that same day, at lunch, I enjoyed another conversation; between two male patrons, thc 18-year-old waitress and the cook-owner (a lady of about 50). Talk hinged around who had announced pregnancy last week and was going to be married next week ...what they had done last night ("Nothing, stayed home then went to visit Nellie.")...wasn't it nice that Sue was getting married at last ("It's too bad, everybody in town knew her.") ...with giggles from one of the men...and a touch of brilliance from the cafe's owner who suggested they all start a scandalous rumor about someone, anyone. This brought four giggles. Then silence as each gave thought to the exciting proposal.

As the old saying goes, "Into every life some rain must fall," I was rained on shortly after lunch and did not even get wet. Exactly at Milepost 426, the three lady school teachers noticed in the restaurant at Tok, were seen standing by the side of the road peering at a flat tire. Sir Walter Carroll rose to the occasion, threw down his brake, and was soon busily engaged in changing one extremely airless tire. That is, I was doing a great job until the wheel wouldn't fit the hub bolts. When I asked the driver if this was her spare tire, she said "I think so, but don't you have the wheel on backward?"

With my red face, and reversed wheel, everything went nobly. In a few minutes the ladies were on their way to the next town to purchase a new tire so they would have at least one spare for the remainder of their trip home to Colorado. They told me they had enjoyed a wonderful time visiting the north and planned to send their car back by ferry from Haines, Alaska. Unfortunately, flood waters so damaged the road that it was impossible to get through and reach the ferry. Then they decided on driving to Whitehorse and riding the train, with their car, to the ferry at Skagway. This plan failed because the same flood had washed out sections of the Yukon and White Pass line four days previously. So they were driving home, disgruntled with being forced to use the same route twice.

Accommodations were in a state of upheaval in Fort Nelson when I arrived. A Mr. Peckett was on hand to inspect the Motor Hotel, one unit of the chain he owned. In addition "The damn tour bus," as one hotel employee described it, had just pulled in with 37 tourists returning to the southern 48. Management had rolled a red carpet from the lobby to near the center of their dusty main street, over which passengers from this last motor coach of the year could enter the hotel. Later the manager told me, "We try to give them the red carpet treatment and be the best hotel on the highway." While I was dining, a charming lady, Judith Kenyon, assistant editor of the local newspaper, appeared with her doctor husband to interview me for a story on the Brasil trip. He disappeared to an upstairs room while I spent more time learning of Mrs. Kenyon's former life in South Africa than explaining my plans for Latin America to her.

The next day, at Milepost 82 with 6,520 miles on the speedometer, we returned to solid footing in the form of asphalt pavement After jouncing and rumbling over Canada's "thousand mile detour" it was a welcome delight to cruise smoothly and silently on a modern highway surface. At Dawson Creek we left the Alaskan Highway for Canadian Highway 97 which lead us toward Prince George and eventually into Vancouver. It was a winding route through some of the most beautiful areas of Canada's British Columbia. And rural it was with an early warning sign slightly after Chet Wynd, reading "Watch out for Moose on the Road." One of the pleasures of traveling relaxed is the great number of pleasantries that occur. Such as in Prince George where I decided to have the front wheels checked for alignment after the severe beating they had taken from the Alaskan Highway. In the morning I parked outside the shop door of the Mercury dealer until the service manager arrived to open up. He gave me the unpleasant news that the shop had no wheel alignment equipment. "But" says he, "Don't worry, I'll call our best local shop and get you in there right away." Which he did. Two blocks left and four to the right and I was in the brake and wheel alignment specialty shop. They found that the right front wheel had gained too much camber and was feathering inside edges of the tire. While corrections were being made, everyone in the shop took the chassis apart with their eyeballs to learn what they could of the first current model they had seen.

An hour later and 50 miles down the road from Prince George, I decided I needed gasoline. While driving through the town of Quesnel, with little idea of how large it was, I proceeded somewhat cautiously while passing only service stations on the wrong side of the road. The first one on the right was a Shell station, in front of what appeared to be an oldish motel. I bought fuel from a charming middle-age woman with marvelous red hair. After we went into the office for a receipt I discovered she also operated a cafe and had fresh baked fruit pies cooling on the counter. Ten minutes later I was happily engaged in working on a huge slab of fresh-from-the-field blueberry pie. She had picked them herself, which meant the blueberries weren't more than a few hours out of the woods. A truck driver sitting next to me, nibbling toast with his coffee, didn't know what he was missing. Personal disaster followed about 200 miles further on. I stopped for lunch but picked the wrong cafe. In addition to serving a well-covered plate of Canadian sausage, the cook ruined my good intentions by opening the oven to remove a brand new lemon meringue pie. Weight control went down the drain as the day's second piece of pie was added to the food bill...and to my waistline.

I'd often wondered why trucks carrying loads of pipe never stacked small pipe inside larger pipe in order to carry more pipe. Usually, all they carry is open-ended cylinders of fresh air. At last my wonderment was satisfied. While running from Prince George to Vancouver, I finally saw such a truck whose driver had nested four sizes of pipe, one inside the other, to make maximum use of tonnage capacity of his semitrailer.

In Vancouver I received a memo that the Ford Motor Company had mailed material about *Aventura.* "Call at the Post Office Customs Station, Downtown," the note read. Following instructions, I entered the office and was greeted by a huge sign: "Go to the Centre Wicket." Not sure what a "Wicket" was I went to a window in the center of a row of windows. It turned out to be No. 7 and was unattended. But there was another sign: "Place Your Ticket in Rotation and Your Name Will Be Called." There were three tickets on the counter so I placed mine in the fourth position, furthest from the clerk's side of the counter. I watched others approach, read the sign and place their tickets in line. All except one gentleman.

He had to cheat a bit and start a new line off to one side. When a clerk recognized the chicanery he promptly put the "fudged" ticket last of all. After my number was called it took very little time to get my material out of customs. It was printed literature of which the clerk said, "You're an American, traveling? This is no problem here. Good luck."

There was equal interest on the part of Vancouver business people to be helpful. I had to send copies of press releases that Ford had mailed to me, to a number of radio and television stations and newspapers. Not knowing whom to call, I telephoned a local public relations agency and asked "Who in town delivers press releases to media?"

The secretary mentioned "Crest Cartage" as the best one they knew. Which, of course, with "Cartage" in their title would have been the last place I would have called. The Crest dispatcher read off a list of press associations, radio stations, television outlets and newspapers that I should cover. The messenger arrived early and when I asked why, he replied, "Well, we thought it might take a few extra minutes to check over your list, to make sure you have all of the important people." We checked and off he went to cover the city for us.

3

RETURN TO THE 48

It took less than an hour, after leaving downtown Vancouver, to drive a modern freeway and cross the United States border into the State of Washington. There was no inspection on leaving Canada and only the usual, "Where were you born, and what did you buy?" questions from a U.S. Immigration and Customs officer. You'll not find much in *Aventura* about traveling in the United States because it can be what you wish: An endless line of concrete Interstates with occasional stops for gas or food. On the other hand there are numerous side roads through the most beautiful parts of our great nation. Because *Aventura Alaska Brasil* concerns itself with travel outside our borders, what follows is somewhat brief..

Such as the frightening sign on Highway 99, between Seattle and Portland, where you can find a town named Vancouver in Washington state. Trouble begins after you pull off the Interstate before you get to this Vancouver, for gasoline or food, then head further south on the same Interstate. Suddenly you see signs reading "Vancouver, 40 Miles Ahead." The sinking feeling is that, by some manner or means, you've managed to turn around and are driving back to where you came from: Like Vancouver, Canada. Worry not, it's really not so, as we learned the hard way.

It will become obvious, as you follow us on *Aventura,* that this book shares the basics of traveling: Gasoline, food, lodging and people. No matter how thin you slice it, a major portion of all traveling hours is spent in these primary areas. Museums, temples and vistas we'll usually leave to Guide Books and tourist brochures. In California Renee met me in San Francisco where we took a day off to visit the city. Then Ford arranged a picture session in one of the parks which was followed by luncheon with a local reporter. From there it was on to Los Angeles for a major press conference in a downtown hotel. All four sponsors (Simoniz, STP, Mercury and Firestone) participated in hosting about 20 reporters interested in what we were doing. After a few days rest at home we packed carefully, telephoned farewell to close friends and enjoyed a solid nights sleep. We were up early to wedge our daughter, Kim, between us in the front seat for a fast trip to her school. There her parting comment was, "Get lost and find your way back home soon." With nose in the air, and declining to look back over her shoulder, she hurried toward school before the tears could begin again.

"Par for the course" well describes the mind-clogging going-to-work traffic that Los Angeles freeways presented during our drive out of town. Instead of 65 miles to 70 miles an hour on open multi-lane ribbons, our departure was controlled by 20 to 30 mile an hour "Stop and Go" for the first five miles. Once we'd passed the center of the city we could cruise at our usual speed. Our destination was Yuma, a few feet over the California border into Arizona and the end of our first day's run of a little over 300 miles. In this area the Interstate rolls across one of its lowest points in the United States, near the Salton Sea, where pavement is 221 feet below sea level. Nearby was one of our photography stops by the remnants of an old wood-plank road which snaked its way across desert sand dunes of southeastern California before World War I.

4

MEXICO

Crossing the border from the United States at El Paso, Texas, into Mexico's Ciudad Juarez, absorbed an hour and five minutes. This contrasts with less than one minute it took to pass into and out of Canada. We drove over the then new Stanton Bridge and, after passing nonchalant Mexican officers, made a sharp right underneath the canopy of their Migracion (Immigration) and Aduana (Customs) station. Apparently it was permitted to park in the center of what appeared to be a one-way driveway, on which we were facing in the wrong direction. By some stroke of more good fortune, I managed to enter the right door of two adjacent offices. After a few moments for document review, a Migracion officer stamped and signed our various papers which allowed Renee and I to visit the Republic of Mexico. After the simple no-cost formalities were concluded, he pointed me in the direction of the other office. Here, our car's documents were cared for by an elderly gentleman who hammered vigorously on a well-used Royal typewriter. His assistant was rather disturbed when we explained to him that there was no serial number under the hood of the Mercury. Disturbed changed to upset when he found the hood would not and could not be opened. Renee did her best to explain that the number plate beneath the left corner of the windshield was all there was on 1968 models. After verifying this against the car-maker's plate in the left door frame he accepted her contention without further complaint.

Inside the office his independently obtained numbers were compared with those I had provided from the registration certificate. Finding them satisfactory, he sent the paperwork, with my signature and registration certificate, to a third office. In moments the documents were back and we were given two "Turista" stickers: Outside, the assistant plastered our windshield and right rear window with the stickers. Another officer looked at but did not open luggage in the trunk to which he affixed tiny stickers which indicated it was permissible for the luggage to enter the Republic. Papers in order, we were wished a pleasant visit to Mexico.

As we prepared to drive off, the messenger-boy assistant began telling me a lengthy story in Spanish, which I was incapable of understanding. One of his companions, who suddenly spoke English, came over and said, "It is customary to make a tip." Accordingly the tip was for services we didn't know we needed, but were apparently "required" as part and parcel of entering Mexico when you speak no Spanish. To the unpaid helper went the very first of our new Kennedy half-dollars. We had obtained them in the expectation that they would be somewhat valued South of the border. The value in this case was a suspicious grunt. I am sure the recipient did not believe that a coin, wrapped in a small cellophane envelope, could be little more than a souvenir of dubious value.

Ten blocks further on, after a number of turns and traffic lights we found a Juarez bank that was open. Inside I went through the formality of identifying myself to exchange Travelers Checks, and all remaining American money, for Mexican coinage and bills. Then Renee skillfully found a way down a narrow street and turned us left onto the main highway which lead from Juarez to Chihuahua. 19 Miles south of Juarez we made two more official stops. Thc first was at a small Migracion station staffed by two officers who inspected our tourist permits. A few feet further on we made a second stop at a similar building. This time to display our permit for the car to satisfy the Aduana officers. Here the permit was stamped. We had passed and entered this Northern area of the Republic of Mexico. No cost, no pain and a matter of two minutes plus time for Carroll's picture taking. 79 Miles south of Juarez a third scheduled stop was made for another official entrance into Mexico. Here an Aduana officer was rcady to check luggage again to make sure it was sealed and properly passed at the Juarez border. However, he only glanced at our tourist sticker on the windshield, said "Okay", and waved us on.

Our first meal in Mexico at Ahmuda did more to shake up the waitress than it did us. Wc long before had decided that the safest way to avoid "Turistas," as dysentery is familiarly called, was not to drink tap water. Accordingly, we ordered a soda and two fried egg sandwiches. They arrived as "Burritos" which were fried eggs rolled in a hot tortilla. Quite tasty when sprinkled with a liberal dose of chile salsa. To the waitresses' frame of mind, our lunch did not go with a soft drink. On the other hand, she had us watching her while we ate. She was seated at the rear of the restaurant, diligently cutting machine-folded paper napkins in half, then refolding each section so that the cut edge wouldn't show. In effect, getting two for the price of one. Before we left Renee returned from the "Sanitario" with tears in her eyes. When I asked what happened, she replied, "I don't know whether I'm crying from too much chili on my Burrito or because of the disinfectant they used in the bathroom."

Renee and I, on our first day in Mexico, reacted like typical (as if we were anything else) tourists. Our desired schedule of up and moving by dawn, then stopping in a reasonable overnight site by three or four in the afternoon paid off. In Chihuahua we were able to change clothes and be wandering downtown streets, cameras swinging, by four o'clock. This was time enough to visit public markets, a few stores, inspect a typical downtown cathedral and plaza, then look for a restaurant wherein we could sit and enjoy a coffee. When we couldn't find such refreshment after three or four blocks of walking, I stopped by a taxi dispatch booth and asked the dispatcher if he spoke English. The answer was "No." I apologized for my poor Spanish before haltingly asking for directions to any nearby restaurant that served good food. For some strange reason he understood exactly what I wanted, talked with a couple of drivers then directed us in simple Spanish that I could understand. Go one block one way, half a block the other way and the restaurant could be seen fronting the post office. As we walked away, Renee said, "My, but you speak beautiful Spanish when you are hungry.?

"Well, if I do," I replied, "why is it I have so much trouble making anyone understand what it is we want?"

Her silent glare was no reward for my poor humor .

We found the restaurant as directed and it proved to be a dandy little place. The waiter parked us in front of a window, so we could watch people traffic, while sipping a cold soda. From our viewpoint, the most entertaining production was a group of spic and span Mexican Army men. They were directly across the street guarding the back door to the post office, below which was their regimental barracks. One was on sentry duty while the others washed or swept the sidewalk. Their effort appeared to be nothing more than an excuse to appear busy while eyeing the many secretaries walking to and from the stamp windows. As Renee commented, "Where you find the Army, you'll find the girls." Later we relocated our car, drove to the motel and tumbled in; looking forward to an early morning start to Torreon, about 250 miles south of Chihuahua.

It's not a bad idea, when traveling south of the border, to always park your suitcases and shoes above the floor, on chairs, tables or vacant beds. Not only does this make them handier, but discourages over-friendly itinerant night creatures from climbing aboard and mixing with your belongings. It isn't that they are angry with you, it's only that they're lonely and seeking a quiet place to spend the evening. Additionally, in more rural areas, turn back your bed before crawling in. You could find other lonely intruders who may object at having their snoozing site disturbed.

Another asset of our flexible planning is that when a scheduled overnight site doesn't appeal, we may have enough additional time to drive further on. On the second night we were supposed to stay in Torreon, which was a large industrialized town in which the "best" hotel appeared to be something left over from the Mexican Revolution. We decided without hesitation to continue for something better. Renee had been reading our AAA guide book, looking for cities near our route that might be of interest. She found that Parras de la Fuente, one of the oldest towns in Mexico, was on our route. Of greater interest to us was the mention of the Rincon del Montero, as a most unique and comfortable resort. Indeed it was. Although few employees spoke English, everyone from clerks to waiters, and the man watering the golf course, went out of their way to be of assistance while adding to our pleasure. After an oversize luncheon we accepted nature's invitation for a 20-minute siesta. This provided enough energy for a 20 mile drive to San Lorenzo, where Mexico's most famous distillery and winery (Founded in 1626.) was located. We were told that the area around San Lorenzo was planted to grapes shortly after Spanish conquistadors arrived. Soon the growing of grapes and production of wine was the sole means of livelihood in the area. Indians who produced the wine, and cultivated grapes for the Spaniards, banded together and declared themselves an independent republic. Shortly afterward the Spanish government decreed that nowhere else in Mexico could others produce alcoholic beverages, except in San Lorenzo, because this was the sole livelihood of its inhabitants. Accordingly, the cellars at San Lorenzo and of Casa Madero, were the first wine cellars in the Republic of Mexico. Renee and I sampled as many products as our equilibrium would allow. This included a fine brandy of the Casa Madero, that seemed equivalent to the best we had enjoyed while traveling in Europe.

Our return was into Parras where we parked by the central square in hopes the Mercury would attract enough attention to produce interesting pictures. While on our way to the bank, to cash Travelers Checks, we passed a school from which we could hear children singing. Inside the surrounding wall there was a conga line of ten second-graders practicing for an upcoming festival. Even the Principal was in the patio, with most of the other students, watching the youngsters prance back and forth. Breaking Travelers Checks at the bank, to obtain the best rate of exchange, put us in the mood to walk further and peer into all the open doors and windows we could find. Such nosiness taught us one thing for sure. The exterior of a house may be a mess, but the interior would be spotlessly clean and, in many instances, beautifully furnished with European-style furniture. Once back in the central square, we benched in a shaded park to obtain interesting shots of the Mercury near horse-drawn carriages. Fortunately, all the pictures included passengers and pedestrians inspecting signs and maps on the car's body.

We left the Rincon early for a fast "milk run" to Saltillo. One of our books indicated there was an interesting open-air market on Saturday. Instead we found a two-storie concrete building in the center of town. It was bursting with food, cooking utensils, low-cost clothing and shoulder to shoulder pedestrians who had bussed to town to do their shopping. Even nearby streets were clogged with traffic, fruit carts and sidewalk food stands. As to being interesting, from our point of view the market was not. Busy it was and certainly symbolic of Saltillo's importance as a trading center for its region. Accordingly, instead of remaining overnight as we had planned, we popped into the Mercury and began a 260 mile run to Zacatecas. The AAA book described the route as an arid, boring drive. For sure, we agreed with this one!

So boring that we prolonged a vicarious thrill that didn't involve us too much. For miles we followed, safely far behind, two Mexican busses about the size of cross-country Greyhounds. Drivers were racing each other on a rolling two-lane road where neither could see oncoming vehicles over highway rises. With black smoke thundering from the poorly maintained diesel engines, windowed tops swaying from side to side high above the asphalt, almost touching each other on wayward swings, it was breathtaking real-life action and so dangerous we couldn't believe it.

While touring in any foreign land there are usually a number of driving hazards which, by their very strangeness, can become a problem of consequence. Earlier this morning I had warned Renee about the vast number of animals wandering about or sleeping on the pavement: Such as mules, horses, cows, sheep and goats. I also pointed out that huge turkey buzzards, often seen picking a meal from animals killed on the road, could be a hazard when they scattered as an approaching car neared. Renee learned her lesson well on this run toward Zacatecas. A large flock of buzzards on the right side of the road were busily working on a small amount of road kill. They scattered on approach of the Mercury but one bird badly underestimated our nearness and flew too close. He/she became frightened at proximity of our wheeled monster and the fear was just too much. With a shrill squawk the bird let go and pooped all over the hood, much to Renee's consternation as she ducked behind the steering wheel and muttered an "Oh sh--." (No pun intended.)

We arrived in Zacatecas in time for Saturday night's action. The place was jumping. There were people everywhere. After finding our motel we walked through what proved to be an interesting and lovely old town of narrow, twisting, cobblestone streets. On hillsides the only "streets" were stairs for pedestrians going from one level to another. Our funny little dinner included a visit from a corps of school girls. They left their adjacent table and came to ours, en masse, to ask a question: in English! They apparently had decided in advance what words they would use, and exactly how each would be spoken, in English of course. I became so upset at being surrounded by such a flock of females that, when they asked me what time it was, I replied, "We're from California." This reply sent all of them into gales of laughter. By more carefully considering their excellent English we figured out what they wanted and re-answered the question. They retired to their table and, for the rest of the evening, exchanged glances with Renee and I while giggling at the funny Americans who didn't know how to tell the time in English.

In Aquascalientes, our next stop, we lucked out. While walking down a side street we saw a sign which spoke of performances at the Rancho del Charro, outside of town. We hurried back to the hotel and obtained directions from a clerk. They brought us to the far side of the railroad tracks where, at "Cowboy Ranch", we found about 300 people bleachered around an old Mexican-style rodeo ring, into which led a 25-foot-wide walled alley about 100-feet long. Inside the ring charros were practicing their skills by roping wild horses fleeing down the alley past a row of horsemen. Instead of roping the horses at the neck, their technique was to throw the rope in such a fashion that it would snare both rear legs. This seldom upset the horse but usually brought it to a neck-straining halt. More exciting was their unusual method of bulldogging. For this, a young bull was chased down the alleyway. As it ran, one of the horsemen would ride behind it and, with his right hand, grasp the bull's tail and wrap it around his extended right boot. By continuing to ride rapidly the charro could pull the bull head-over-heels onto its back. The moment the bull fell the charro would free the tail and continue toward the bull ring. At the last minute he'd stop by sliding his horse on its haunches, directly toward the seating for about 30 of Aquascalientes fairest female teenagers. They would clap with pleasure while the audience roared approval of the rider's daring and skillful bulldogging.

The next event was bull riding. The first young man did a good job of holding on, most of which appeared being done with his eyes closed. He rode the bull to a standstill. After resting a moment, the bull went wild a second time and succeeded in throwing the now tired rider. Three charros came out and, while two of them played with their lariats, one roped the bull around the neck and proceeded to lead it around the ring for edification of the crowd. One of the lariat players then succeeded in accidentally roping the back legs of his own horse, which amused the audience greatly. They laughed even more when he attempted to retrieve the lariat from underneath the bull's feet. The lariat had somehow managed to tangle with strands under his entangled horse which were also bothering the bull. Finally the man succeeded in roping the legs of his companion's horse which charmed the audience into rude and noisy comments about his lack of skill.

The second bull rider gave his animal a magnificent ride. When it tired he spurred it directly toward a steel gate where another charro roped the legs and brought it to a standstill. The rider calmly peeled off the beast's back, unloosened the belly thong and walked away amid cheers of the crowd. Only then did the action slow to the point where we realized that riders were holding with both hands as compared to the American one-hand hold. The animals were not stupid and after the bull had been ridden, roped and hazed to the point of tiredness, it sat and refused to move. Riders untied their lariats to better push or pummel the bull into action again, while the crowd cheered and booed with equal gusto. Eventually the bravest charro twisted the bull's tail and give it a swinging kick in the rump. This sent the animal to it's feet and back into the pen for another ride. "Wild" horse action followed. The wild horses being relatively tame animals that had been abused to make them almost unrideable. Following a skillful riding exhibition by one man, four horsemen attempted to lasso the now-ridden "wild" horse. They were so totally unsuccessful and inept the crowd cheered the horse in hopes it could continue to evade capture by the Keystone Comedy quartet.

On return to town we parked the Mercury in front of our hotel, which was on one of the city's main streets. With both signs in the windows, engine running and parking lights on, it soon became a center of attraction. From our second-floor balcony we watched older pedestrians walk slowly past and look at the Mercury enviously out of the corner of their eyes. Young adults stopped, inspected everything, walked around the car once or twice to examine the styling, and occasionally read the window signs which explained that the test engine was operating continuously. Teenagers were the ones who explored most diligently. A great number of them stood carefully distant, with hands in pockets, to consider everything they could see. Then the eager beavers, who might qualify as juvenile delinquents, would casually look around to see if anyone was watching and equally casually inspect each and every lock on the car. All door handles would be tried, as would trunk lid and hood, to determine if they were secure. The Mercury eventually attracted two local newsmen who took pictures of Renee and I, after interviewing us for a story to be carried later in the city's daily newspaper.

When we came downstairs early the next morning, it was easy to see that every speck of dust covering maps on doors and trunk lid had been wiped aside by what must have been hundreds of tracing fingers. The hood showed marks of hands and ears of pedestrians who'd made sure the engine was running. And side windows were covered with prints of greasy noses that preceded staring eyes pointed toward the car's interior. We loaded the Mercury and eased into traffic. There, while spending too much time reading a highway map, we learned that the fastest thing in Mexico is the horn of the driver behind when a traffic signal changes.

By watching Mexican farm boys we learned about two ways to ride a burro. One was somewhat conventional, in which the lad sat astride the sagging center part of the animal. This made it appear as though the combination was a six-legged quadruped with legs of a tall boy draping sides of a short burro. On the other hand, some Mexicans sat far back on the haunches and, in effect, used the burro's back legs as an extension of their own. From a distance we would see a burro with a boy aboard, but with only four legs extending to the ground.

Though it was mid-October the closer we came to Mexico City the more spring-like the countryside. Beside the highway were mile after mile of charming wild flowers of orange, blue, purple, light yellow and white. There were areas where the entire countryside was rich with green cactus, grass and fat cattle, while frequent streams were flowing full from recent rains. This made us feel so good that in Guadalajara we decided to live it up and registered into the best motel we could find. But we knew we were in Mexico when the typical Latin management procedure of saving money resulted in tepid "hot" water that afternoon, and only slightly warmer "hot" water for the following morning. After showering and shivering, we checked out the lunch department on a lovely patio spread with colorful tables near the swimming pool.

Have you ever been to a cockfight?

Neither had we.

That night we decided to attend one because Renee read in a guide book that cock fighting was a typical sport in Jalisco, of which Guadalajara is the capital. She also discovered that the arena had scheduled fights that night. We left the Mercury outside our motel room and went to the front office for a taxi. Unfortunately, there were none. Fortunately, the hotel's musicians, the Mexican Jets, were leaving for their more modest diggings and fresh clothes for the evening's performance. Lucky us, they were using the motel bus; a stripped Volkswagen van minus doors. We sat on its hard bench seats and hung onto the great outdoors as it whistled along while the motel driver scared us to the nearest taxi stand. The Jets practiced English with us and acknowledged that they too would like very much to visit Brasil. In the words of one musician with wanderlust, "Este una muy bueno pais." We didn't do too well trying to tell our cab driver where we wanted togo. However I had written our destination address and, after reading the name of the arena, he grinned and acknowledged that this was it. Then began the somewhat frightening ride through central Guadalajara. The taxi was threaded through a maze of pedestrians, bicycle riders and itinerant drivers to emerge on the far side of the city at the door of "La Tapatia," a restaurant. Adjoining was the Plaza de Gallos, a little arena in which cockfighting would take place. Both were within the same adobe-plastered enclosure under a roof of corrugated plastic sheets, surrounding a roofless central patio. Though Renee's information indicated that cock fighting began at 7:30 PM, we were told it really would not happen until 8:30. We were about two hours ahead of time and rather wisely decided not to taxi back through the city. We went into the La Tapatia area, found a booth and ordered dinner. A thin "bistec" with frijoles and tortillas made a dandy, stomach-filling meal. Meanwhile, at the bar, a Mariachi band played both loudly and well. Between waitresses and female customers who could sing, restaurant and arena customers were thoroughly entertained during a nontypical fun-type Mexican event. While eating, the ticket-taker appeared, sold us two tickets for ten Pesos apiece and retained both Pesos and tickets in the same pocket. Meanwhile, it began to rain buckets. We could hear water bouncing off the roof, running down a Rube Goldberg gutter and watch it wash through the open patio which soon became a mass of fresh mud. A little after 8 PM the bar crowd began thinning into the cockfight building. Taking the hint, we finished dinner, followed them and found seats in the stands. The arena's circular dirt floor, about 30 feet in diameter, was surrounded by solid fencing about three feet high. Behind the fence were three rows of folding theater chairs, the second and third rows higher than the first. This was seating for those of us who had bought the right tickets. A circular walkway behind the theater chairs separated them from rows of benches for low-cost watching. Off in a far corner, near the roof, was a crude bandstand on which the Mariachi band soon appeared. Two girl singers were with the band to belt out numbers and fill time whenever ring action slowed, which proved to be not often enough to give them many opportunities to perform..

Inside the ring about a dozen men were circulating while shouting and holding up card-tickets with large numbers on them. One, who spoke English, explained that this was a form of lottery. Patrons could buy a favorite number for 100 Pesos and after 12 tickets were sold a winning ticket would be drawn. Holder of the lucky number would win 1,000 Pesos and the house would keep 200 as a commission. Fairly soon lottery judges were rattling 12 numbered dice inside a leather bottle. One at a time, die were tossed from the bottle into the center of the cockfight ring. Die One, Two, Three and Four were discarded. The Fifth die tossed from the leather bottle was declared the winner and within seconds vendors were back in the ring seeking buyers for a new set of raffle tickets. They went through four raffles before a fighting bird appeared in the ring.

Immediately the raffle vendors changed their tune and began selling bets on the bird. As explained to us, the bird with a red thong holding a newly-sharpened spur on his left leg was usually a bird who has fought before and won. He was defined as a "Champion". The other bird, with a green thong holding its spur, was a newcomer and most likely to lose. In the course of a Mexican cockfight, losing meant becoming a tough chicken dinner for some fortunate attendee. Betting on the outcome was simple. The champions, or red-thonged birds, carried a 200 Peso price the night we attended. This amount was printed on a blackboard hung from the arena's roof post. Patrons could bet with a champion or against him, with odds changing radically depending upon the direction of betting. As nearly as we could determine, to bet on a champion to win, would gain only 16 Pesos for our trouble if he won. If we bet against him, and he lost, we could earn 200 Pesos. Of the four matches we watched, champions won four times.

To cover the house, a seven percent breakage fee on every bet was declared by a sign hanging from another post. Of all notices in the Plaza de Gallos, the most interesting was near the entry door. It advised everyone that "The management prohibits anyone from bringing guns into the building." We were not sure whether the problem was the shooting of birds for dinner or shooting of patrons over a lost bet. Nevertheless, the whole purpose of cockfighting events appeared to be more gambling than sport. Matches seldom lasted more than a minute or two, while gambling and raffle ticket vending seemed to go on for hours.

Each fight was a highly formalized event. Action began with appearance in the arena of two cocks and their handlers, one wearing a green badge the other a red badge. In addition, two other men had the sole function of attaching spurs to the birds. A fifth man, the judge or referee, completed the group who were officially involved with the cockfight. When a bird was first exhibited by its handler, it was soothed and held close to the handler's body to keep it quiet. They frequently moistened the bird's head and preened its feathers before placing it on the ground to strut for inspection by the audience. After a few minutes of this procedure, in which both cocks wandered around the vendor's who were selling bet tickets, handlers would hold their cocks up so spurs could be attached. Those for the red cock always appeared to be freshly sharpened. Those for the green cock appeared to be spares taken from the handler's pocket and strapped in place with the green identifying thong. Once spurs were in place, and had been inspected by the judge, activity of the part of the bet salesmen increased.

When a third cock was brought into the circle, a one-minute warning whistle sounded. This third bird, held by its attendant, was used to irritate and excite the fighting cocks. These later would be faced off with the newcomer, feinted forward then pulled away to encourage anger. Another method the handlers used to irritate their "pets" was to pull neck feathers out of the bird they were holding at the same time they forced it toward the decoy. Apparently the fighting cock believed the decoy had attacked and would in turn begin to attack the decoy, which would be pulled back to safety. This was done to both cocks in turn, until each was fighting mad. Then handlers picked them up and soothed their anger while turning toward the audience so the two fighters could not see each other. The decoy was removed and the fight was almost ready to begin. A final warning whistle sounded while bet salesmen made their last round of the arena before leaving the ring. Only the judge, two handlers and two angry cocks remained. The birds were placed on the ground, about ten feet from each other, inside a square scratched into dirt of the arena floor. On signal, they were allowed to fly toward each other amid a flurry of flapping wings, pulled feathers and cheers from the audience. The birds would be spurring and cutting their opponent until such time as one cock had enough and would play dead in hopes the fight would stop. Handlers and the judge would allow the possum playing to continue for a short time while the weaker bird rested. Handlers then separated the cocks, held and soothed them before facing the birds off to begin fighting all over again. It was noteworthy that the more tired the birds became, the more carefully their handlers worked with them. One method of cooling a tired bird was for a handler to fill his mouth with water and blow it on the bird's comb, toward its face and in the rectum. Another method appeared to be holding the back of the cock's head in the handler's mouth. After three or four fights the animals were bone tired and lying quietly in a mass of feathers and frustration. Now the cock fight became a matter of which one retained the greatest aggressiveness. In one match this was decided when the judge scratched two lines, about three feet apart, across the center of the ring. Each bird was placed behind its opposing line. On signal they were let loose. One was so tired it couldn't move. The other leaped forward and was declared to be the winner.

Because it continued raining, and we had no car, we decided to leave early and make certain of reaching our motel. One of the street policemen found us a taxi so that during a break between fights Renee and I could leave. We swished through water and mud to a sedan already occupied by the driver's two girl friends in the front seat. We were pointed toward the back seat of this Guadalajara taxi that should have been declared a national disaster area. It was one of the most decrepit ten-year-old vehicles we've ever been in. While we were crawling inside the driver was outside, in pouring rain, soliciting a push from the vehicle behind because our car's tired battery couldn't turn the engine over. He finally arranged the push and we began vibrating through Guadalajara in all directions at once. There were no windshield wipers and it took a full turn of the steering wheel, from right to left, just to keep the thing headed between the curbs. I am thoroughly convinced that brakes were more a matter of faith and prayer than existence in fact. As we sluiced through a sequence of flooded streets the driver and his two companions maintained a continual flow of conversation, little of which I could understand. By the time we finally arrived at our lodgings I had all fingers crossed for fear he'd stall the engine and be stuck by the lobby door for the night; with Renee and I blamed for littering the motel driveway.

Our following day's overnight stop in Morelia involved bedding in a hotel, originally the Spanish Viceroy's palace, supposedly built in the early 1800's. The walls were about three feet thick which meant that to look out a side window, we had to climb a narrow flight of steps to better lean over the window ledge and view passersby far below. While I wandered around nearby streets and took pictures, Renee changed clothes. We then began a two hour walking tour of the city. This included both parks, sidewalk markets, an old monastery that had been reopened as another hotel and the main street. Dozens of pretty female teenagers made eyes at this tall American, much to Renee's disgust. I had been told some years before that for a Latin woman to enjoy a tall man is to enjoy a virile man. Apparently they continued to connect tallness with goodness and presume I had both qualities. I should be so lucky.

This was where I purchased my single Mexican souvenir, a hand woven sombrero of the type worn by the charros of Aquascalientes. It is an unusually well styled sombrero weighing about twice what one would imagine because the weaving is extremely thick and the straw has been filled with a clay-like substance to produce a smooth appearance. It fit well and Renee said it looked "interesting." Hanging on the wall will undoubtedly make it look much better. We had lucked out and, with the help of the hotel staff, used a parking place at their front door. This mean that almost every resident of Morellia poked at our maps or fingertraced them in the dust. From the time we parked until we retired, around 9:30 that evening, 10 to15 people were always around the *Aventura* Mercury.

Between Morelia and Hidalgo, on our way to Mexico City, we crossed a mountain range which took us up to 9,272 feet. The highway was a twisting two-laner with only a moderate amount of traffic. According to our AAA guide book there were 310 curves. I am convinced this must be an understatement. All day long the steering wheel was being twisted back and forth as rapidly as I could turn it. After we passed through Toluca, a clean modern city, we found a vast complex of automobile assembly plants including Chrysler, Rambler, General Motors and a number of automotive parts suppliers. "This Highway Is Not For High Speeds" filled a large sign as we left the industrial area and entered the dual-lane highway between Toluca and the Mexican capital. Both sides of the highway were sprinkled with tiny rural houses. Their occupants were usually sitting in the front yard or washing clothes in a water-filled drainage ditch. An occasional animal or pedestrian wandered across the pavement, as though it were just another wide spot in the land, to make the 45 mile an hour limit well justified. It took nearly an hour before we reached the outskirts of Mexico City which was hidden in a veil of smog. It was later described to us as being "Just like air in Los Angeles." One minute we were driving through farm land, then suddenly found ourselves on beautifully landscaped streets amid expensive homes of the Reforma district. We were stopped by a smiling policeman "To take a census," so he said, "of strange cars entering the city." Then we wandered through more of the proverbial mad Mexican traffic to eventually find our Hotel Regis with little or no trouble. I laid the Mercury against the curb and left Renee to guard our goods and smile prettily should anyone complain. The hotel clerk sent me to a convenient garage in which to park the car and settle down for five days of pleasure and relaxation in Mexico's capital city.

Our room, the most unique we had ever been in, was on the seventh floor facing Avenida Juarez, one of the city's main boulevards. But this was an old hotel built prior to modern construction methods. There was not a single thing in the building which was plumb, square or level. The floor of our room tilted so much that from the front of the suite to the bedroom was an uphill hike. Going into the bathroom was a question of reducing speed before your head hit the door jamb, which was six inches lower than any other doorway in the room. This was demonstrated by abrasions applied to the hairless scalp of unsuspecting Bill during the simple process of seeking a hand washing. The head of our beds was so much lower than our feet that our faces were red every morning. As Renee said, "If an earthquake happens, I don't know whether to jump out the window, sit and pray, or ride the bed as it skids along the floor when the outside wall falls off." Like many tourists, we spent our first night on the town by seeking some form of a "magnificent" dinner. Without mentioning the name of the place we must report that the surroundings were fabulous and prices more so. The food mediocre. Somewhere near three in the morning I dropped Renee off in the hotel and walked to the garage to check our car. As I returned to the hotel, I passed one of Mexico City's specialists. He was standing in the shadow of a doorway, hands in overcoat pockets with slouch hat pulled down to the eyes. As I approached, the hat was lifted, a smile broke the face and a deep base voice murmured "Hey mister, you want'a meet my sister?" I explained that I had no interest in his relatives and proceeded to the hotel elevator while considering the lengths of Mexico City hospitality.

Renee wanted to get her hair done, because we were going out again the next evening, so I suggested she try one of the Americanized tourist hotels. She had no trouble making an appointment for nine in the morning because most Latin American females seldom stir until mid-afternoon. This left mornings relatively free for early-bird appointments. As Renee reported her visit, the hairdresser spoke English, knew familiar terms such as "page boy, under-combing and back of the ears" and responded well to instructions regarding height of the hairdo. What did we do while there? One event was Grand Prix auto races on Sunday with seats over the finish line. Later it was a drive to the pyramids where it was discouraging to discover that many sites had been over-restored to the point that they appeared new. However, those features which seemed original were indeed beautiful. Many colors in the paintings were bright far beyond expectations and their years of aging. Dinner in a wonderful restaurant with dancing, cocktails, wine and flaming fish. Walks around town and visits to small museums at no charge. Plus a visit to the cathedral and Juarez museum off the Zocalo, eating plantains, the sweet cooking banana, purchased from sidewalk vendors and finding funny little candy on a stick, made of chocolate rice crisp formed into the shape of a man's head. And becoming lost an average of four times each day, at no charge for missing the street signs. We found that many wide streets included what was called "Topes," or as Mexicans colloquially describe them, "The sleeping policemen." Topes were a row of large traffic buttons placed across the street. Vehicles had to slow to bump over them or they shook driver and car but good. There was no way to evade Topes. On the other hand, we have been told with good authority that they do absolutely no harm to tires and only manage to inhibit eager drivers.

A business associate told us a delightful story about statuary bordering the Avenida Reforma. It seems that some years ago Mexico ordered a statue of a Mayan Indian chief to place on a pedestal in the center of a "Glorieta" or traffic circle. Near the same time the Republic of Peru ordered a statue of one of their Peruvian ancestral chiefs. Both orders were placed with the same foundry in Paris. Unfortunately, at shipment time the Parisians were not quite sure which statue belonged where. They did the best they could. Though this happened over a hundred years ago, it was only in late 1967 that Mexico discovered that their statue was that of the Peruvian chief and Mexico's Indian ancestor was peering grandly toward the Andes of Peru.

While continuing *Aventura*, through mountains between Mexico City and Pueblo, our car's gas tank became rather shy of fuel. We'd been told of a small town, Rio Frio, where food and fuel could be obtained. The food was great. But fueling in Rio Frio proved to be most unique. The town bordered the old or Libre (Free) highway which featured a multitude of narrow curves, hundreds of trucks and cost users nothing. The American-style toll road on which we were traveling, was separated from the town by both barbed-wire fencing and rock walls. There was no gasoline station on the toll road side. The only station was on the Libre side of the barriers. Mexican ingenuity solved the problem. While we drove around the toll-road cafe's parking lot, seeking access to the town's fuel supply, a small boy came running toward us while waving a funnel made of an old Pemex (The petroleum cooperative of the Republic of

Mexico) can to ask if we wanted gasoline. After saying "Yes," he lead me to a corner of a large dirt field by the barriers. Here a man with a tired five-gallon can indicated that he would lead me to the gas station. We hiked along a dirt path, climbed over a brick wall, wandered through random bushes, passed an abandoned service station, crossed the narrow "Libre" roadway, eyeballed the general store and eventually arrived at a one-pump station. The rusty can was filled, fuel paid for and we returned to the Mercury where our guide poured gas through the small boy's funnel to nourish the engine.

Mexican toll roads were somewhat different than those in the States. Though fenced and separated by a divider, their builders were not too concerned with length of the trip. There were few off- or on-ramps and no way to turn around. You just drove from one town to the next with no stops between. Because everyone paid the same fee there was no posting of prices. For tourists it was a question of asking each booth attendant how many Pesos he required for passage.

Along this portion of the highway we saw frequent shrines dedicated to a selected patron saint who was believed to protect local citizenry from harm. One of the most unusual was serving a specified purpose. As we approached a small town between Mexico and Pueblo, workmen had half the roadway blocked while they constructed a pedestrian overpass above the highway. As part of the construction, built upon a mound of excavated earth, there was a temporary and very lovely shrine. The wooden framework of rude two by fours was covered with brilliant cloth and paper. On its raised platform, some 30 feet above the roadway, was a religious statue in front of which were numerous vases of fresh flowers. We decided that it was constructed by the workmen to watch over and protect them as they risked their necks climbing back and forth on steel girders high above the busy highway.

After dropping out of the mountains past Rio Frio we stopped in Pueblo to fill with additional gas, following our earlier one-can fueling. On learning that we were headed for Oaxaca, the service station attendant suggested an alternative route. This, he said, was very lovely, only forty kilometers longer, and well worth its slight extra trouble. It was the first time on this trip that we seriously considered the advice of anyone who suggested alternative routes. As Renee expressed it, "I'm interested to see what happens, particularly in view of the fact that a Mexican, who is fueling his family car, indicated that this would be a wise alternative."

South of Pueblo we almost immediately entered into a tropical land. As far as we could see there were broad fields of sugar cane or grazing cattle. And the highway was frequently over-bordered with lush bushes, old palm trees and anything else able to find a foothold beside the pavement. A few miles east of Veracruz we turned right through a never-ending vista of more beautiful scenery. The Gulf of Mexico was on our left with, for part of the distance, a huge lake on our right. Many times the highway, which appeared newly built, had been cut out of a hillside behind nearby villages. Accordingly we could look down into many a rustic Mexican backyard from heights of the embankment. As we passed through an area of coastal towns late in the afternoon, we saw farmers and field workers walking home with a machete at their belt while chewing on a length of sugar cane. In one small town three field hands were carrying single-point wooden plows on their backs as they left the fields. In this same area we learned about three types of highway rock piles. The first pile or row of rocks placed across our lane in the road was often painted white. This was put there by the road crew to advise drivers that somewhere immediately ahead, a portion of the road is going to be missing. Drivers had better stop, find the detour, or swing into the opposite lane. A second type of rock piling was more informal. This generally consisted of two small pyramids, six to eight inches high, placed about the distance separating a pair of car wheels. These we usually found on hills. They were used to block rear wheels of a tired truck or car to keep it from rolling downhill while being repaired. Once repairs were completed, drivers would rush madly off to make up lost time; leaving rocks in the road as a potential hazard for following travelers. A third type of rock pile was often spaced along the shoulder of a new road at somewhat regular intervals. These advised that the shoulder was newly constructed or freshly oiled and not to be driven on. For variety, Mexican road crews occasionally placed palm fronds or weed cuttings as "Don't drive here" warnings.

The porter at our hotel at Coatzacoalcos told me their parking lot was under a public market down the street. I found it quickly and drove down the ramp and went to the office to be advised that the place was open day and night so that I could leave as early as I wished. When I asked about where to park, the attendant said "Follow me." He walked ahead. I followed rather slowly. We made a sharp left between parked cars where he pointed to a space that appeared open. One look convinced me that you couldn't have gotten a Volkswagen into the hole with a shoe horn, much less the wider Mercury. After some conversation, be agreed that I was right and pointed to another space. “This one,” I said “is also much too narrow.” He proceeded and pointed to a larger open slot. I watched while he moved a pickup truck. Only then did I notice that the Mercury was being showered with water from leaky sprinkler pipes overhead. I turned on the windshield wipers in anticipation of this being a good chance to wash off the now-dirty glass. Then it struck me that this situation was rather unusual. A fire sprinkler leaking in a concrete building. I looked further to discover the fire sprinklers were not leaking. In fact, there were no fire sprinklers. What was leaking was sewage plumbing draining toilets in the market above. I quickly backed out but not before the Mercury was laced from one end to the other with drips and splashes from overhead sanitary facilities. If the Simoniz people were really concerned as to the ability of their product to protect a paint finish, we had inadvertently given it the ultimate test. More ultimate than fresh buzzard droppings from Renee’s frightened bird. The new parking slot had no sewage drips and the Mercury was locked safe and sound for the night. Retrieving it from beneath the market place only involved an early morning walk to the garage and shooing away a flock of vagrant chickens who found our car a convenient place under which to roost themselves.

Between Coatzacoalcos and Tapachula, while crossing the Isthmus of Tehuantepec toward the Pacific Ocean side of Mexico, we passed a small building on the left side of the roadway. In front was a uniformed officer who, as we sailed by, began playing a commanding “Stop” tune on his whistle. We backed up to present our tourist papers and waited while notations were duly made in the officer’s log book that the *Aventura* Mercury had passed. Another Migracion officer, much younger and sharper, talked with us in Spanish that was so clear that even I could understand much of it. He was interested in the automobile, our trip and Renee’s ability with the camera. As a gesture of good will, he told me about a bypass shortcut to Tapachula but emphasized that it was “Muy importante” to inquire in the gas station, at the main corner of the next town, as to condition of the short cut before we took it. It was sometimes very bad, he pointed out.

Like other tourists, our two day run from Mexico City to Tapachula by way of Veracruz and Coatzacoalcos reminded us of a lesson we should never have forgotten. Both Renee and I knew from previous experience to consider local guidance with suspicion. Our gasoline-supply friend at

Pueblo had given us two pieces of information. One was that the Pacific Coast trip was beautiful. It was. The second information said it was Cuarenta (40) kilometers longer, which is about equal to 25 miles. It wasn't. It was closer to 160 miles. As a result of extending an already tight two day schedule, we were faced with driving for extra hours to reach a reasonable hotel in preference to sleeping in the boondocks. And driving at night in southern Mexico was a study in patience. Not only were vagrant animals wandering or sleeping on the highway, but locals were walking on either side of the road while facing in that direction which pleased them most. Both animals and humans seemed firmly convinced that if they were within five feet of the edge of the pavement, they were completely safe. Our problem being that about the time we were giving a wide berth to men, women, children or animals on our right, a huge lumbering truck would appear in what would be described as the center of the roadway. We moved far right…fast.

Our arrival time in Tapachula, which is by the Guatemalan border, was about six in the evening. After stopping for another Aduana and Migracion inspection we headed in the general direction of what we hoped would be a comfortable hotel. Renee spotted its sign high on a hill and we turned up a steep dark road which appeared to lead somewhere. Fortunately it terminated at the Camino Real, one of the Western International Hotel chain which also operated the Century Plaza in Los Angeles. Here in complete American-style comfort, Renee and I had an interesting dinner: Made so because the hotel manager joined us to talk about the *Aventura* run. Later, while discussing the tremendous overpopulation problem in Latin America, he said "The biggest trouble the poor people have, because they can't afford contraceptives, is the church bells. They start ringing in most towns at 5:30 or 6 o'clock and accordingly wake everyone whether they have to get up or not. This makes it fairly difficult for the poor to practice birth control."

The following morning we enjoyed two pieces of very good news. One was provided by a hotel employee who washed the Mercury. Only then did we know for sure that possible paint spotting of "poopy" water from leaky sanitary facilities under the market had washed off without harm. The other piece of good news began with our second border crossing. From the hotel we drove ten miles to Mexico's Talisman frontier station where an officer pointed us into a parking place under shade of the station's canopy. We took our passports and other papers into the Migracion office where Renee and I signed exit permits. An officer stamped the documents and waved us toward a room marked Adauna. The Aduanero inspected export papers of the Mercury, said that everything was "Okay" and we were free to find our way across the Rio Suchiate bridge into neighboring Guatemala.

5

GUATEMALA

It was a slow departure from Mexico because we had to thread through pedestrians boarding or leaving an assortment of buses and trucks, then around their heaps of luggage cluttering the bridge. On Guatemala's side of the Rio Suchiate we parked in front of their Talisman Migracion station. An officer told us that the first thing to do was to pay the bridge toll: Twenty American cents per person. I had no Mexican Pesos or Guatemalan Quetzals but an American half dollar proved completely satisfactory. Our second stop was in the office where passports were inspected, stamped, and our entry listed in a large ledger containing thousands of names. Somewhere in the process, at the Migracion office, I was asked what my profession was. I replied "Editor." While listing Renee's name and passport number, the officer came to heading marked "Profession." Without being asked, I said "A good wife," which cracked up the officer and Guatemaltecans waiting to have their passports listed. Step number three was to visit offices of the Guatemalan National Police. Passports were inspected again and we were listed in a second large book to the tinkle of a badly played guitar. It was here that we heard the first questions about our license number, I replied "It is 48."

The officer grinned and asked "Is un placa oficial?"

"Yes" I replied in English, "I am a very small politician."

After the National Police were satisfied, I was directed to drive up a small hill to the Aduana offices. Here, the car was formally entered into Guatemala, which included attaching tourist license plates (No. 309) and effectively covering our "official" No. 48 Alaskan plates.

Customs formalities for passing personal luggage into Guatemala were simple. Our bags were laid on a bench for inspection while an officer poked through the car's trunk because we had previously agreed that it would be too much work to unload the entire thing. Someone asked if we had any guns. We did not and I explained we had two cameras, with which we did all of our shooting. All was satisfactory and, after visiting three more desks and meeting four Aduaneros, we were finally ready to go. The most important item being a paper pass to be given to a police officer guarding the single road in and out of the Aduana station. About five miles further on we stopped for another small roadside police booth. We were asked "Where to?" and after answering with "To Guatemala City," we were wished a good trip and waved through. The stop was repeated ten miles further on but this time the license plate, automobile papers and our passports were carefully inspected by the officer. He too advised us that everything was correct and we could proceed. A few miles after this third police booth, we were stopped for the fourth time; this by a military policeman carrying a submachine gun. His concern was twofold: Do we have a gun? Do we carry any tequila? Our answer to both being "No" we were passed without further formality. In Quezaltenango we stopped for lunch at the first of what undoubtedly will be many "Pensions," which in Latin America were boarding houses most of which fed travelers at low cost. This was the Bonifaz; a lodging house hidden behind a tired façade on a dirty street of nearly unwalkable inclination. Inside we found a lovely patio, beautiful tile floors and immaculate surroundings. The dining room was occupied by eight local couples enjoying lunch. We joined them and ordered the meal of the day. Immaculately dressed Indian girls, conveniently short enough to serve at table height, started us off with soup and concluded our meal with a delicious dessert of tree-ripened bananas, chopped Jell-O and fresh cream: Plus strong black coffee. The desert sounds rather prosaic, but believe me there is little more tasty than a tree-ripened banana as compared to tasteless long-haul green skins we buy in the United States.

After lunch at Quezaltenango, while on our way to Chichicastenango, we traveled a beautiful new paved highway marked "Central America No. 1." This was the Inter-American Highway as designated by all Central American nations. The twisting section of asphalt passed through some of the most intensely cultivated farmland we have seen. In addition, at almost every corner, Indian boys or girls would suddenly leap from crevices in the rocks and wave food, homemade weaving or pottery as we drove past. But our greatest delight occurred as we slowed for two Guatemalan boys tending a herd of about twenty goats wandering along the highway. But goats be darned. The boys were dancing to the tune of their own whistling, laughing and joyfully bouncing as they waved to us in sheer youthful exuberance. This was our first experience with a unique factor we saw much of in Guatemala: that was the level of happiness among the children. Even adults evidenced great animation and laughed often at each other's stories

It was only a two hour drive from Highway No. 1 to the small town of Santo Tomas de Chichicastenango. Much of the rural road was a dirt trail which switchbacked down into deep valleys before climbing up the other side to enter the town. It is known throughout the world as where Indians pray to pagan gods on the steps of a Catholic Church. Here we overnighted in a Pension I had visited previously. It was the Chuguila which served Guatemalan travelers and tourist-car chauffeurs. Their guided visitors and motor coach groups were separately lodged at the nearby Mayan Inn which catered to the tourist trade, most of whom were Americans. The Mayan was thoroughly modern with a grassed patio, Mariachi band in the evening, and a bartender who spoke excellent English and served complimentary Bacardi cocktails on the house.

But our Chuguila was the real fun spot as a typical middle-class Guatemalan Pension. It was built around a lovely cobblestone garden, toward which all rooms faced and in which cars were parked. After checking in, Renee changed clothes and we walked around the central plaza area of Chichicastenango. It was rather late and most Indians in town for the following day's market had retired. They were lying on the ground, or under canopies on the sidewalk, with blankets or pieces of canvas over them, sound asleep while waiting for the morning sun so they could begin their market day of selling village products to each other and tourists.

Back at our Pension we headed into the small dining room with all of six tables. Each was covered with a woven checkerboard cloth from which two Indian boys had cleared used dishes after other lodgers served themselves from an old fashioned buffet with the meal of the day. So what did everyone have for dinner at the Chuguila? It was an assembly that tasted and looked like Beef Stroganoff without noodles. Next to it was a pile of whipped potatoes. On the other side was a huge pile of fresh string beans. All of this preceded by an unidentifiable soup, both bowls of which (Renee's and mine) rapidly disappeared. For dessert, we had an unidentifiable pudding which really wasn't quite like a pudding. Included was "Cafe con leche" which is superstrong coffee laced with hot milk.

That same evening Renee had her most bride-like (which she's not) treatment so far. A small Indian boy arrived at our door after dinner, knocked quietly, entered noisily and built a charming fire in the fireplace. The next morning at 7 o'clock he again appeared (as he had promised) and built the morning fire for her. For those of you who have never had the pleasure of retiring with a fire in the fireplace, or waking up to find a new one busily warming the room, it is indeed only second best to making love under the sound of rain on a tent roof.

During our day of shopping in the Chichi market, one of the many elderly women selling Indian goods kept approaching me time after time. She was beautifully dressed in a local costume with basket-balancing pad on her head under a great basket of wondrous goodies saleable to tourists. Renee asked how it was that I knew it was the same woman each time and would speak with her in such a friendly fashion. During the next sales pitch, I showed Renee that my typical Chichi Indian, selling goods from her village, was wearing on her left thumb, presumably for protection of a hangnail, a brand new and beautifully sanitary Band-Aid.

One of the nicer things, about our subsequent drive from Chichi to Guatemala City, was the frequent friendly horn-tooting by tourist guides we had met in the Chuguila. Most of them spoke English very well and we had enjoyed dinner and breakfast conversations about the Mercury, purpose of our trip and need for careful driving on Guatemalan highways. Accordingly, on the following day, as guides and Carrolls passed and repassed each other on the highway, there was arm waving and tootling to commemorate our previous relationship. At one point, as we were rolling down a long hill nearing Guatemala City, one of the guide cars and his load of Americans was in front of us. Suddenly the driver's arm popped out his window opening as he made frantic signals which I interpreted as "Slow down and pull to the right." With good reason. Just a few yards ahead was a parking area from which we had a magnificent view of the valley in which Guatemala City was situated. The guide's tourist passengers evidenced little more interest than to glance out a window at the sight. Renee and I parked for five minutes to marvel at the panorama.

The balance of our run into Guatemala City was uneventful until we reached the downtown limits where all direction signs suddenly vanished. They were replaced by unreadable dull green wall plaques indicating which street we were on. With Renee's unusual knack of navigation and good fortune, we found the street on which our motel was located, drove in and asked about our reservations. As is common in hotels throughout the world, no one knew anything about us. Finally, after much commotion and Latin excitement, they decided to again search through a list of room reservations. Lo and behold, there we were. We were given a suite on the ground floor from where we could watch over the Mercury parked a few feet away. Like other Latin American hotel/motels, this one was protected inside a walled compound with gates closed and guarded at night. To get in, one sounded the horn. If the guard recognized you he would open the barrier and let you enter. No recognition, "No pasar."

Before retiring, we asked the desk clerk if he could find a boy to wash our car. In the morning we peeked out the window to see how the Mercury was doing. A youngster, around ten years of age, was scrubbing away on the car's dirt stained coral finish. It turned out that our car washer, named Raul, had borrowed the hotel's only plastic bucket as a water supply, an old towel for drying, and a patio chair so he could reach the car's top. It took about two hours for him to go around the Mercury and he did a beautiful job. Then he rapped on our room window to find out if we wanted our shoes shined. Needless to say, after tramping around Mexican desert areas and Guatemalan highlands, Renee and I had shoes that needed more excavating than shining. Raul came into our room to set up his equipment and, while I did some writing, commenced to polish shoes. Then he stationed himself outside the front door to our room and did a pair of Renee's slippers, her boots and my boots. Later I learned that Raul was in the Fourth grade and would pass into the Fifth in January. He said he wanted "Mucho" to learn to speak English because it would help him do business with tourists. But despite his attempt to convince us he was an old hand, we had a sneaking suspicion that he was a new boy on the route. His shoeshine box didn't appear as though it had more than a week of very little use.

Downtown Guatemala City, specifically that portion which we visited, was a modern bustling capital only slightly more rural in atmosphere than Mexico City. Perhaps its most unique feature was the many narrow, one-way streets aglitter with neon signs. Most of these extended completely over the pavement so that night traffic moved under a tunnel of brilliantly illuminated signery. How this promoted safety was unknown but it certainly provided above-average street illumination at no cost to the city. After our walking tour, dinner and subsequent taxi back to the motel we decided to call home to our daughter, Kim. Then were slightly shocked when moments after the phone connection was completed, the desk clerk banged on the door. He wondered when we were going to pay for the call. We had run up a "talk" bill of $25 (US). I shouted through the door that we would take care of it in the morning. He clumped off down the hall as I vowed to never again let such an expensive thing happen.

By now we were not too concerned to find there was no water in bathroom pipes around 2:00 or 3:00 in the morning, when a refreshing splash of cold water on the face feels so good. About 6:00 or 6:30 A.M. we could usually hear thumping and clicking in the pipes, plus a tremendous splash into the vanity bowl, when water was turned on by the morning porter. When we wanted to mail letters from Guatemala City, the most friendly advice was "Drive to the airport and mail them there." This, our friends said, insured speedy escape from the sluggish Guatemalan postal system. We easily found the airport only minutes from the city. A polite clerk weighed everything, accepted money and ran our envelopes through a postage meter. He assured us that our mail would be in the air that same day and be delivered in the United States on the morrow.

We asked one of our business contacts in Guatemala why it was that most people drove at night with interior lights of their cars turned on. He replied, "This is only new. It started about three weeks ago while a Salvadoranian was in Guatemala City for a family wedding. While driving home from the reception he didn't hear a whistle from one of our many policemen stationed at traffic points surrounding the city. The policeman raised his submachine gun and sprayed the car. He killed the driver, injured the man's wife and nicked the arm of a priest in the car. "As a result", our friend continued, "all of us now drive at night with interior lights on so the police will know that we are not guerillas or robbers. We don't want to frighten them because they are so trigger-happy."

Here Renee was introduced to what city residents called the "Submariner". This Guatemalan drink was most unique. A shot glass was filled with vodka and, while held in one hand, an upside down water glass was lowered over the shot glass until the inside bottom of the water glass was supported by the smaller glass. Both glasses were quickly inverted so the shot glass was upside down, resting on the bottom of the larger glass. But the vodka could not run out because its glass was sealed inside the water glass which was then filled with beer. In effect you had a submarine (glass) of vodka at the bottom of a glass of beer. While drinking, the vodka dribbled into the beer to modify its flavor and, in its own ungentle way, relax the bodily constitution.

Renee, being a woman of many single purposes, frequently made up her mind to do something then did it. This was our introduction to "Parvesa" which she spotted on the menu and ordered. Little did we know what was going to be served. It turned out to be boiling hot bouillon or onion soup that had been poured over a fresh egg broken into the bottom of the bowl. Thus the steaming liquid cooked the egg. Croutons floated on top of the soup which was sprinkled with freshly-grated cheese. The combination of soup, cooked egg, cheese and toast was delicious. Try it!

Our one Saturday in Guatemala City was devoted to visiting Antigua, the second or third capital (depending upon how you count) of Guatemala. In 1717 it was almost totally destroyed by a series of earthquakes. Huge churches with walls four, five or six feet thick tumbled down as their roofs became piles of debris in the aisles. Practically the entire city was destroyed to the point where the government, then under the aegis of Spain, moved to what is now Guatemala City. The current government had carefully refrained from restoring the ruins to a like-new conditions. Visitors could easily imagine themselves back to the day when terror of an earthquake, striking death and destruction, trembled the land. Antigua's narrow, one-way, cobblestone streets, fabulous University of San Marcos (The first in Central America) with its magnificent colonial facade bearing the coat of arms of King Philip of Spain on its front, contrasted with Antigua as a busy town. It was also the site of a major market for Indians living in the area and guides made it a point for each tourist in Guatemala to visit this activity. While wandering through the San Marcos Museum we gawked at two rather incongruous sights. One was the many museum guards or policemen armed with carbines, pistols and billy clubs which they seemed well prepared to use. The other unusual sight was a barefooted Indian lad wearing horn-rimmed glasses and carrying a small Kodak. His mother carried a transistor radio as they walked among exhibits and solemnly inspected the religious artifacts. Every now and then mother posed dramatically in the courtyard while son took pictures of her amid the colorful bougainvillea which charmed our eyes.

Aventura Alaska Brasil

We also found a colonial Guatemalan house where we could wander through every corner of its immense gardens and fabulous vaulted rooms loaded with ornate carved furniture. Even the kitchen was of intense interest to me. There was no stove as such. The cooking department was a series of grates built onto the top of a brick counter beneath which a charcoal fire could be lit. As you can imagine, the ceiling was dark with the smoke of many years. We saw no sink but were told that dishes were washed in the backyard where there was a large pool with laundry slots on the side walls. Next to the kitchen, and entered through a mammoth archway, was the dining room where each corner had a small waist-high fireplace for warmth. Summertime diners, seated around the broad wooden table, could look out past magnificent double doors that opened toward a courtyard where flowers waved in the gentle breeze

It was in Antigua that Renee saw her first Latin funeral. The procession's black coffin, gaily decorated with gold paint, was carried by four strong men. And followed by a half-dozen barefoot members of the family, walking along the side of busy streets on their way to the cemetery. We also bumped into one of the tourist guides, leading his American flock, who we had met previously in Chichicastenango. He greeted us as long lost friends and insisted we accept his business card. Then we met Lupe, Constantia and Maria, all because of Renee's persistence in obtaining information from every available source. She had disappeared for a few minutes and, when found, had cornered every official Guatemalan tourist executive and was extricating reams of information from them. Their primary suggestion was that we should drive about 5 kilometers out of town to the "First" capital of Guatemala: At this time a small and unimportant village. This we decided to do. Only a short distance along the suggested paved road we saw a direction sign and turned up its dirt lane between columns of trees overhanging the route. We drove further than expected before realizing that we were on the far side of a village. It seemed we had missed the earlier turnoff and would eventually come to a second entry road. As we approached this intersection, two attractive Indian girls rushed madly onto the road and began waving their arms, indicating we should stop. We did. Almost in unison they shouted "Buenos tardes, Senor" and launched into a rapid and thoroughly incomprehensible speech in Spanish, while pointing toward a magnificent display of hand-woven goods hanging from nearby trees. They hadn't finished when an Indian woman showed up to address us in Spanish I could understand.

We parked in the shade and walked over to the grove. On ropes strung between tree limbs were some of the most beautiful Indian weavings we had seen in Guatemala. The girls and lady assured us that all were made by hand. The girls showed us how they wove while the woman exhibited the wares, including shawls, skirts, blouses and napkins. But none of these were completed. What she held were pieces of hand-woven cloth of the size and shape to provide the item or the garment you wished to make. Six napkins were woven in a row as one piece of cloth. Buyers would have to cut them apart and hem each individually. Blouses were woven in the shape of a gigantic cross with a hole in the center. By putting one's head through the hole, and allowing the blouse to fold over, it became a T-shaped garment with woven designs in the proper place. Among miscellaneous bits of information we picked up, was the point that many Guatemalan Indians have abandoned their national costume by virtue of economic necessity. It took so long to weave costumes on a home loom, and the cost of living had become so high, that Indian women seldom took time to work their looms. Instead they assisted their husbands in farming or other income-producing tasks. Male costumes being the most difficult to produce, were said to be the soonest replaced with western-style clothing which was much less expensive. She told us that many children were going directly into western clothing and never passed through the stage of wearing traditional costumes.

For many this was said to be logical progress because Indian youths were known to leave their homes in mountain villages for the lowlands or small towns and seek employment as laborers or factory hands. They quickly gave up native costumes as soon as they could afford western clothes which were more suitable while making a living away from home. They would speak Spanish at work and only use their Indian language around the house. Eventually, it was suggested, regional costumes and languages would pass into history to be replaced by a massive wave of western clothing. One local observer pointed out that much has been made of the effect of the transistor radio on the ethnic and sociological background of the natives. "However," he added, "I believe the cotton loom has done more to level their society and change their method of living than anything else. It has provided low-cost clothing which does not in any way represent regional choice or custom."

Later we stumbled onto the most obvious way in the world to make sure we had pictures of ourselves together. It was quite easy for me to take a picture of Renee; equally simple for her to take a picture of me. Getting the two of us in the same photograph had required diligence in the order of a self-timer and camera support. While visiting ruins of Antigua, we noticed that families were usually faced with the problem of father taking all the pictures and, of course, never appearing in any them. A nearby Mexican family had this problem so I offered to take a picture of the family, with father in it, so that they could all be seen together. He, out of courtesy, offered to do the same for us. Which was what I wanted to have him do in the first place.

Finding our way out of Guatemala City on Sunday morning, for the drive to Salvador, was no problem at all. We merely read the AAA instructions, applied them onto a convenient map supplied by the hotel and promptly drove the wrong way. Renee suggested we turn left. We did, found the proper street, turned right, and proceeded along a back alley which had a stop sign at every corner. This lasted about 15 stop signs before we dead-ended into a multi-point intersection with six streets all coming together, none of them marked. The question being, which of the six was Central American Highway No. 1 leading from Guatemala City toward El Salvador? We asked a nearby policeman. He looked at us as though we were crazy. We could almost see the wheels turning as he must have thought, "Everyone knows which is No. 1". When we repeated the question again, he flapped arms in the direction of what did not look to be a highway to anywhere. Away we went. The first mud colored marker by the side of the road indicated we were already 5 Kilometers from the center of Guatemala City, a few hundred feet past our helpful policeman, and pointed toward El Salvador. Whereas the northern section of the nation, nearest Mexico, was extremely hilly with every mound extensively cultivated, this southern portion of the country was a contrasting flatland which dropped rapidly down to green tropical lowlands. Though there was some agricultural activity it appeared to us that cattle raising was the most important activity. At the San Cristobal border, departure from Guatemala began with parking under a concrete shed and taking our papers into Migracion where Renee and I were stamped out of the country. Across the aisle, at Aduana, they released the car and removed tourist plate No. 309 after asking me to sign a blank form recording that I had left the nation. In another office, at the National Police desk, our names were listed in a huge register and our passport numbers noted. Exit formalities were less than 30 minutes for Guatemala.

6

EL SALVADOR

It was a drive of less than 50 feet across the frontier into El Salvador. There, underneath the roof of a double-arched building, we were the only car passing in either direction for over a half hour. First the Migracion officer checked passports and listed us into the country. Then the National Police officer checked passports and listed us in their registration book. Finally the Aduanero did his car entry bit. Here, as in Guatemala and Mexico, we were given a large carefully typed form which listed characteristics of our automobile and options built into it: such as radio, air conditioning, etc. Our final stop was for a second Aduana inspection by army soldiers. They did a thorough job of asking about every box in the car and inspecting everything we opened but were nice enough not to bother when we slightly protested the opening of sealed packages. Total time through both Guatemalan and Salvadorian stations was a little less than one hour, about the same as from Mexico into Guatemala.

The run from the Salvadorian frontier into the capital city of San Salvador was an uneventful tour over the somewhat narrow, winding road. At first traffic was light. But the closer we came to the capital, the more large buses, small jitneys and private cars clogged the thoroughfare. At one point we turned onto a small side road to look for a ruin signed as the "Taz Muhal." It was not like anything found in India. The site in El Salvador was a lump of Mayan-type ruins surrounded by a gated barbed-wire fence. We left the ruins for San Salvador and booked into the Hotel

Intercontinental, situated high on a mountain slope near an extinct volcano which in ancient time had destroyed the entire city of San Salvador. From our friendly little Motel Plaza in Guatemala City to the Intercontinental involved a little less than 200 miles of driving. The difference was 1,000 miles apart. In the Plaza, we enjoyed Guatemalan travelers, a number of delegates to an economic conference concerning all Central America, a group of naval officers, a few army officers, a Central American electronics businessman, a retired TWA pilot waiting out the growing of rubber on his 6,000 acre plantation and random locals of the city. In the Intercontinental we found retired American school teachers and well-to-do tourists. We were greeted by a doorman, a porter, a boy to wash the car and a desk clerk who spoke enough English to handle room negotiations. However, everyone's comprehension failed miserably when informed (in English) that continual operation of our Mercury engine was to be expected. This matter surfaced about 30 minutes into our room when the taxi dispatcher called to tell us the engine was running. Because we had explained this so often in Spanish, which seemed to work rather well, we were able to get the message across. "There is no problem with our Mercury: It just sits there and operates and operates and operates."

Rejoining the world after a night's sleep at the Intercontinental wasn't difficult. Surrounding the structure were a number of private homes, all of which had the most confused chickens in the world. Because the hotel was brilliantly illuminated at all times, the chickens assumed it was daytime all night. For awake they were, roosters and hens alike, one crowing or replying after the other. In the middle of the night it was ludicrous to hear one cock crow and hundreds more join in a rhythmic symphony of barnyard commotion. In addition to chickens, each house owned at least one dog. As pedestrians passed each dog would set up a howl of warning to indicate a stranger was near. Added was the frequent blowing of police whistles to create a night-long commotion that was not only unique but fell far short of "jungle noises" Renee had been hopeful of hearing. On the positive side, I had turned my bed completely around, end for end, so that when I sat up in the morning, I faced the beautiful San Salvador Volcano, on the tip of which was parked a fleecy white "stocking cap" of a cloud.

Later that morning, prior to our Salvadoranian press conference, I drove to a nearby Esso station to have the Mercury washed. The new station, only five months old, was beautifully clean and magnificently laid out. In front two magazine racks were loaded with American automobile magazines. Next to them was a shelf of freshly baked bread and cookies. Inside there was another rack of Spanish-language pocket books, comics and three used tires. For Kim I bought a copy of Archie and one of Batman, in Spanish and printed in Mexico. I'm sure they confused her completely.

Although El Salvador is one of my favorite nations, perhaps because it is so small, it was a study of violent contrast. There seemed to be factories of every size and variety here, including many producing brands we were familiar with in the United States. There were many new cars and buses though we were told that the import duty on a car priced in excess of $4,000 was 100%. One young man told us the import duty on his $3500 Pontiac amounted to $1400. There were several television stations, numerous radio channels, and daily and weekly newspapers. But outside the city limits the nation was intensely tropical rural: Mud huts, tin roofs, ox carts, barefoot adults and pantless children.

Our wildest day in El Salvador included the press conference with a half-dozen non-English-speaking journalists attempting to communicate with two some-Spanish-speaking travelers, a trip around town, luncheon at a delightful Indonesian restaurant and visiting a Central American art exhibition which included a number of extremely good paintings. Plus changing our dollars for the nation's Colons. The evening was equally different. A local automobile editor arrived to have dinner with us and brought along his Cuban girl friend, a cabaret singer at the hotel.

While billed as "The" luxury hotel of Central America, the International was locally famous for a lack of an acceptable dining room and modestly incompetent service. We thought it was one of the funniest chain hotels we had visited. Examples? We requested reservations for a further hotel of the same chain but no desk clerk was really sure how that matter could be accomplished. Up to the time we departed, word was not available as to success or failure of this service (?). On return from our first trip downtown we failed to find a single sign directing traffic to the hotel driveway. A local Spanish-speaking business contact spent 15 minutes trying to locate us in the hotel. Neither the desk clerk nor telephone operator were sure where we could be found and claimed they had been ringing our room for the total time. Our telephone rang once, at the end of his 15 minute search, when our friend finally made contact. In later discussion, he said, "They have no competition which makes it easy for them to do as little as they wish".

At one time, El Salvador could boast of having one of the few active volcanoes in the world, Izalco. Familiarly known as "The lighthouse of the Pacific," it was used by mariners to navigate nearby Pacific ocean waters. A few years ago, an enterprising hotel chain decided to build a modern establishment near Izalco so visitors could enjoy both tropical scenery and thrill of an active volcano in their front yard. The hotel was completed and ready to open when Izalco stopped functioning. It has not done any more than produce a few puffs of smoke since. One Salvadorian lady expressed concern by saying that when the volcano does blow, it is quite likely to result in a severe earthquake. Superstitious locals were said to believe that volcanic Gods became angry because, with the hotel overlooking them, they could be spied upon. Accordingly, they turned themselves off and volcano'd no more.

We did our part to balance the Colon budget of San Salvador when we left the next morning about 7:00 A.M. This early start enabled us to escape some downtown traffic while allowing opportunities to take pictures as we headed south on our way toward Nicaragua. Nevertheless, the narrow busy highway outside of town was thick with morning buses traveling in both directions, walking field workers, ox carts and stray dogs. Livestock must have been more valuable here than in Mexico for most pigs and cattle were on halters to prevent them from being damaged by passing vehicles. When there was a car a short distance ahead of us, walkers would hear that first vehicle but did not always hear us following. Unless warned they stepped back onto the pavement directly into our path after the first car passed. Practically every rural bus was overloaded and many carried passengers and huge bundles of cargo on roof racks, plus extra passengers standing on the rear bumper. One young man leaned around the edge of his bus to watch us coming toward him in the opposing lane. He maneuvered himself as far out on the bumper as he could and then projected his foot in an attempt to kick the Mercury. Considering that the two vehicles were passing at a velocity approaching 100 miles an hour, he certainly would have suffered a broken foot or broken leg had he been successful in his sporting gesture of derring-do.

We spent nearly an hour passing controls of El Salvador and Honduras though the Salvadorian portion was quick and to the point. There was no inspection of luggage. Only registration of our passports and inspection of papers covering movement of the car through their nation. We then crossed the Puente Goascoran into Honduras.

7

HONDURAS

Although we were going to pass through Honduras within not more than four hours on the run to Nicaragua; our passports were listed by Migracion, the national police registered us, the traffic police registered us, the car received a registration certificate adapted for transiting the nation and an Aduanero inspected the back seat to see what we were carrying.

No matter how you slice it, two border crossings in a day was almost one too many. Or to put it the other way, going from Honduras into Nicaragua was going from the sublime to the ridiculous. As compared to time consuming paperwork of entry, the Honduras exit was quick and efficient. They checked passports, listed us as leaving the country, accepted our paperwork identifying the car, stamped it out and gave us a pass to leave their frontier compound.

That was it.

8

NICARAGUA

We rolled about 200 feet down a slight grade into Nicaragua, parked and I went into the border station to stand in the line for Migracion. The standees were somewhat orderly but passport handling was utter confusion. There was no order or routine. Ours, and several others, were on top of the stack to begin with and at the bottom near the finish. It was just a case of too many hands in the soup and no one watching the fire. The next stop was at Aduana for documents to move the car across the country. The young man in charge of the desk apparently had no taste for his job or couldn't read or write. He would pick up pieces of paper then lay them down, open passports and close them, inspect driver's licenses and find them difficult to decipher, or act as though it were impossible to discover a motor number on papers printed in Spanish. In addition, he was so completely slow that when he left his desk for a few minutes the locals around me broke into conversation about the boy's complete and idiotic inefficiency. I was lucky because I was able to hand our papers to his helper who moved to another typewriter and prepared an impressive set of paperwork. One set to enter our car into the country and the other to leave. This took longer than expected inasmuch as he couldn't believe the Mercury had license No. 48. Then he had to see the car before he realized it wasn't a (19)'48 model. This took a little explaining but the next point was even more confusing. He wanted to know when the license plates expired. I told him in May of the following year. He found this equally difficult to believe and inspected the front plate through the office window to decide for himself. What he finally typed I never knew. All in all, it took us an hour and a half to get into Nicaragua. With papers completed it was time to drive on. I got into our Mercury and an armed guard came over, said "No" and me pointed back to the Aduana. Using my head for a change; I insisted that he come along with me. A dripping ice cream cone was in his right hand while the left hand caressed the gun on his hip, perhaps to impress me. Once inside we bellied up to the table of the Aduana officer where "Ice cream cone" began to sputter that I did not have the proper papers for the car. By now I realized what his problem was. I showed him papers at the same time the Aduanero told him to get his fat can back outside, because I do have all the papers. It seemed that the guard causing this minor disturbance was the one who inspected cars. Whether he now felt a little abashed or whether his cursory inspection was normal, at least all I had to do was open the trunk while he looked in then said to close it. As I opened the driver's door, he mumbled "Good-bye" and walked away.

Renee had noticed that a Nicaraguan woman, also doing baggage inspection, not only went through luggage with great thoroughness but took time to read newer books and magazines belonging to bus passengers that preceded us. Certainly a high spot of informality in customs inspection which I was pleased that we had escaped. In addition, Renee had entered into conversation with a salesman traveling in the same direction that we were. Somewhere along the line, she mentioned that we planned to stop in a Nicaraguan town called Tipitapa for lunch. It was on the edge of Lake Managua and was noted throughout Central America for the number of restaurants serving fish dinners. Her English-speaking acquaintance replied that he too "saved his dinner" until he arrived there. She mentioned the specific restaurant which featured fish swimming in tanks from which patrons could select their meal. That one, he said, was particularly favored by tourists but he had never eaten there. He preferred another place that appeared bad on the outside but served fine fish.

We had not driven far inside Nicaragua when Renee had her first taste of a tropical rainstorm. We had stopped for fuel, underneath thumping clouds and thunderless lightning, at a small station where the attendant warned us that within a very few minutes rain would be coming down quite heavily. Right he was. It hit so hard that we could barely see 50 feet in advance. The relatively flat roadway became inches thick with water and puddles sprayed over the car as we forged ahead. Other traffic, perhaps less confident than I, hogged the middle of the road and crawled one step faster than parking. Nevertheless, we maintained forward movement during the entire storm with both of us driving. It was as frequent for Renee to say, "Dodge that cow," as it was for me to say, "Damn, we sprayed another pedestrian," when we splashed man or beast. There was nothing we could do about people caught walking in the rain. Adding to the confusion, at the crest of one hill we saw a dim object ahead in the center of the road. It turned out to be a motorcycle rider and his girlfriend, sans taillight, chugging along in this tremendous downpour. We slowed and passed gently to ease their discomfort. After about an hour the rain had slowed to a strong drizzle as we rolled into Tipitapa, the little town where Renee had been told we could find excellent fish dinners.

We selected the "Alpine" as cleanest appearing of three restaurants. It seemed to be a family operation because a father-type came to our table to ask if he could help us. His English was little better than our Spanish and accordingly it took a combination of both of us to order dinner much to the amusement of a number of Nicaraguan families in the dining room. Every window and door was open to keep the place cool, although one sign listed it as being "Air Conditioned" which I guess thus it was. We ordered what was named Pescado Sin Espinas, a local fish from Lake Managua with a head half the size of its body. All bones and backbone were removed, the fish baked and then covered with a sauce which included thin sliced tomatoes across the top. It was served with thick Nicaraguan tortillas and rice. The cook had used a small apple corer to cut the center out of a lemon (or lime) then notched both ends to make a decorative and seedless method of providing lemon juice for fish lovers.

We left Tipitapa while it continued raining and slushed the remaining six dark miles to Nicaragua's capital, Managua, where Renee's uncanny sense of navigation paid off again. Although it was so clouded that we could only see about a block ahead, she pointed us up the proper avenue on which our Gran Hotel of Managua was located. The entrance to the foyer was blocked by a tiny car half in and half out of the rain but the exit was wide open. We drove to the exit and backed under the protective canopy. Renee went to our room while I circulated eight or ten blocks of the city before finding the hotel parking lot hidden behind a nearby service station. The Mercury was parked and the damp attendant given to understand that it was all right for the engine to run day and night with parking lights on. Nevertheless, we were not in our room ten minutes before the telephone rang. The hotel operator was helpfully telling us that our car's engine was operating and parking lights were on. We explained to her that this was right and proper. A few minutes later the telephone rang again. This time it was the owner of the service station in front of the parking lot. He re-explained that lights were on and the engine was running. He too was assured that this was satisfactory as it was a "Test" car. When the telephone rang a third time, we decided not to answer and rolled over to sleep in hopes someone would read one of the signs on the Mercury which explained the engine-test situation.

Our Gran Hotel was an archaic hacienda-type hostelry with the oldest rooms faced inward to the central patio. Though the name may sound upscale impressive, the residents appeared tired, disillusioned, hot and sweaty with rumpled open shirts, unpressed trousers and a never-ending supply of tall drinks on their table. As Renee saw it: "This place looks more like a tropical hotel than those shown in motion pictures." This was the same hotel in which, during the civil unrest of January 1967, about 50 tourists were held as hostages by individuals objecting to the then current form of Nicaraguan government. As told to us, the insurgents holed up in the hotel while bargaining tourists in return for safe conduct. During some 36 hours of sporadic fighting, battle tanks were said to have parked in surrounding streets and peppered the hotel with nonexplosive shells. Two businessmen from the United States reported lying on the floor of their room, at the same time shells were flying in the windows to wreck the ceiling and shower them with plaster. One man said he heard violent knocks at the door, which he refused to open, then heard other doors being kicked open amid the sound of machine guns. However, clearer minds have said that rapid-fire sounds he heard were from fighting outside and not from insurgents destroying hotel guests.

Managua was everything a tropical capital city could be. Busy, bustling, hot, humid, noisy, and often funny. Where else in the world, but in Latin America, could you see a horse cart blocking traffic after the signal light glowed green while the driver patiently waits for his horse to relieve it's kidneys to the noisy accompaniment of impatient taxi horns and laughing pedestrians. Hopefully the horse was as relieved to be relieved as traffic was to again be on the move. The narrow sidewalks of Managua were not only crowded with pedestrians but we usually had to dodge drippings from air conditioners which hung from every window.

Jaywalking was common, usually accompanied by thc screech of brakes as unschooled farmers and their offspring attempted to dodge unfamiliar vehicles. We were told of a game called "Nicaraguan Roulette" played by Managua's motorcycle riders. Though some one-way downtown streets were controlled by traffic signals, or stop signs, most of the busy intersections were not. Accordingly it had become a great sport among younger motorcycle riders that, when riding home late at night while feeling no pain, they paid no attention to signal, stop sign, oncoming traffic, or uncontrolled intersections. It was considered a form of heroism to ride thusly without stopping for anything. According to reports the average fatal collision between rider and vehicle was less than one motorcyclist a month. Nicaraguans considered this a good average for such a dangerous sport.

A less violent major sport of Nicaragua was the raffle. Almost every store we passed was raffling off rooms of furniture, television sets or cameras. On one street a new Mercedes was the raffle prize, with ticket proceeds given to a local charity. One resident said it was common for businessmen to select products that couldn't be sold and donate them to a charity at cost. This put the merchandise into circulation and deprived a businessman of the pleasure of losing money on merchandise that had been a bad buy or had been returned by the purchaser.

While in Managua we were fortunate that one of our business contacts was able to take time to show us much of the area. One of the first places visited was a lovely park overlooking the city. Though tiny, it had two wading pools and two exhibits. One was an old steam locomotive about which I knew nothing. The other was a Douglas A26 Attack Bomber built with a 75MM cannon to chase Rommel across the desert when his battle tanks were overrunning the sands of Africa. Then we visited the Nicaraguan Army Officers' Club, located in front of the Presidential Palace, and took pictures from its magnificent balcony overlooking the city. Next was luncheon in a luxury restaurant said to be the finest in Managua. As we dined, tropical winds blew across our table and kept us comfortable and cool. Sissies among the restaurant's patrons were chilling in an "Air-Conditioned" enclosure inside the building.

Later we toured a hill behind the President's Palace, the rear of which was protected by a large lake. The point of interest being that the Palace was said to be connected with the American Embassy, three blocks away, by an underground passage. In the event of internal upset the President could flee to a safe refuge. The lake was a popular laundry spot for “muchachos” of nearby houses. At the time of our visit the shore was shoulder to shoulder with these women doing their washing. Shoreline bushes were winter-white with drying laundry. It was obvious from our viewpoint, high above the water, that excess soap was threading and coloring the water from areas where the women were washing. We then drove for about 45 minutes to the town of Granada which, like its namesake in Spain, is an ancient collection of historic colonial buildings of which many were obviously tired. After threading our way through central Granada, we toured a few miles along the shore of Lake Nicaragua before boarding a launch for a trip to view tiny islands dotting the lake. About half were equipped with ornate summer residences of ten to fifteen rooms; others hosted simple bachelor shacks for weekend fun and games. Each had a boat slip to which was moored water transportation ranging from the latest Chris Craft launch down to one-lung punts which had been hammered together to provide basic transportation services. To build a swimming pool island lovers merely dug a hole in the ground and lined it with concrete or dammed off a portion of the lake front. The area was so charming that Renee wasted no time picking her vacant island and suggesting a credit-card down payment for future residence.

The next morning we rolled out of Managua toward Costa Rica, our next scheduled destination. “Quickest inspection yet,” was Renee’s comment after we passed through Nicaraguan and Costa Rican frontier inspections. Leaving Nicaragua, required little more than a visit to Migracion for registry of our passports, typing of a short form by the Aduanero to release the car, and back to Migracion to find someone to approve the form the Aduanero had typed. This took about ten minutes.

9

COSTA RICA

After about 300 feet across what appeared to be No Man's land between the two nations we pulled into the Costa Rican frontier station. There a Migracion officer registered our passports and directed us toward the Aduana. Here a simple form was quickly typed for my signature. The form approved circulation of the Mercury within the country for 15 days. At the same time, a second officer prepared a multicolored certificate which he pasted inside our right rear quarter-window. Including a short break for a cold soda at the frontier restaurant, Costa Rica's total time was 35 minutes and involved no inspection of luggage. When I commented on this to Renee, she told me that other cars passing through, licensed to nations of adjacent countries, had been thoroughly inspected.

After leaving the border area we drove about 60 miles before stopping for lunch in Liberia. This was at the El Brahmador, a small roadside restaurant and motel famed throughout Central America for the quality of its accommodations. We had a simple lunch of roast beef sandwiches and soda. In addition to good food, a unique aspect was our impression of the other patrons. Most of them seemed to be cattle ranchers from the area who wore expensive wrist watches and dangled heavy decorative gold pieces on belt chains which led into their pockets.

A few miles past our lunch stop I jokingly remarked that I'd like to start back for Alaska because driving had become much too boring. A few miles later I was at a junction leading to the Pacific Ocean port of

Puntarenas where the highway changed. What had been boring pavement became endless miles of broken surfacing, pot holes, chuck holes, no pavement, missed pavement, washboard, gravel and ruts. For nearly 100 miles we bumped and thumped along in a manner strongly reminiscent of the "1,000 mile detour" which Canada had labeled the Alaskan Highway. Suddenly we zoomed onto a four-lane toll road leading from the national airport to Costa Rica's capital, the city of San Jose; a distance of 16 kilometers. Unfortunately our entry into the city coincided with the entire population either heading home or going shopping. Every narrow, three-car wide, street was totally blocked with crawling traffic. In some instances, parking at both curbs limited car movement to one center lane. Mixed well with buses, small trucks, dozens of motorcycles, frequent imported cars which take little space plus an occasional large American car; it was complete and utter confusion. We found our downtown hotel and a parking space at the same time: Luckily. Bags were unloaded into the Royal Dutch lobby from where we were escorted to one of their 60 rooms. After dinner we moved the Mercury off the street to a public garage where it was securely locked in a stall. The attendant was given instructions that it was important for the engine to be kept running and if it stopped would he please take a taxi to the hotel, wake me and explain the problem. San Jose, unlike other cities in Latin America, had no laws, or did not enforce existing laws, regarding the use of auto horns in downtown streets. All day, and far into the night, vehicle, bicycle and motorcycle horns mingled into a continuous symphony of transportation, although true music lovers may feel this was not much evidence of talent. From our vantage point, six floors above the street, it was quite something to watch a traffic jam develop at the major intersection below and then hear horns sounding from a block away to keep company with noisemakers on vehicles involved in the blockage.

On the other hand San Jose traffic police appeared to have been instructed to be helpfully efficient. Like traffic officers in Mexico, they were equipped with screw drivers to remove license plates from offending vehicles. But I saw one traffic officer, with captive license plate in hand, helping a lad push his failed motorcycle across the intersection into a parking place. On another street I saw an officer pouring gasoline into the carburetor of a stalled car while its owner attempted to start the engine. Additional traditional hospitality of the Costa Ricans popped up one morning while I was wandering about the city while photographing.

I had stopped on a corner to survey the area for pictorial possibilities. While there, a man walked out of a nearby six-story building and addressed me in English, saying, "Oh you are taking pictures. If you'd like to use the top of our building you are welcome to do so."

Later, while taking my usual siesta, I was awakened by a siren below our hotel window. It was from the initial vehicle of a ten-car parade for one of the "Queens" of Costa Rica. The siren was from a city ambulance followed by a public address truck wearing the signs of a major laxative manufacturer. Each of the two following cars carried a "Princess." The Queen, wearing a wildly colorful Paris-type creation, was sitting atop the seat back of the third convertible while waving to the crowd. Walking on each side of her were Boy Scouts, Cub Scouts and members of other youth organizations throwing confetti and handing out leaflets for whatever charitable cause the queen was espousing. The next vehicle was a huge semi-truck carrying a Boy Scout band playing Costa Rican tunes. This was followed by a soft drink truck making further public announcements over a vibrating speaker system. Bringing up the rear was a unit of the radio patrol police. Few leaflets reached the hands of those on the sidewalks. Most of the confetti went into the hair of young female passersby which makes it worth noting that throughout Central America, Costa Rica is noted for its beautiful women. And indeed they are taller, of lighter complexion, more graceful and usually prettier than those of most other nations through which we traveled. It is not that other nations do not have beautiful women, it is just that there seems to be an eye-filling abundance of them in Costa Rica.

Later we asked a Costa Rican businessman, who had been educated in the United States, for his opinion of American women. He said, "Though American women do not have good manners, nor do they understand and appreciate good manners, they are easier to get to know. You can know much about them in one weekend. But Costa Rican girls lead such sheltered lives, and live so close to home, you could go with a girl for three years and never really know her." His sentiments were echoed by a second businessman who pointed out that in the U.S., one can date a girl for many months without feeling any obligation toward marriage. He explained that in Costa Rica, if you take the same girl out twice discussions and rumors immediately begin to fly that a marriage is involved. He said that no matter where you went, the mother or father of the girl would eventually show up to make sure everything was all right.

While Costa Rican girls are beautifully educated to be hostesses and housekeepers, they seldom were aware of business problems and importance of developments that could influence their husband's business, he concluded.

In Costa Rica we had our first conflict with national affairs while obtaining visas for Panama. Months before, in Los Angeles, the lady Panamanian consul declined to give us a visa valid for more than 30 days. Unfortunately, our trip from Los Angeles to the Panamanian border was scheduled to take 34 days. This meant we had to get an extension in Costa Rica. But our arrival in San Jose, and appearance at the Panamanian consulate, coincided with a Panamanian Independence Day. Now the consul, like all good men, could have very easily closed up and remained at home. On the other hand, the need to make an extra dollar and be helpful to travelers prompted him to remain open. Outside his office door was a large sign which stated, in both English and Spanish, that visas during Panamanian Independence Day would cost five American dollars each. He told me that it was not possible to extend our old visas at no charge and the only thing he could do would be to give us new visas. When I asked for a receipt he wrote into the passports that I had paid the requested $5 fee for each one of us.

So far we had been the subject of a number of press conferences since leaving the United States. They produced considerable useful local publicity for our sponsors: Mercury, STP, Firestone and Simoniz, as well as business enhancement for their local representatives. It was most interesting how different the conferences had been. In Mexico City the conference was an evening cocktail party with considerable drinking, modest amounts of food and everyone standing. A few reporters informally asked questions though most were content to take the press release and relax with ice cubes surrounded by liquid refreshment. In Aguascalientes, a reporter and his photographer, while driving about town in their official car marked "Prensa", found us in our hotel just as we sat for dinner. Nothing would do but we must go to the street, be photographed and be interviewed by them next to the Mercury. To make up for the intrusion they brought us ten reproductions of their paper the following day. In Pueblo one of our most amusing press incidents occurred in this land where the Carabina watches over morality of her female charges with a wary eye. One elderly reporter, who apparently had a number of young daughters at home, asked me how it was I had this young girl traveling with me on such a long trip. After I explained that Renee was my wife, I couldn't be sure whether his responding wink meant he was proud of me for having such a lovely wife or he suspected I was living it up a bit and explaining away my "Companera" the easy way. In Guatemala City a Ford public relations representative took Renee and I to one of the major newspapers. There, in a second floor editorial office, we were interviewed with the aid of a translator. Then we all trooped downstairs to be photographed where the car was parked next to an unfriendly parking meter. The photographer placed the reporter in the foreground as the most prominent part of the picture. Nevertheless, his story did run and provided good publicity to all four sponsors of our trip. In El Salvador the Ford representative called a press conference at which eight representatives of national papers appeared. Interviewing was accomplished in the lobby of the hotel. A semicircle of folding, theater-type seats held media people, who faced Renee and me sitting on a couch. A few pictures were taken here before we wandered outside to the parking lot, for additional questions and extensive picture taking. In Nicaragua, the local Firestone representative was kind enough to invite us to lunch at a delightful restaurant. Almost before we could order our lunch, a photographer appeared and we charged outside to where the car was parked on the street. It was maneuvered for the best lighting for pictures taken of us with the Firestone man. These pictures, we were told, were going to be used for future release to the local newspapers. In San Jose, Firestone and STP representatives merged forces and called a conference for the national press at the Union Club which was, so we were told, "The" club of San Jose. About a dozen reporters, including one female, showed up. They were seated at a rather formal U-shaped group of tables facing Firestone and STP representatives. Renee and I were at a separate row of tables across from both groups. After a brief presentation the reporters asked questions before the conference broke up. We then merged into informal groups for detailed discussions about the trip. While this was all going on, every few minutes Renee and I would be called outside for pictures with the car or to pose with an STP or Firestone representative displaying product samples. Meanwhile waiters were constantly at hand serving drinks and pleasantly hot Bocas. In addition to reporters, I was surprised to learn later that two representatives of the Costa Rican government tourist department had attended. Both had been concerned about our experiences while crossing their frontier and said that border controls were their major problem area for visitors driving personal cars.

While buying gasoline in Costa Rica we were again involved in a situation that happened often during *Aventura.* The owner of the station appeared and asked what the car was doing. We explained: "Number One, it was on a long trip from Alaska to Brasil. Number Two, it is a test car (in which the Mercury engine was operating continuously) using STP in the oil, Simoniz on the finish and Firestone tires." This is all we would say. Within a few minutes, when the typical and usual crowd appeared, the station manager delivered a full-bore five minute lecture on the Mercury's activities. He did an excellent job of "selling" the *Aventura* project to curious Costa Rican citizens.

During an evening out in San Jose we passed the central plaza with its many small restaurants and coffee shops. In front of the restaurants were gathered free-lance musicians, each dressed in his best. Some were wearing a typical Costa Rican costume, others sharp night club clothes or tuxedo trousers and gold lame' jackets. All had at least one instrument, usually a guitar or brass horn. As we were told: When San Jose residents plan a party they drive to the plaza and bargain with musicians until they have assembled a combination at a price they could afford to pay. The musicians were taxied to the house where they entertained for the agreed upon length of time and were eventually driven home. In the morning they usually reported to more stable jobs and used musical moonlighting as additional income.

Political stability of Central America, often considered a joke by North Americans, was in fact at a higher level of permanency than most people believe. A good example of this was Costa Rica. At one time local papers and a number of smaller radio stations broadcast reports that a revolution was imminent in the nation. The President, instead of throwing the journalists in jail, as might have happened in other years, called upon the newspapers to report the facts. "Although there is always conversation about overthrowing the government by irresponsible people," the President said, "in fact there is no problem at all. Accordingly, would irresponsible journalists please check their stories before broadcasting them to the nation as a whole. Because," continued the President, "you are not only disturbing the peace of our country, but you affect the good economic relations we enjoy with other nations."

It may be of interest to know of the method by which we handled the many rolls of film exposed on this trip. Our procedure was to retain all such film until we reached a capital city, such as San Jose. We would insert two rolls of color film in one sturdy Kraft envelope from the supply carried with us. Our collection of numerous envelopes containing film were then airmailed from the central post office or airport. This insured the most rapid delivery to the United States. More importantly, should an envelope go astray it would only be a loss of two rolls instead of the ten or more that might be shipped in a larger package.

Instead of writing notes as *Aventura* progressed, a tiny Stenorette tape recorder was always on the front seat of the car throughout the trip. As events transpired each situation was recorded at the time it affected the *Aventura* run. Every tape from our electronic notebook was repackaged in its own box which was then tucked into a Kraft envelope. These were also mailed from a capital city. On arrival in California, the tape cassette was transcribed in our office so the completed manuscript would be ready to be edited and reduced to book form when Renee and I returned to the United States. This is why so much of this material is reportorial in nature because we recorded events at the time they transpired.

While in San Jose we were honored by two automobile clubs. One of them, RODA, gave Renee and me a delightful little plaque commemorating our visit to their city. The second, Association Costarricense de Automovilismo, invited us to a cocktail party at their club headquarters near the civil airport. Both clubs, each with about 75 members, were heavily engaged in promoting automotive sporting events such as rallies, road races, modest track races, slaloms and gymkhanas.

To begin our last full day in San Jose, we rolled out of the sack early and left the city a little after six on our way to Irazu, the nation's now dormant volcano. A few years before we arrived, on the very day of former President Kennedy's visit to the nation, this volcano erupted. Clouds of ash had filled the air and dominated the landscape while hot lava flowed down the mountain slope to damage crops and villages. For a while it appeared as though the Costa Rican economy was doomed for ash even deluged San Jose. Our drive to Irazu was up a twisting, mostly one way, paved road. Near the top brilliant green shrubbery of the tropics suddenly gave way to a desolate landscape where nothing lived and little, except a few tourists, moved. There were no birds, no wild life, nothing; just a massive gray blanket of lava ash. To watch over this sleeping giant, and warn of impending danger, there was a small barracks on the hillside from which members of the Guardia Civil maintained an observation post. We parked at the rim of the volcano, did pictures then threaded our way over broken landscape down into the crater. From its edge, by using binoculars, we could see clouds of steam escaping through open fissures in hot rock far beneath us. By the time we left the entire volcano was beginning to be obscured by clouds of moisture settling over the mountain tops. How did we feel? Relieved that it had not decided to explode while we explored the rim and crater.

Leaving our hotel at 4:30 the following morning to pick up the car, before we departed toward Panama, involved walking about five blocks through nearly deserted streets. It was interesting to find a policeman in every block. In five blocks I said "Good morning" to four of them. Three of the four replied with an English "Good morning" and one with "Buenos dias." The fifth appeared sleepy and may not have heard me. Our reason for leaving so early was that portions of the roadway to Panama were under construction and one long section through the mountains was said to be closed beginning at six every morning. We planned to head through that section prior to the closure time. Our only hindrance was the great number of narrow one-way bridges, leading in and out of San Jose. They created a minor traffic problem that Costa Rican police solved in an interesting manner. At one end of such bridges they placed a "Stop" sign. If you were approaching from this direction it was obligatory that you stop and observe bridge traffic. Anyone coming from the other direction had the right of way and need not stop. Nevertheless, it was pleasantly disconcerting for us to be driving the "right" way and watch a huge bus or truck screech to a halt on the other side to give us freedom to proceed.

Our major headache was that the road map was not clear, nor were there direction signs in Cartago which was the turnoff point for travelers seeking the Inter-American Highway southward. So we missed the intersection and drove 15 miles out of our way. After returning to Cartago we found a bus driver who told us, "Seven blocks ahead, turn left and follow your nose." By following his instructions we had a few miles of pavement before beginning hazardous miles of gravel and road construction under the haze of almost continual rain. The road was so high, along a mountain ridge ranging between nine and eleven thousand feet, that much of our travel was through thick clouds with visibility limited to a few hundred feet. Nevertheless we passed frequent buses, more frequent pedestrians and an occasional truckload of coffee or cacoa bean. As we neared the road's crest, more dense clouds were blowing across the way further reducing driving speed to about 25 miles an hour.

Soon we reached the summit, the highest point of the Inter-American Highway in North and Central America, at 10,930 feet. It was in this area that one of our luckiest breaks occurred as we descended from the highlands near the village of San Isidro Del General where a construction crew was busily engaged making a new cut for the thoroughfare. In so doing, they had completely destroyed the original roadway with a mass of boulders, mud, dirt and squirming bulldozers. More disconcerting was an effective steel cable stretched across our way. We asked the flagman when he expected the highway to be open and he said in about four hours. However, one of the bulldozer operators noticed the *Aventura* Mercury and decided that it would be a nice gesture of friendship to make us a way to pass. He and the other operator went into action with a roar of diesel exhaust and big blades flying. They soon carved a new path for us across the mountain of rubble. Then one man backed his huge machine, with the blade dragging, to smooth the surface and smash larger stones level with the dirt. The other operator followed and kept the tracks of his machine in a straight line to press the soft dirt and rocks into a somewhat firm pathway for our tires. Satisfied with their work, both grinned broadly and waved us on. With shouts of "Thanks" we bumped across our first "non-road" and continued south toward Panama.

A bit further we passed through that section of the Inter-American Highway of which the AAA guide book advised, "Watch out for landslides." We didn't have to watch for them. There were two right in front of us. One was so recent that a bus, which had passed in the opposite direction only minutes before, was the first vehicle to leave tire tracks over the rubble. We were the second to roll over the earth fallen from an adjacent cliff that had almost completely blocked the way. As we bumped across the dirt and tree limbs we could hear them scrape and jar the chassis. A rock banged our muffler so hard we began to sound somewhat like a tractor. After regaining the graded road, I slid under the car and, with the aid of a big foot and handy rock, forced the muffler back onto the exhaust pipe from which it had parted company. It took about as long to replace the muffler as it did to drive another 200 yards and face a second landslide hidden around a corner. We had little trouble driving across this one but it's presence made it obvious that some portions of the Inter-American Highway lend themselves to adventuresome dangers not common when traveling in the United States. As we continued I had Renee avalanche-watching out of the right-side window toward the cliff area, with instructions to make loud noises if dirt or rocks were tumbling down. My hopes were that she wouldn't shout, "Duck! Here comes another one." What I would have done, had a landslide started, wasn't decided. Probably "stand on it" and drive like hell in hopes of out-speeding boulders or a dangerous flow of loose wet rubble.

After piloting the Mercury for 14,841 miles it suffered its first flat tire. This was after the landslides and while we were bumping through additional construction areas. As we rounded a curve I felt the car begin to sway a little and guessed that one of our tires was soft. After we stopped I looked to the left rear and there it was: As flat as a tire could be. Don't laugh, but our first reaction was to find convenient bushes on opposite sides of the road to pass along excess cups of coffee enjoyed for breakfast. Once nature was cared for, we turned to the task of changing wheels. Due to an agreeable amount of forethought, which included storing the spare tire somewhat uncovered in the trunk of the Mercury, it required only 21 minutes to handle nature and switch the spare with the left rear. The tire's problem was a big fat nail which had let air out of the casing. Beyond this one could describe the run from San Isidro Del General to the Panamanian frontier as a never-ending detour. Frequent and serious chuck holes, inability to maintain a reasonable forward speed and multiple landslides were genuine hazards to passenger and driver safety.

In retrospect this section to the frontier with Panama was the most tiring drive to date. We were literally beaten to pulp during the six hours of traveling only 141 miles. For the benefit of mathematicians this figures out to a little more than 23 miles an hour. By the time we reached the frontier neither of us were talking. We were not only not talking to ourselves, but we were not talking to each other. Crossing from Costa Rica into Panama absorbed a modest 45 minutes. On the Costa Rican side we were promptly checked out by Migracion before the Aduanero accepted papers describing the car and license data. While this went on, a radio operator in a third room attached to the same building was shouting at headquarters to check our license number with someone back up the line. The communications equipment was so tired we had the feeling that his voice was carrying the message rather than electronic waves. Once approved, we bumped across the line into Panama where a 20 foot wide strip of concrete circled the Panamanian frontier offices. Here were police, a tourist assistance office, immigration and customs inspectors.

10

PANAMA

An over-friendly Panamanian Aduanero took charge of Renee (and got stuck with me) to teach her Spanish. We three wandered in and out of offices having our passports validated and paperwork prepared for the Mercury. After completing a cursory customs inspection that included the car trunk and inquiring as to whether we had any fruit, we were waved onto a good paved highway toward Panama City.

After that bustuppy ride from San Jose to the frontier, newly concreted pavement toward Panama city was one of the softest lengths of highway ever encountered. And we hadn't gone far before I was made to feel completely at home by a Panamanian driver. As most of us know, it is a common sport in the United States for aggressive drivers to speed up when someone tries to pass them. The Panamanian in front of us kept slowing and slowing until it was necessary for me to pass. Then, as we began to pass, he would stand on it and fly away in his Jeep station wagon. Since we drove at a rather stately speed, commensurate with the legal speed limit in each area, he easily outdistanced us to make himself happy.

We were so tired that finding our hotel in David, Panama, was a complete fiasco. There was a sign on the Inter-American Highway which pointed toward David as being somewhere at the end of a narrow paved road. After wandering through back country for a while it led us into a small Colonia or subdivision which I recognized as not being David. Somewhat over Renee's objections, I U-turned into a dirt road and found what appeared to be another main road. Turning right on this one we proceeded a few blocks and bumped over railroad tracks into the center of town. Both of us were grumbling at each other while looking at a map neither of us was alert enough to read. We managed to find our way to a Plaza from where we spotted our accommodations a block away. A quick U-turn in the center of the street and there we were. The Hotel Nacional turned out to have accommodations equaling those of any previous overnight stop. Dead tired, we hadn't arrived until six that afternoon.

There was a beautifully modern concrete highway from David to Panama and we made the best of it during the next day. The wandering ribbon passed through fabulous cattle raising country and small sugar cane or banana plantations, separated by an occasional village. As the highway rose and fell with the terrain, we were sometimes cloud high, then down at sea level where tropic breezes were welcome. It was a pleasant and fabulously beautiful drive. Along the way Renee had her first view of a "Chiva" or home made bus. It had a gaily painted body mounted on a truck chassis for rural transportation and random use in Panama City. A few miles before reaching the line between the Republic of Panama and what was the U.S. Canal Zone, it began to rain. By the time we reached the Zone it was pouring cats and dogs. Windshield wipers could not clear the water away fast enough to allow us to see clearly where we were going. As we turned one corner there were five Panamanian boys in bathing suits, sitting on water covered pavement, enjoying the warm tropical rainfall.

Our "Welcome" to Panama, by way of the El Panama Hilton Hotel, was an afternoon of total bewilderment. A chronological listing of events would go something like this: After the pleasant 250 mile drive from David over modern paved roads, we pulled up in front of the Hilton. A uniformed porter, standing on the walk, reached over and opened the car door on Renee's side. She said "No," so he promptly slammed the door. I exited and began to unload. While I piled luggage at the porter's feet he maintained a post-like posture against which the luggage could lean. Suddenly realizing that we had more luggage than could be carried, he disappeared and returned with a small cart. We locked the car and went into the lobby where I approached the registration desk and waited. There was a gentleman clerk tending to the needs of another guest and a young woman sorting mail.

The young lady asked what I wanted and I replied that the hotel had reservations in the name of William Carroll. She said, "Oh," and explained that it would take a minute to look. Inasmuch as she was working with mail I said "Would you mind seeing if we have letters?" She didn't mind and searched through the pile to find a welcome letter for us. Meanwhile the clerk had completed negotiations with the other guest who departed to leave the clerk and I staring at each other. The clerk then shuffled papers, walked ten feet away and deposited the papers. He returned, talked to the young woman handling mail then left for the cashier's desk. By the time he returned there was another gentleman standing next to me. He was well dressed, which I, after a day's driving, was not. Instead of attending to my needs, the clerk cared for the gentleman first. In the middle of their conversation I became upset enough to rudely interrupt "You have reservations in the name of Carroll?"

The clerk smiled, said "You will have to wait a moment," and walked away.

Meanwhile the woman continued shuffling mail. Noticing me still standing nearby, she asked "Is there something else I can do for you?"

"As I mentioned to you before, we have reservations in the name of William Carroll."

Finally she realized that there was a potential guest on her hands and something must be done. So she thumbed through a list of registrations. After a few minutes of going up and down the list she explained that she had no reservation in my name. I repeated the name, the spelling and explained who placed the reservation. Back she went and looked again. Still no reservation. She checked with one of the managers and another of the clerks before returning with "I'm sorry, but we have no reservation but I will give you a room anyhow."

While I'm filling out a room card, a second woman came over, asked what the problem was. She was given the word that William Carroll needs a room and has no reservation. She brightened and told us "Oh yes, there is a reservation for a Mr. Carroll," pulled up the list and extracted our reservation. It was for William Carroll, not Carroll William as the first woman had been searching for.

I completed registration and gave Renee change so she could tip the porter. His tip, I suggested, should be no greater than small because I object to seeing a car door slammed in my wife's face. The porter told her he would meet her on the second floor. This left Renee alone to find her way upstairs and, hopefully, locate our room though she didn't have the room number. First things being first, upon sitting I called room service for two sodas and chicken sandwiches. After several telephone calls to business associates, and 20 minutes had passed, I rang room service again. At the other end of the line were great commotions in Spanish, most of which resolved around "Someone wants two sodas and chicken sandwiches, where are they?" With other shouts of "We haven't gotten to them yet." This shook me to the point where I called the manager's office and asked them to please do something about room service. Five minutes later the manager's secretary called back and said our order would be on the way, and lunch did arrive soon afterward. Minutes after this happiness, like ten or 15, there was a knock at the door. A solemn-faced maid marched into our room, placed a bowl of flowers on the table and walked out. We never did find out from whom. During my earlier telephone conversation with the Firestone Tire and Rubber people, I was told that the hotel had been asked to see that we had fruit in our room when we arrived. It arrived, an hour later, with a card from the hotel manager. Adding to our delight with "graceful" service of the El Panama Hilton was our post-dinner return to the room. None of the beds were prepared. I called the housekeeper and was told "Oh yes, Mr. Carroll, the maid is supposed to make up the beds. You don't have to do it. She's somewhere in the hall outside." (In effect, if I wanted a maid, I could go look for her.) Unfortunately I didn't accept this information happily and noisy chipping of the teeth produced an unhappy maid. Our beds were soon made up.

Before holding our prearranged press conference at the Hilton, the next day, when the Mercury was to be displayed in the lobby entrance, we drove to a Firestone Service Center to rotate tires. This we had been doing at 5,000 mile intervals. We also had to repair the tire which had been punctured in Costa Rica. While switching tires, we discovered that another tire had a similar nail. Tire service was almost completed when Renee appeared on the scene. "We must hurry to the Venezuelan consulate right away, otherwise our passports won't be ready in time."

By dropping tools and cleaning hands in a hurry, we arrived a half hour before the consulate closed that afternoon. The secretary had promised Renee that passports and necessary car papers could be processed that same day. After tire shifting and Venezuelan consulate arrangements were completed, I drove back to the hotel, parked and collapsed for a late and much needed nap before the press conference.

The following day, which was a third Panamanian Independence Day celebration during the month of November, most businesses were closed. However Panama Agencies, the representative of Grace lines, was open for business. Arranging shipment of the car to Venezuela was far easier than we had imagined. As we had already booked passage on the *Santa Flavia*, the shipping line quickly organized our requested on-deck shipment of the Mercury. Papers were signed and the car was listed on a "Uniform Bill of Lading." We were told that this was extremely important for three reasons: Number One There is little trouble with customs because the car is on the ship's manifest and a declared part of the cargo. Number Two. The Bill of Lading describes the car accurately and when it leaves the ship on a foreign land it is traveling on documents that local custom officials are familiar with. Number Three. The car was, during shipboard time, covered by the insurance and responsibility of the shipping line until it's returned to the shipper's hands.

Bright and early the following morning I took the car to the local Mercury dealer so that he might display it. While I was doing this Renee, in a private car with driver, was touring the city and photographing points of interest. Meanwhile I was attending a Panama City Rotary Club luncheon where local students provided an exhibition of national dancing. At 1:30 I ducked out of the Rotary meeting to pick up our car at the auto dealer's and by 2:00 P.M. had delivered it to the Grace Lines terminal on Canal Zone Pier 18. We found the shipping line representative on the dock. He, with an assistant, inspected the car and made a list of equipment it contained as well as "exceptions" to its condition. The exceptions included stone bruises, chipped paint from highway adventures and gravel nicks on the wheel discs. They also listed interior equipment, accepted a key to the car, gave us a receipt for it, a copy of the Bill of Lading and a receipt for our money. Their staff member assumed responsibility of checking the Mercury and Carrolls out of the country. At this point, the ever-running engine had to be turned off because the *Santa Flavia's* Captain was concerned about a possible fire hazard.

The next day we visited the home of a Panamanian journalist who lived about 15 minutes out of town. For luncheon our hostess prepared Sancocho, the national Panamanian soup-stew which can be made with fish, fowl or beef, plus any variety of local root-type vegetables. It was a delightful climax to the Panamanian portion of *Aventura*. After lunch another friend drove us to Balboa Pier 18 and the *Santa Flavia.*

11

THE *SANTA FLAVIA*

The *Santa Flavia* had arrived through the Bay of Panama and docked at Balboa early that afternoon to load its cargo. About dusk we were allowed to board and find State Room No. 2 on the second deck. Within a short time we met the Master, one of the stewards and, more importantly, the man in charge of feeding us. Ray was 65 years old, on his last voyage. He was an amiable, grouchy, black gentleman whose hobby consisted of keeping passengers fat, happy and contented. The first thing he did was show us the location of the mess hall refrigerator and display its contents of milk, fresh fruit, cheese and sliced meat. Bread was in a corner box and we were welcome to help ourselves. At the far end of the dining room he introduced us to the coffee maker and a little gong with which he announced meals. We were, from thence, on our own. A few pictures were taken before the sun went down as we wandered around the ship while making ourselves at home. Lashed on the rear deck we discovered a beautiful green "Chick Sale" riding in solitary splendor as possible deck cargo. Because the Mercury was also traveling unprotected on deck as part of evaluating Simoniz Master Wax, it was to be one of the last items loaded. Discussion with the ship's crew indicated that it would not be on board until after midnight. Accordingly, we went to bed early and set our alarm for twelve. As a backup, the deck officer promised to call us prior to loading. Unfortunately, the seaman sent to bang on our door found the wrong stateroom and woke passengers who knew nothing about a car.

After our alarm went off we hurriedly dressed, romped on deck and discovered that loading was complete. Our Mercury was safely and securely lashed on the left side of the forward hatch cover, where it would cruise all the way to Venezuela. We remained awake about half an hour while inspecting the now almost deserted ship, then watched the rigging crew secure hoists and leave the ship in the darkness of one o'clock. After discussing the canal operation we went back to bed and, this time, set the alarm for four-thirty. After the clock went off, what seemed like ten minutes later, we looked out the porthole and saw the *Santa Flavia* was being slowly pulled backward from its Dock 18 berth toward the center of the Panama Canal channel. For the second time that night, we upped, dressed and rushed on deck. What a sight there was!

The sun was just rising over Quarry Heights, a lump of rock overlooking the Canal. Three cruise ships, which had arrived during the night, were ablaze with lights. And the *Santa Flavia* was thumping slowly along the channel toward the first set of locks. The sun continued its slow colorful climb into the tropic sky as we entered the locks at Miraflores to begin our ascent through its water "steps."

No operating feature of the Panama Canal attracts more attention than its massive locks. They total six double chambers which act as stair steps to lower and raise ships over the Continental Divide. On the Pacific side, high tide averages 11 1/2 feet above sea level and low tide averages as much as 11 feet below. The two double-lift Miraflores locks lead into a short run through Miraflores Lake to the single double-lift Pedro Miguel Lock which raises or lowers transiting vessels 31 feet. From here vessels are passed into the Panama Canal's often pictured Gailard/Culebra cuts through Gold Hill and the Continental Divide. At that point transiting ships are about 15 miles from water of the Pacific Ocean at the south canal entrance. They then sail through a connecting series of water filled valleys to pass Gamboa and enter Gatun Lake. At the north end of the lake they pass through the three double-lift Gatun Locks which lower or raise vessels 85 feet. At this point users of the canal are about seven miles from the Limon Bay breakwater ands the Caribbean Sea outside the coastal town of Colon by the northern canal entrance.

As a matter of comparisons, the Gatun Locks on the Caribbean side form one continuous flight of three chambers which raise incoming or lower outgoing ships approximately 85 feet. The Miraflores Locks at the Pacific entrance, have two chambers which lift or lower ships 54 feet.

The Pedro Miguel Locks raise or lower ships 31 feet in a single chamber. Water required to operate the Panama Canal is stored in Gatun and Maddon lakes during the long tropic rainy season. Each lock chamber holds about 8,800,000 cubic feet of water, or 26 million gallons. The principal involved is simply that of allowing water to drain from lake reservoirs through tunnels 18 feet in diameter, located in the center and side walls of a lock, to fill the chamber and lift the ship(s) inside. To empty a lock and lower the vessels, water drains through openings in the floor of the chamber, back into the main tunnels and down into the lock chamber below. Lock gates are steel structures 65 feet wide and seven feet thick which vary in height from 47 to 82 feet and in weight from 390 to 730 tons. Each was built of steel plates riveted to a girder framework, similar to methods of ship construction. These "leaves," as the gate sections are called, are watertight compartments which make them buoyant to relieve stress on bearings in hinges attached to the lock chamber wall. A remotely controlled 40 horsepower electric motor, turning a gear drive, can open or close a pair of leaves in approximately two minutes.

At each end of every lock chamber are "fender" chains to prevent a ship from ramming the lock's gates. The chains weigh 30,000 pounds each and, when lowered, drop into slots in the floor of the look. They are hydraulically tensioned in such a manner that if struck by a ship the chain would lengthen and bring the ship to a gradual stop without damage to ship's hull or lock gate. Vessels of the greatest length to have passed through the canal were 835 feet long and 106 feet wide. This is only four feet less than width of the canal's lock chambers. Ship tolls for transiting the canal were based on each 100 cubic feet of space useable for revenue purposes. The rates were 90 cents for each 100 cubic feet for laden vessels, 72 cents for vessels in ballast, and 50 cents for dredges, floating dry docks and warships based on per ton of displacement. We were told that even if only one ton of cargo or one revenue passenger is aboard, the transiting vessel would be assessed the laden rate toll.

An impressive sight it was as we entered the first lock. Its huge gates closed behind us and water began to flow into the chamber at the rate of eight million gallons a minute. This raised the *Santa Flavia* upward at what we estimated to be about 12 feet a minute. After passing through the two steps of Miraflores Locks we sailed into Miraflores Lake. This was a small mile-long lake at the other end of which was the Pedro Migual Lock. Its one-step lock lifted us to the level of the canal's central channel. Soon we were sailing, under sunlight and random clouds, through Contractors Cut, Culebra Cut, past the Continental Divide, and eventually into Gatun Lake. We, and ten other passengers aboard the Santa Flavia, took this opportunity to rush the mess hall where Ray was laying out breakfast. All we had to do was select from the menu and Ray would practice magic while evidencing high concern over acceptability of his skills. Breakfast was soon hurriedly over and we all ran back on deck to "Oh" in awe as our ship sailed between jungle covered banks of the channel. It's almost impossible to describe our reaction, and that of other passengers, to the spectacle of traversing this unique waterway. Islands and jungle were on every side, plus trestles of the Panama Railroad which operated coast to coast on an almost hourly schedule. Ever-present navigation towers and flashing beacons were an equally important part of the waterway. Following us was a former "Liberty" ship of the U.S. Maritime Service, now operated by South Korea. Coming toward us was a freighter belonging to the German Democratic Republic, followed by one from Rotterdam and another from Helsinki. Alongside scooted a tiny tanker of the Panamanian Maritime Service. Anchored ahead were two Shell Oil tankers, registered from London, which left their site as we approached Gatun locks near the Caribbean coast.

While transiting the canal we had an opportunity to talk with the Canal Zone pilot assigned to guide the *Santa Flavia* through. He explained that he functions as an advisor to the Captain, by using his piloting skill and knowledge of Canal channels. The Captain remains fully responsible for his ship and should the Canal Zone pilot bump it into a channel bank, it would be considered to be the Captain's fault. The pilot told us that providing guidance in the Canal was nerve-racking and that some of the larger ships were "ulcer producers". He'd been with the Canal Zone about a year and every few months had been "graduated" to piloting larger and larger ships. As he expressed it, "Just about the time I become comfortable with a ship the size of the *Santa Flavia*, they'll allow me to handle even larger ships. And that's what I'll be assigned to next." Of all Canal Zone employees aboard the *Santa Flavia*, he alone was dressed in a blue business suit and appeared to be more a young businessman than a pilot. Other members of the Canal Zone staff included line handlers and a foreman whose job was to control ropes and heaving lines passed from the Canal Zone docks and locks to manhandle the ship as it passed through the narrow waterway.

When we asked the pilot what his most serious problems were, he replied, "We really have only two. The first is weather. During heavy fog or rain, visibility is almost impossible. The second" he continued, "is old ships which have unresponsive equipment. In some instances the steering gear is so sloppy that by the time I issue an order, and the ship responds, we're far past the point at which it should have turned." Other problems he mentioned included ships which had power failures. Month's before, as his vessel was passing another, all the electric lights on his vessel went out leaving it in total darkness. In effect, the pilot of the other vessel could not see opposing traffic while passing it in the channel.

The transit list for our November passage provided an idea of Canal traffic. There were 19 north bound (Pacific to Atlantic) and 23 south bound (Atlantic to Pacific) ships passing through in one day. Among those using the canal during our transit were vessels from Britain, Panama, United States, Korea, Norway, Libya, Sweden, Japan, Netherlands, Germany (East and West), Denmark, Finland, Russia and Ecuador.

We had to anchor in Gatun Lake for about an hour and a half for the *Dubuque*, a United States Navy helicopter landing ship, to arrive. It was 570 feet long and 104 feet wide, which is only six feet less than width of the Canal's lock chambers. Accordingly, there would be only three feet of clearance on each side when the *Dubuque* transited. After she cleared the area, and we could move, the final locks at Gatun needed little time to drop us three levels toward the Caribbean Sea. A few minutes later we were sailing past Cristobal and Colon to clear the breakwater. At four minutes past two that afternoon, ten hours after backing from the Balboa dock, we were out of the Canal and on our way to Venezuela. Minutes later, Renee and I were sound asleep. We'd been up almost continuously since the day before and were somewhat tired from rubbernecking and photographing our transit through the canal. We napped until five, ate a huge dinner and ended up on deck chairs equipped with cool beverage glasses and ice cubes. Our sole activity became watching moonbeams play on the Caribbean while warm tropic breezes wandered across our faces. If there was ever luxury in a small package it was the delights of this tiny freighter, the Grace Line's *Santa Flavia*, on which Captain L.S.R. Engberg and his officers treated us as welcome additions to their family.

One of the more interesting things we learned the next day, was found in the mess hall. It was the United States Coast Guard Forecastle Card displaying a resume of the "Articles of Agreement" between Master and Seaman of the *Santa Flavia.* In part it read as follows: "It is agreed between the Master and Seaman or Mariners of the SS *Santa Flavia* of which L.S.R. Engberg is the master, that it will call in certain ports in the Canal Zone via Pacific Coast and/or Mexican Ports in any order and then at the Master's option to one or more South American and Caribbean Ports and return to such other parts and places in any part of the world as the Master may direct and back to a final port of discharge in the United States exclusive of Alaska for a term not exceeding nine calendar months." The card also listed all items the seaman will receive; including five quarts of water a day, a half pound of biscuit, a pound and a quarter of salt pork and other items such as fresh and preserved food including, "mustard, pepper and salt for seasoning." One of the more interesting comments was "...no grog allowed and none to be brought on board by the crew." Above the card was a notice pointing out that going on shore in foreign ports "is prohibited" except by permission of the Master.

Available to the ship's crew and passengers was a "Slop chest" which sold "items of necessity." It was maintained for the benefit of the crew, as per agreement with the ship's owners. Merchandise was sold on a profitless basis to supply the seamen with their needs. Shopping was allowed once a week. Among the stock was: Toothpaste, razors, tissues, socks, undershirts and shorts. Tobacco was sold on shipboard tax free, candy by the carton and soft drinks by the case. Luckily for us, the slop chest was open for passengers whenever we could catch the purser which was quite easy as he dined with passengers and other officers. Shopping by the crew was allowed once a week. On the notice, which listed prices of slop chest items, was the following important point: "The fastest way for this ship to get into trouble is to have customs officials see longshoremen or merchants leaving the ship with cartons of cigarettes sticking out of their pockets. All fines levied against the ship for infractions of regulations will be passed on to those crew members involved."

The *Santa Flavia* was 459.2 feet long by 63 feet wide and sailed at a speed of 18 to 20 miles per hour. According to Captain Engberg it carried a crew of 52 people, "Including me," he added. Some idea of informality on board is that our Captain wore delightfully oversized sport shirts while the Chief Mate dressed in khakis befitting his authority. We were told that the working crew of seaman is replaced at a maximum of every seven months to spread work among all maritime union members. The kitchen crew changed every year while officers, who were employed by and through the ship's owner, remained with the vessel as long as they or the owners wished. Rotation of personnel maintains a spread of work and also a somewhat higher level of efficiency, according to the Captain. Our fellow passengers included a Canadian lady traveling to South America, a retired ship's steward and his wife, a young woman taking a two week Jamaican vacation from her Canal Zone job, a businessman who represented the Grace Line in the Canal Zone and two Carrolls.

Although passengers and officers ate in the same dining room and were supposed to mix, it appeared that we passengers were somewhat intimidated by the ship's staff. We usually ate at one row of tables, ship's officers at the other. Mealtimes were: Breakfast, 7:30 to 8:30. Lunch 11:30. Dinner at 5:00. Our menu for one day began with a breakfast which included fruits, mush, cereals, bacon, eggs, omelets, hot cakes, jellies, preserves and all the fresh milk one could drink. Lunch: Carrot sticks, cucumbers, split pea soup, roast leg of pork, brisket of beef, chicken liver omelets and assorted deserts. Dinner: Grilled tender veal chops, beef livers, braised ox chops, with the dessert being baker's cake and fresh pineapple chunks. Seconds were on the house. There was coffee in the mess room 24 hours a day and we understood the officers took a coffee break at ten in the morning and three in the afternoon with passengers invited to drop in and visit as often as they wished.

We caught the Captain on deck one day and asked about the purpose of the green "Chick Sale" lashed on the after portion of the deck. He told us that this was a separate latrine carried for the benefit of foreign-port stevedores. He said it was far better to keep the latrine there than it would be to have them using the ships toilets particularly because in some Latin American nations workers had the rather unpleasant custom of tossing used tissue on the floor rather than into the bowl. He also mentioned that in a few South American countries the stevedores were so particular they would not work unless the latrine had been freshly cleaned. Accordingly the ship's crew used a fire hose to wash this unusual ship's accessory after a day's use in a foreign port.

Through Captain Engberg's courtesy, Renee and I were able to make an almost complete tour of the *Santa Flavia* during which we visited the bridge, engine room, propeller shaft tunnel and kitchen. Our escort for the tour was Glenn, a sophomore at the U.S. Maritime Academy, serving as an officer cadet on the *Santa Flavia.* As he explained his entry into the maritime service, "When we first arrived at the academy, our class was literally locked on the school's grounds. For 180 days we were not allowed to leave. During this time our senior classmates were telling us about great trips they had taken and hazing us unmercifully.

"However, one thing about it," Glenn continued, "in this first year we found out which men could handle the isolation of sea duty and who could not. During our sophomore year we are all sent to sea. The ship lines pay part of our wages and the Government makes up the rest. We serve as cadets on United States steamships and have a chance to visit far parts of the world. It's really exciting, and when we return we'll be more than ready to swap stories about the places we've been." We asked Glenn for his impression, so far, of seagoing life and he said that he liked it and intended to make a career of serving in the Merchant Marine. On graduation from the Academy it would be as a third officer." (From what Captain Engberg told us later, such graduates were in great demand.)

Before visiting the bridge, Glenn told us there are three unwritten rules of conduct: 1. No one sits down. 2. You never enter a closed door without warning because one of the officers may be working on navigation charts and have closed the door to keep valuable papers from blowing out to sea. 3. Only the Captain uses the Captain's binoculars and they are always in their own special hanger. On the bridge Glenn showed us radio-navigation instruments that could instantly determine the ship's location. And next to them was the chart room stocked with charts of all seas the ship sails and some on which it does not. Far more detailed than road maps, these pilot charts show depth of the ocean at specified points, location of light houses, contour of coastlines and the exact location of radio direction beam stations. On one wall Glenn pointed out the "Stool Pigeon" which was a constantly unwinding roll of paper which continually recorded the direction the ship was traveling. This was connected to the automatic pilot which steered the *Santa Flavia* on open seas. At such times the wheelman paced back and forth in front of the wheel to inspect both sides of the ship while watching forward. Should the automatic pilot fail it would emit a loud, clicking noise to warn the wheelman to disconnect it, take manual control and maintain the ship on the proper course. The *Santa Flavia* was also equipped with radar which enabled officers to watch other ships in dense fog or evaluate its position from nearby coastlines. In the radio room there was enough expensive communications equipment to enable the operator to reach any point in the world. Much of its business communication was done with a "key" and Morse Code to insure accuracy. However the radio operator told us he frequently made voice communication with "Ham" operators in the United States and foreign ports. A complete record was maintained of every contact the radio room made. It was in scheduled operation between nine and twelve in the morning, two and five in the afternoon, and seven and nine in the evening. By noting this three-shift schedule, outside sources always knew when the *Santa Flavia*'s radio room would be receiving communications.

Glenn then took us down into the engine room where a 130-degree blast of heat met our faces as we stepped along steel ladders, about 30 feet above the boilers. None of us could hear another's speech because of the tremendous commotion and rush of power in this heart chamber of the ship. We gingerly picked our way down continuing steel steps, which were coated with grease and soot, to reach the floor of the engine room that was about 15 feet below the ocean's surface.

The *Santa Flavia* was powered by steam turbines fed by two oil-fired boilers, each of which was about three stories high. They produced steam at 400 pounds per square inch pressure which was released to a high speed turbine spinning at nearly 7000 revolutions per minute. After steam passed through the high speed turbine it was piped to a low speed turbine, where it expanded a second time to spin the second turbine at about 700 revolutions per minute. Both turbines were driving through separate speed-reduction cases which contained clusters of gears. These reduced the enormous speed of the turbines to not more than 120 revolutions per minute, the maximum speed of the huge propeller shaft. This shaft, which turned the single fifteen-foot diameter propeller, appeared to be about 12 inches in diameter and something like 200 feet of bolted together ten-foot tubular sections. While the ship plowed through the sea at its scheduled 15-1/2 knots, the propeller shaft was turning an indicated 86 revolutions per minute. Renee and I were lead down the shaft gangway so close to the rotating shaft that we could touch it. At this point we were about twenty feet below the ocean's surface. Further along, at the rear of the ship, we could touch both sides of the hull at the same time where the propeller shaft passed through the stern plates and exited into the sea. It was there, down in bowels of the *Santa Flavia,* that carefully lettered chalk on the blank steel bulkhead, carried the admonition; "Please refrain from shaving or peeing in this hold."

Another surprise was the engine room telegraph. Its dial and indicator system was connected with the bridge and through it engineers received their power-output instructions. On the bridgc the telegraph indicator could be moved to select the specific speed the Captain desired. The engine room's duplicate unit advised the engineers of the order. But it took about two minutes to provide the desired power due to the time involved in manually adjusting numerous steam valves and control levers.

One engineer was always stationed in the center of the engine room from where he could constantly monitor temperature gauges for the boilers, speed of the steam turbines and watch the unbroken flow of oil from an 800-gallon tank which was constantly circulated to lubricate turbine-wheel bearings and gear drives to the propeller. He told us this lubricating oil was never changed but was filtered and cooled continuously. Another unusual set of devices was a pair of mirrors and peep holes which allowed instant inspection of the amount of fuel consumed as shown by color of smoke from the funnels. This, he emphasized, is most important because many cities have air pollution control regulations and ships that do not conform have been known to be fined. In one California port, another shipping line's Captain objected to an air pollution control officer telling him how to manage his fuel consumption. The result being that the Captain was arrested and jailed overnight: A situation in which the Master was not really the master of his own ship, much to his chagrin and embarrassment. The engineer on duty also showed us a chemical analysis kit which was used to make frequent tests of boiler water. He said testing was important to eliminate scaling that is somewhat like the coating inside a teakettle. Similar scaling could coat the inside of the boiler tubes and seriously reduce their ability to efficiently create steam.

After this eye-opening trip through insides of the ship, Glenn lead us up other flights of steel steps into the crew's quarters. A short walk down a companion way, cool by comparison to the engine room, brought us into the kitchen. Johnny, one of the cooks, was busily cutting steaks for our evening meal. He stopped and entertained us with a good half hour of detailing the proper means of running a ship's kitchen. Among Johnny's more interesting points was, "On board ship, food is one of the most important things. Boy, when we make a mistake in the kitchen, do we ever hear about it! Those crewmen come in here and you'd think we'd fired every one of them."

The kitchen which served crew, officers and passengers was large and spotlessly clean. As we were leaving, the baker entered. Renee and I both complemented him on the delicious lemon pie, which was actually as good as my Aunt Margaret used to make. "It's just that I like to cook, and I'm sure happy you like my pie." He grinned and left us with Glenn.

Cargo of the *Santa Flavia*, which was everywhere on deck and in the hold, was a marvelous collection of almost anything one could think of. On deck were huge frame and wheel assemblies for building oil-well trailers, stacks of lumber, a collection of steel light-posts and a beautiful double deck cabin cruiser for some fortunate person. Plus our Mercury. Inside the hold were passenger cars, canned fruit, mail and an unusual experiment. It seems that in Oregon the ship had loaded over five hundred tons of fresh apples. These were segregated into a separate hold then sealed under a plastic tent into which chilled air was being blown. If the experiment was successful it would be a low-cost method of shipping fresh fruit. Captain Engberg said that chilling would hold the fruit at the as-picked ripeness and eliminate the need for freezing or expensive shipping in a "reefer" ship. An even fuller understanding of the variety of other cargo on board was from listings on the cargo plan. This plan was a large blueprint of the ship which showed where each and every item was stowed. Such a drawing was necessary so that stevedore crews could quickly locate that cargo to be off-loaded at a specific port. Shipments carried inside the hull included: A trailer and boom, five boxes of machinery, more boxes of machinery, an antenna for a commercial radio station, 120 cartons of beans, 400 cartons of unnamed contents, 869 cartons of peaches, 50 drums of oil, 1490 chests of grapes, 1906 sacks of frozen peas, 50 barrels of lubricating oil, 3,583 cartons of nets, 811 cartons of nuts, 14 barrels of special lubricants, 600 cartons of dates, 511 sacks of malt, 75 cartons of paper, two mail vans, 2,100 sacks of onions, seven barrels of fiber material, raw paper pulp, 4656 boxes of pears and apples under the chilly tent, more paper pulp, wood pulp, Masonite, phosphate, 1500 sacks of flour, chemicals, more wood pulp, bales of wood pulp, bags of beans, lentils, shipping vans, 40 pallets of talc, cartons of paper board and 378 bales of alfalfa. And this was only about a fifth of the cargo onboard which included our *Aventura* Mercury.

The ship's officers and passengers, all of whom selected as much bunk time as possible, were somewhat aghast at our practice of being awake before the sun arrived. We usually stomped around on deck to amaze at awesome sunrises over the ocean and, when the light was sufficiently strong, go onto the deck's cargo area to photograph the Mercury as it sailed over the Caribbean near the bow of the ship. Best of all, in the morning our car's body was covered with salt spray. Glistening sunlight on the big bubbles of moisture made an unusually expressive picture. Such photographs were the record-making part of our continuing exposure of Simoniz to climatic conditions providing maximum abuse. To date, the Mercury's finish had been subjected to extremes of the Arctic where we washed it with glacier water, suffered the arid dry sands of Arizona and northern Mexico, tropical humidity and frequent thundershowers of Central America and paint eroding salt moisture of the ocean. Certainly we were involved in one of the most unique tests of car-care finishes that had ever been undertaken. When we first came aboard the *Santa Flavia*, and met the Captain, he told us about a planning discussion with his chief mate, Samuel L. Petty. While discussing the on-deck location of the Mercury, Petty was told that one of our needs was to subject the paint to the elements, including moisture on the high seas. Petty, so the Captain reported, replied by saying, "Well, if we don't get enough moisture on the car that way, I can always turn the fire hose on it." When we met Mr. Petty a bit later we explained that a fire hose wouldn't be necessary but, nevertheless, he offered again. The following day at six o'clock in the morning, the ship was drenched from stem to stern by a tropical thundershower. At breakfast we thanked Mr. Petty for his efforts on our behalf. He and all the ship's officers laughed as he replied, "It took a bit of doing but I hope you found the shower useful."

For some pleasantly relaxing reason or other, what we usually did really boiled down to sleeping, eating, looking and listening. Although neither Renee or I are doing any work, except for taking neccessary pictures or dictating this book, we too seemed to be sleeping much of the time while catching up on hours lost during the Mexican and Central American portions of *Aventura*. Wandering consists of walking from one deck to the other, a distance of about seventy feet, and peering seaward to find an occasional ship or one of our frequent views of land. We have seen islands large and small, coast lines with towering snow-covered mountain peaks above the clouds and other areas which featured desert or jungle reaching down to the sea. We even passed Aruba, the Dutch oil concession and island loading area, where the seacoast was lined with oil docks and storage tanks. One continuing event we always enjoyed during this trip was hearing the sound of the sea as it was cut by the bow and crashed against steel plates of the hull.

Before retiring for our last night aboard the *Santa Flavia*, we set the alarm for five in the morning because we were told the ship would be docking at six. Up we were bright and early in the dark, showering and hurrying to be on deck as the ship came to life. We made it and watched Captain Engberg, on the bridge above us, using his walkie-talkie to pass docking commands to the crewmen. Soon he ordered the propeller to be powered astern so his ship would back while the bow anchor was raised. Then his order was for part speed ahead. Within 40 minutes we were berthed alongside a dock at La Guaira in Venezuela.

12

VENEZUELA

Here our gangplank was dropped and 12 people came aboard. They were the doctor of the port, a port officer, three armed Venezuelan policemen, several merchants who had business with the ship, two Grace Line executives and a gentleman who described himself as "Chief of Turismo" for the Venezuelan government. He explained that he or a member of his staff met all the ships, their job being to help those visiting the nation. Into our room he came, inspected passports, stamped both, and on being advised that we had a car asked for the vehicle entrance forms. Only then did we learn that the Venezuelan consulate in Panama had not given us an entry permit required for the Mercury and one was required.

Courtesy of the tourist official rose to solve our problem. "Do not worry," he said. "I will write the letter for you. That is all you'll need. Come to my office in an hour and I will give it to you." Then he rushed away to meet a liner with 150 incoming passengers. We enjoyed a quick breakfast then hurried back on deck to take pictures while the Mercury was being unloaded. I waited at the bow, far forward and out of the crews way, for about 20 minutes before stevedores arrived with a cargo sling designed to hoist automobiles. By 8:30 our car was waving around in mid air, about 50 feet above the deck and half over the water while I frantically took pictures and prayed they wouldn't drop it. The Mercury was no sooner on the dock than Renee was back from the tourist office where she had gone to collect our entry letter. She did not have my passport with her and because the Mercury was registered in my name, they had to see a passport visa before they could write a letter. She headed back with the passport while a representative of the Grace Line went along to help get our car through customs. After Renee returned we left our luggage on the deck of the *Santa Flavia* and car on the dock, both actions causing backward glances of concern, while we hurried to the port's Adauna. While waiting there I read the letter the Turismo official had given us. In effect it said that we were genuine tourists and, under Venezuelan law, could be allowed to enter the nation for a period of 30 days without payment of import duty on the car. This on condition that we would leave the nation with the car at the end of that period. This letter was acceptable at the Aduana and they issued another document which gave us permission to drive the Mercury in the country. Should a policeman investigate our registration, this was the piece of paper which would do the job. At the Aduana the Grace Line representative told us about Venezuela's rather sensible method of controlling importation of vehicles. Only one person at the La Guaira port possessed authority to sign custom's documents permitting importation of a tourist vehicle, and allow its circulation and eventual export, without a major fee. As explained, the theory of this procedure was that a single official can only have so many friends. This reduced the potential for illegal activity should his "friends" lean too hard to import cars for their own use. As a backup system, should this solitary official become sick, a second in command could then, and only then, allow importation of cars. Our Grace Line representative now drove us back to the dock's passenger terminal where everyone entering La Guaira had to pass through luggage inspection.

While he disappeared around the corner to handle more of our paperwork, Renee and I cooled off with tall beverages. Soon he returned to tell us it was now time to process our belongings through the dock's Aduana. After wandering around through a remote section of the pier we found, among nearly 50 baggage carts, our luggage. Though stacked helter-skelter it was all in good shape. With the aid of a porter, the cart and our luggage were added to a lineup of similar carts pointed in the direction of the inspection counters. Waiting was not a waste because we had time to observe one of the world's most mixed-up affairs. At the far end of each luggage line was an inspection counter staffed by a crew of four inspectors who had honed the art of opening bags, satchels, trunks and boxes to absolute perfection. They usually managed to extract all the contents and never put anything back. While this was accomplished, they would point, with joyful glee, at interesting items found among personal possessions. In one instance, a large box from Italy attracted a dozen officers who examined in detail every item and snickered happily while exploring its interior. A gentleman from China, with a great mass of luggage found his boxes torn open and contents exposed to the rest of us. Then it was time for a gentleman with three large trunks, of fresh cheese, nuts and chocolates, to be inspected. All food items were unceremoniously pulled from his cases and tossed into a nearby refrigerator. Renee said that it appeared that the goodies were being held for later distribution to official "friends." At noon we seemed to be clear and free. Inspection of our property was simple. Everything had been opened, looked at and lids replaced. In fact, compared to others passing through the same inspection crew, we were treated most gently. Once we had everything repacked and ready to travel, our porter was able to stand still and receive a useful tip for services which may well have included the more comfortable inspection.

Then we bumped into our first stone wall.

It was 12:15 by the time our baggage cleared customs but the office to finally approve release of the Mercury closed at noon and would not reopen until 2:00 P.M.. Reason and time enough to have lunch. We invited the Grace Line representative to join us. He spoke little English but managed, by speaking Spanish very slowly, for the three of us to enjoy a very pleasant hour and a half exchanging information about our countries. Throughout I worked on rabbit stew which was surprisingly good because it was loaded with tiny diced mushrooms and balled vegetables in wine sauce. Renee had red snapper which had been partially steamed, heavily marinated, then served as an impressive portion. Lunch finished; the Grace Line representative excused himself to visit the customs office. We needed that final-final rubber stamp on the piece of paper which would release our car. His "visit" was an hour and 45 minutes. "They made a big production of this at the office", he said. "I'm sorry I took so long." It was no problem with us. We had somewhat enjoyed waiting in the passenger terminal while watching the random confusion of returning Venezuelans greeting long lost friends and family. And clucked with sympathy for the confused, harried and lost tourists obviously wishing they could find someone speaking English to tell them what to do next. Ready at last, with our final approval, we scooped luggage, found a taxi and were driven to our car, which had been parked about two miles away. We arrived to find the Mercury impounded with about 50 other cars in a guarded parking lot. Several officers were inspecting the car closely, obviously impressed with its gleaming coral finish and fresh styling. We signed another document to release the car and were then told that no one had a key to open the doors It had been locked when placed in the yard, but the key I had given the dock people had become "lost." I grumbled and moaned loudly to see if someone would produce it from their pocket. A key was not forthcoming but there was no real problem as a spare set of keys had been taped under a front bumper bracket. In an emergency such as this, either Renee or I could unwrap the spare keys and drive off without further trouble.

Accordingly, in a few minutes we were ready to leave. The Grace Line man headed back to his office after pointing us toward the Autopista leading between La Guaira and Caracas. We drove into the toll booth, paid a fee and accelerated about ten feet further before a police whistle chattered. We looked around and saw an officer waving at us. So we stopped. This was not the right thing to do. The whistle sounded again as he indicated we were to pull off to the side of the road. His problem: Where are the car's registration papers? We showed him documents from the Adauna. He inspected them closely, smiled that all was well and waved us onward. The toll road to Caracas, from La Guaira, was a relatively new three laner in each direction. Although steep and twisting it was good for 50 miles an hour without problems. Unfortunately it dumped the entire traffic flow into the civic center. And Caracas, an impressive historic city hemmed in by high mountains, had not been planned for any great number of vehicles. Most streets were narrow, twisting and one way. Everyone drove and no one walked. We were told there were more taxis in Caracas than in New York City. And, as far as we're concerned, they and 10,000 buses were all on the streets at the same time.

Our Hotel Tamanaco was easily found by following a map given to us by the La Guira tourist office. As usual with chain hotels, the answer was "We're sorry Mr. Carroll, we have no reservations. We did not know you were coming." I had them check under both William Carroll and Carroll William. To no avail. There was no reservation. This despite the fact that we had asked a previous Intercontinental hotel to process a reservation. As we learned later, our Firestone contact in Caracas had been calling the hotel for three days to find out when we were arriving.

However our arrival-day room clerk must have believed that we were sincere, for after a small amount of gossip, he indicated that he might find a room for us. He did and we were soon lodged. Although it was continually frustrating to enter a hotel where we thought we had reservations and find there were none; we had now come to the conclusion that this situation could only be accepted as hopelessly funny and fully expected. Accordingly, we no longer presumed that we had lodgings where we thought we're going to stay. If the hotel had reservations, so much the better. If they didn't, at least we were prepared to complain bitterly until a room was produced.

Early the next day the Mercury was cleaned, washed and fueled to be restarted on its ever-running engine operation. This was in preparation of a scheduled press conference held at our hotel the evening of our first full day in Caracas. But the spark plugs were badly in need of cleaning and there was no cleaning machine at the Ford agency. They lead me to a second agency, but it had no machine either. At a third Ford service center we found a brand new spark plug cleaner. But for some strange reason it couldn't clean the electrodes. I opened the abrasive reservoir and found that, instead of emery granules used in such equipment, someone had very carefully filled it with nice clean brown dirt which is not sufficiently abrasive to clean dew off a pat of fresh butter.

One evening later we were taken to dinner at a lovely Caracas restaurant named "Hector's." And unique it was. The owner (Hector) was the Maitre d', menu reader and Bon Voyageur; if there is such a thing. The evening began while we were all seated in the foyer enjoying cocktails and chamber music of talented musicians. Hector, a charming gentleman of indeterminate age, appeared with an impressive menu of billboard size. It was the only one the restaurant possessed. He passed it around. After everyone in our party had decided what they would order, Hector retrieved the menu and proudly announced, "Now that you've had a look at the menu, I will tell you what we have." Hector described every appetizer, soup and entree. Those of us who inquired were told how each item would be prepared, how much we would enjoy it and emphasized that he would have it cooked especially to our order. Hector made no notes, though our party of five placed orders that were varied and totally unrelated. Yet he repeated them perfectly and there was not a single mix up during our perfectionist service. While we were dining Hector circulated the room with a handful of roses. He handed one to each lady, together with a pin, so she could enhance her dress. As we left, all his musicians lined the walkway and serenaded us to the car.

The following day I had Renee obtain final travel verifications for us. First she visited the Columbian embassy to be certain we had all documents and certifications to enter that country. "No problem" they told her. Then she checked with Venezuelan offices of the Tourist bureau to make sure that our import certificate was adequate to both use of the Mercury within the nation and to leave when we desired. Again she was told it was adequate. But automobile insurance proved to be something else. We had been totally unsuccessful in obtaining South American coverage from any agency in the United States and there had been no time to inquire in any Central American nation. Insurance questions in Panama were met with "You can buy this in South America, we do not sell it." In Caracas the story was more interesting. It seemed that, at least in Venezuela, there was no one company selling insurance for all South America. We were advised that after entering each country we should visit a local agency and buy insurance for the length of time we would be within its borders. This meant that after we entered each nation, and while driving to the capital city where the insurance companies were located, we would be without insurance. Then we could buy coverage for the few days we were circulating and while leaving the nation, only to repeat this "No insurance and some insurance" performance each time we visited a different nation. Our decision was to forget it. If a fender were bent it would have to be fixed by us because we would not be in any one locality long enough to fight through a collection battle with any insurance company. In short, why bother?

Renee was able to take time off to visit the city. While downtown she managed to find Bolivar Square, considered the nerve center of "old" Caracas. It was formerly the "Plaza Mayor" where executions ordered by the Spanish Captain Generals took place during colonial times. Now it was the site at which the municipal band played musical programs near the gilt-domed capitol building dedicated February 19, 1873. Surprisingly enough when Renee walked by with her camera, one of the guards thought she wanted to take pictures. He approached and explained in Spanish, which she understood by watching his hands, that it was not allowed to take pictures of the building unless one had written permission. Instead, her camera found its way to tiny alleys bordered with ornate wrought iron balconies in the French tradition, red-tiled roofs in the Spanish, and traffic-clogged streets of today. In one area she watched a huge truckload of green bananas that was gradually easing its way downhill through a narrow alley. The truck was so wide, or alley so narrow, its sides almost touched the buildings. When the truck reached the bottom of the alley it exited onto a main boulevard. Hidden behind the bananas was a procession of motorcycles, scooters, bicycles and cars which had been waiting for the truck to complete its downhill crawl. As Renee explained, "It was like emptying a water jug to watch all these tiny vehicles flow madly out of the alley once the (banana) plug had been pulled."

That night was capped by an eleven-minute ride on del Teleferico Mariperez, an Alpine-style funicular car which provided a thrilling experience. The tiny car rose from the Caracas terminal station, at 3,264 feet, to Pico Avila which is 6,925 feet above sea level. There we found a complete recreation center with restaurant, bar, soda fountain and ice skating rink. From any one of these travelers could enjoy a breathtaking panoramic view of Caracas. The incomparable night scene was illuminated by myriads of city lights below and the fantastic snaking pattern of moving automobiles: Red in one direction and white in the other. From the other side of the peak we could look north down toward the Caribbean Ocean and La Guaira. In the Hotel Humboldt, near the Teleferico's upper terminal station, we found the bartender mixing something called "The Bomb" for other guests. We decided to try one. His "Bombs" began with pouring half a cup of pineapple juice, a jigger of dark rum, a jigger of light rum and a pony of vodka into a blender. This was thoroughly cooled with ice. Then a small amount of green crème de menthe was added and the concoction poured over fine crushed ice in a super size brandy snifter. The taste: Worth the effort. The results: Bombed!

Inspection of the dinner menu indicated that pricing was a bit rich for our budget so we walked (?) slowly toward the terminal station. With such a libation managing our equilibrium, swinging in the cable car while coasting down the mountain slope was almost terrifying. Here we were, a bit unsteady and high above the ground, in the dark, and dangling from a thin strand of steel in an experience totally unlike that of flying. There was only the slightest sound of rushing wind as we peered hundreds of feet below to watch the ground rushing upward. Then we caught our breath when, unexpectedly, the cable zipped over one of its several towers in a burst of noise that was somewhat like a subway train rushing through a tunnel. Again all was silent, with only whirring wind and bright lights of the city coming ever closer and closer and closer. We were both glad to exit the cabin car at the bottom station where we caught our breath and found a taxi for a quick ride to the hotel. Soon Renee was enjoying the fat juicy cheeseburger most American tourists dream about. We had so much work to be done, such as dictating this book and writing reports to people concerned with our product evaluation (Mercury, Firestone, STP and Simoniz), that we decided to leave Caracas and its busy commercial activity early the following morning for a few days rest.

Our first stop after leaving Caracas was to be at the Ford guest house in Valencia. We cruised along the Autopista and soon noticed that wherever there was a shady spot, such as a bridge, single tree or collection of trees, there would be one or more people waving at us. At first we thought they were just being friendly. Soon we realized they were entrepreneurs. One of the peddlers was managing a unique three-people flea circus. A tiny child was sitting between the knees of its mother. Mother was picking fleas from the child's hair. At the same time elder daughter was standing behind mother cleaning nits from mother's hair. They were much too busy to wave merchandise. And for obvious tiny reasons we did not stop to shop. Later we saw a number of vendors holding almost identical packet's of white paper. They waved with a motion indicating we were to pull over and stop. At first Renee and I spent drive-time guessing what was in them. Sandwiches? The packet's were too large. Candy? They were all the same size and appeared to have no exterior markings. Finally in desperation we pulled over, inquired and bought. The contents were Panecillos: a form of sweetbread midway between white bread slices and pound cake. At the end of the autopista we paid the toll in small change, much to the disgust of the attendant who grumbled mightily as he counted our coins. We circled Valencia by following a friend's map, drawn on the side of a paper bag, to arrive in good shape.

It was an extremely late start the next morning for no better reason than I overslept. About noon we're both hungry and in need of a place to eat. But having many times traveled across the U.S. by car we're leery of signs advertising a coming restaurant as being "The Greatest" place to eat. By the time we reached Barquisimeto we were famished and nearly out of gasoline. We also wanted pictures of one of the unusual bar, restaurant, gas station and repair garage combinations which were a feature of this area. None such appeared until, on the outskirts of a small town, there was a large sign "10 Kilometers for Don Carlos Service

Station with Good Service. Restaurant with good food." We continued on in hopes of finding a picture site, but all we saw were Don Carlos' signs. At the advertised 10K we crested a hill and faced a billboard telling us "Aqui es Don Carlos": And there he was. The service station offered three grades of Shell gasoline. "Extra" which was 93 octane, "Popular" at 84, and "Corriente" which was reported to be useful for lighting bonfires. After gassing we drove a few feet to Don Carlos' restaurant and were pleasantly surprised to find shaded car parking beneath a tin roof, a scrupulously clean patio and a dining room which was as open to fresh air as the patio. After liquid refreshment, avocado salad, beef stew and steak, served with "Apares," the Venezuelan equivalent of a tortilla, but hard as a rock and tasty as a maiden's kiss, we felt better.

After lunch we headed across the Venezuelan countryside toward the Republic of Colombia. A heavy rainstorm slowed travel and by the time we arrived in Valeria it was almost 8:00 P.M. Luckily the Imperial Hotel found us a room with only modest difficulty and great courtesy. Such as from the porter who explained where the dining room was, why the elevator didn't work, why our room cost so much, ("If you stay three nights, if will be less per night.") and expressed sorrow that it was raining to cause us so much trouble. While at dinner, Renee and I gave the back of her hand close inspection. On the previous day it had attracted an insect bite that was beginning to swell to the point where I was alarmed. After dinner we decided to do something about it. We asked our porter if there was a pharmacy open in the evening. He thought for a moment, dialed a telephone number, discovered there really was someone at the other end of the line, then lead us out to the street. "Seven blocks that way," he said, "Three that way, and turn left." It continued to pour so we ran for the Mercury and followed directions. When we finally turned left, in front of us was the pharmacy. Perchance you question seeking a pharmacy instead of a doctor, it should be explained that doctors in Latin America were primarily surgeons. If locals have only a reasonable problem, they visit to the nearest pharmacy because the town druggist is the person who really knows what to do about it. The Valeria pharmacist was seated behind the counter reading a newspaper while two boys waited on customers. He came to us, inspected Renee's hand and began to question us rapidly. As usual his Spanish was far ahead of ours. After much slower questions he came up with a simple word we all understood, "Insectos." This we agreed was the cause of the problem. He retired behind his shelves and reappeared with a tiny aerosol spray can of material Renee thought was made in Germany but later turned out to have come from New Jersey. Sprayed on the skin it instantly reduced the itching and calmed our nerves. Now came time to buy. The price: seven Bolivars. Unfortunately we had run low on local currency. Our pockets contained adequate American dollars but only five Bolivars. He couldn't accept American money but sold us a "short" can, from which he had been spraying other clients, for our five Bolivars. Delighted, we headed back to the hotel. The rain was coming down quite hard so we tumbled into bed for what I hoped would be uninterrupted sleep. About 1:30 I awoke to the sound of rushing water. I went to the window to observe the rain and discovered there was none. Not a drop was falling. But the street in front of the hotel was awash from curb to curb with a small river flowing off the nearby hillside. The next morning the pavement was thoroughly cleaned and dry.

Speaking of the next morning, when Renee's hand was much better and the swelling half gone, we ran into our first instance of studied discourtesy on this entire trip. Two cars were parked in such a fashion that they both blocked the Mercury. Moving either one would have freed us so we could have left the parking lot early in the morning and been on our way. One car owner was asleep in the hotel. The driver of the other car was busy, key in hand, taking stuff out of the trunk so that he could wash his car. But move it he would not. Under no circumstances would he move it. I asked him, "I said please" and I threatened to poke him in the nose. Move the car he would not. The parking lot guard talked to him without avail. His friends talked to him. Finally an attendant from the hotel came and talked to him. But rude he was and rude he remained, more unhappily so by the minute as pressure mounted. But he would not move his car. The only recourse was for a porter to awaken the owner of the second vehicle who kindly dressed to come down and moved his Mercedes so the Mercury could leave the parking lot.

Several of our business contacts had recommended vacationing in the Colonia Tovar, an unusual resort in Venezuela and only a two day's drive from the capital city. After departing Valeria, civilization dropped far behind us leaving nothing but beautiful scenery ahead. Eventually we had our heads in cloud mist which slowed our pace to that of a snail. With headlights on, we crept around one curve after another, unable to see more than a white center line. Suddenly the clouds broke and we were awed by sunlight lighting mountain tops that glowed with trees, underbrush and flowers. The rest of the run to Colonia Tovar, 3000 feet cool in the mountains, was a continuation of occasional clouds, fog and brilliant sunlight. When we finally drove into the village its narrow streets proved no hazard because there was no traffic. And so few signs we circulated through town before sighting the entrance to our destination. It was the tiniest of hotels whose name, Selva Negra, translates into "Black Forest".

Our host spoke excellent English as well as Spanish and German. He appeared to be a young college boy from the United States but was as Venezuelan as Caracas. Our cabin with living room, bedroom, kitchen and bath was next to a happily noisy river. Amid the unusual Bavarian surroundings we enjoyed farmer's plates of sauerkraut, sausages and ham chops, as well as dinners of stroganoff, goulash and other forms of Germanic cooking. All being liberally enhanced by Venezuelan beer served in chilled stoneware mugs. Other guests included Americans working for a tire manufacturing company and members of the U.S. embassy staff. They, like us, were in the minority for Tovar was heart and soul to vacationing Venezuelan escapees. A feature of the hotel was a large beamed living room with a huge, wood-burning fireplace. A large round coffee table centered a dozen comfortable chairs. Our first night found every chair filled with locals discussing the state of the world amid warmth of their surroundings. Outside, our Mercury could be heard chugging quietly away as it continued its unprecedented durability test of continuous 24-hour operation. We were told that the beginning of El Tovar was about 150 years earlier when enterprising settlers arrived from Southern Germany. They soon found this part of the wild Venezuelan highland and reproduced a small edition of their homeland. In the current village, its residents ground flour, made jams and jellies and were expanding an arts and crafts section that was recreating the fine ceramics of their former Bavarian highlands. The community's four tiny hotels catered to visitors and a number of El Tovar households accepted guests. Architecture was almost totally Germanic as were decorations in hotels we visited. Here too was the unusual situation of Spanish-speaking blue-eyed blondes.

Our map showed a back road from El Tovar which would eventually lead us to the next overnight. Accordingly, one morning we departed up a narrow back street with deeply ridged pavement to provide tire traction on its steep grade which seemed to be in the 15 to 20% range. After a mile or so the pavement deteriorated into a dirt trail, which wandered across the highlands. As we bumped along the lane of farm tracks we again pierced clouds hovering over Venezuela. Then began a breathtaking downgrade on which the Mercury's automatic transmission was locked in first gear to reduce our speed to a safe level. As we rolled down toward La Grita we could look down into the distant valley with its tiny homes and ranches scattered on sides of the hills. Toward each was a track but from the distance we couldn't tell if it was suitable for vehicles or only for walking. As we squeezed by a parked jeep, where the driver had stopped for nature's call, he shouted that the road ahead was extremely bad. We thanked him and kept going. And was he right! It immediately became an even more dangerous downgrade of deep water-washed ruts. For the first time in over 15,000 miles we could smell the Mercury's brakes overheat as we used them almost continually to maintain our speed at a safe level. It took an hour and forty five minutes to bump and thud 15 miles over miserable dirt during which we dropped about a half-mile in altitude. At the bottom the track leveled along the tiny valley. Where it forded a shallow river I let Renee out of the car to take off her shoes and wade through cold water and take pictures as I drove through the river. As the Mercury plowed into the rushing water she caught spray in all directions.

Soon we reached an area where the valley roadway became two cars wide and slightly less miserable, with shallower ruts and less effective potholes. Working in front of a small house beside this later section of the valley, in which foot steps stirred a dusty haze, was an entire family busily engaged in washing a car. It was so old, so battered and so tired it appeared as though it wouldn't even run. Yet children were carrying buckets of water from a nearby stream so their parents could diligently refresh the family's prized possession. A few more miles of dirt brought us to La Grita from where we gained speed for about 15 miles to the entrance of an Autopista. At the interchange were services we never expected to find: Several drive-in restaurants, three service stations and two bars for the traveler in need of refreshment. We collected a ticket (Courtesy of IBM) and spent the next few minutes sorting a pocket full of change to come up with the necessary Bolivars. Travel differences included signs indicating each lane was a "Canal," a speed limit of 100 kilometers per hour (65 mph) in the left Canal and 80 kilometers (50 mph) for the right Canal; plus big billboards, small signs, pedestrians, bicycle riders and an occasional animal wandering along as though it too had paid the toll charge.

The balance of our run toward San Cristobal was a pleasant six hours over extremely good highways. The scenery was almost totally tropic: Bananas, bananas, bananas and villages with bare-bottom babies and pregnant females on every side. Soon we became hungry and searched for lunch. We stopped at the Hotel La Pesina, a typical tropical motel built around a central patio with everything open to the four winds. We found a corner table from which we could watch the Mercury parked outside. At first it attracted nothing more than a hoard of shoeshine boys. Then came the town unemployed and finally a number of local businessmen. Meanwhile we were busy inside. The waitress, who apparently was also wife of the owner, said they had no menu but kept telling us something again and again. We didn't get the message until she literally took me by the nose to point my eyes in the direction of the wall. There, neatly lettered on a soft drink blackboard, was her menu for the day. We shocked everyone by ordering steak, spaghetti and soda. One of the town's businessmen asked me, in broken English, why we were allowing the engine to run. We explained and he replied, "This is a very important thing. Thank you very much for telling me your information."

After we lunched the manager declined to accept traveler's checks or American money. He said "Only Bolivars" and would not touch anything else. And he was kind enough to alert us to the fact that many other business people felt the same way. In short, it would be critical for us to have an ample supply of Bolivars to travel within Venezuela's back country, into more of which we were heading. We decided to repair the Bolivar deficiency at the first bank. Luckily too, as it turned out to be the only one we saw all day. It was the Banco Union in a small unnamed town on the highway between Valeria and San Cristobal. We presented traveler's checks to a cashier who, without ado, went to a communications set and radioed headquarters in Caracas. His question concerned the proper rate of exchange. Once obtained he made payment on the checks and we were happily on our way with the Bolivars which every Venezuelan accepted.

After driving more miles through tropical banana land, we began to climb into highlands leading to the Colombian border. Just outside the town of San Juan de Colon we stopped at a fork in the road to obtain directions from a Guardia Nacional officer standing nearby. He provided both directions and a request for a lift to San Cristobal where we were going anyway. For the only time on this trip, we picked up a hitchhiker.

There were two reasons for breaking our "No Rider" rule. Number One: We wanted to talk with him. Number Two: He was thoroughly sober, well-dressed and a member of the nation's respected armed forces. Believe me, we enjoyed having this man with us though he spoke no English and our Spanish was not competent for a detailed conversation. We did learn he was a second grade sergeant, married, father of a boy and a girl, liked the Guardia Nacional and was taking a correspondence business course from a United States school because someday he would like to be something other than be a soldier. As we neared San Cristobal he recommended we stay at the Hotel El Tama which he said was the best hotel in town. But he was not quite sure where the El Tama was located and soon all three of us were lost. We stopped four or five times for guidance to the El Tama and when we finally arrived were not completely certain because there were no identification signs. After registering we drove back to the center of town where our soldier was deposited in front of the local headquarters and his barracks.

It was a wet winding road that lead out of San Cristobal toward the Colombian border the next morning. The further we drove the higher it climbed. Often we could see the paving ahead twist and turn up the side of the mountain and disappear behind a cloudbank. For the first time since our arrival in Venezuela, we saw barefooted Indians walking on the cloud-wet roadway. There was also a barefoot Mercury tiptoeing through the same clouds when visibility dropped to about 25 feet as we crept along, for about an hour, over a mountain range. Occasionally the dull yellow beams of another vehicle's headlights would approach and slowly creep by to disappear into the mist behind us.

Venezuela was said to be noted for the number of Guardia Nacional, transit police, city police, tax collectors, and custom's stations on highways leading from one part of the nation to another. We'd been warned to be certain we made a complete stop at all of them, or at least wave to the officer. This we did. Sometimes they waved back and sometimes they glared at us for disturbing them. The basic idea was to make yourself known. The warning sign for such action usually depicted a peaked-roof guardhouse from which projected a jagged bayonet. We couldn't miss it! Accordingly it was not totally unexpected when, about a mile out of the clouds, we rounded a curve into a village and found the road barred to passage. Guardia Nacional officers had stretched a steel cable from inside their guardhouse to a solid post on the other side. A tired red flag sagged from the center section. We stopped. Officers peered out of their hut. We looked back. The cable dropped. And *Aventura* passed without a word being exchanged. Leaving Venezuela was only complicated by making two U-turns on the main street of its frontier town. We wanted to buy a can of Venezuelan coffee and, a block from the border crossing, sighted a grocery store. Quick U-turn No.1 brought us to the store where coffee was purchased. U-turn No. 2 headed us back toward the border station where a guard pointed toward a parking space. Both passports were stamped and we passed through minus baggage inspection or any time-consuming formality. A total of less than 15 minutes, including photographs of Renee inside the Customs station.

13

COLOMBIA

It was a quick drive across the Rio Apure bridge into Colombia where an officer merely looked at our car and told us to check with Migracion in the next town, Cucuta, 17 kilometers further. His tiny frontier community, adjacent to the border with Venezuelan, was only a two-block long collection of shacks on each side of the roadway. Occupants of the huts appeared to specialize in selling meat and vegetables. It's worth noting that Colombia had the first border crossing in Latin America with information signs in both English and Spanish.

Our first obligation in Cucuta was finding Migracion where papers were checked, passports stamped and we were waved on to Aduana. Directions were given and we started off in search of what proved to be an unmarked building. An urban renewal project had managed to eliminate most street signs so that when we finally found the Aduana we were on the wrong side of the wrong street. They had to inspect the car, so we circled four other blocks to head back in the right position. The car was examined and papers stamped, then we went to a second office in the same building to obtain an approval signature for the inspection. This was our first use of the Mercury's Carnet de Passage, the document from the AAA in New York. It certified that our car would be re-exported from the nation involved and was based on a letter of credit deposited with the AAA. It was instantly recognized by Aduana and we sailed through their processing with a minimum of difficulty. The next project was changing our money before we went further. The first bank said "Nix" as they did not accept American Express Traveler's checks. "The only one to do it is the National Bank," said the clerk. Finding the National Bank wasn't difficult. It was across the street. Inside were five armed guards and one customer: Carroll. But it was necessary to wait because the man in charge of exchanging Travelers Checks for Colombian money was elsewhere. He showed up 15 minutes later, accepted a check and gave me a bundle of Colombian currency in exchange. But he could not take any Venezuelan money. That had to go to another bank or one of the money changers on the streets. Across the park I found one money changer who offered the legal rate of exchange. I accepted and swapped leftover Venezuelan money for additional Colombian currency. Now our only remaining objective was locating the Tourist Office because we wanted a map. Despite a dozen different sets of instructions we could not find their office in Cucuta. In desperation, we stopped at a service station for instructions about leaving town. They were simple. "One block that way, turn right and follow your nose." This we did and were soon on the way to Bogotá, Colombia's capital city.

Just outside of Cucuta we passed a most unique bridge repair project. One boy worker, about 16, was being supervised by another boy of about 18. The first boy was repairing the bridge with a length of well-used rope which he was tying around a section of broken railing. We were more than happy that the one-way bridge was made of steel with a thick wooden floor that did not need the support of more rope. Within the next 20 miles we checked through no less than five traffic control points. The first involved a guard monitoring vehicles on the road. He was recording license plate numbers. The second was manned by both policemen and the Guardia Nacional. The third was manned by Aduaneros who were examining truck cargos and car papers. The fourth set of officers examined both car papers and passports. A fifth set of officers stopped us to inspect car documentation then waved us around a pair of waiting trucks. At this latter Aduana the officers were taking no chances. The somewhat empty truck in front of us, carrying only two sacks of grain, was thoroughly and completely inspected. All loose material on the truck floor was lifted and each sack punctured many times with a long screwdriver to determine if contraband was hidden in the grain.

A few hours later we were in what was one of the prettiest towns we had seen. Pamplona, a community of 25,000 people, was nestled deep, and we mean deep, in a surrounding circle of brilliantly green hills. Everywhere they were covered with small ranches and wood cutter's homes. Capping the hills were fleecy clouds in a sky of brilliant blue only found where industry has yet to take a stand. It was about two in the afternoon and we saw nothing resembling a reasonable restaurant. Near a corner I stopped to ask a pair of policemen. Neither one was quite sure where to send us, but one exhibited an unusual courtesy. He said "Come with me" and down the block we walked. Soon we came to a restaurant, he walked in, looked around, decided it could be satisfactory, invited me to inspect the interior of the Cafe Monaco and told me that I could park right in front. Unfortunately it didn't work that way. While circling to make legal use of one-way streets, we found a sizeable hotel. There we had what could properly be considered one of the most unusual luncheon appetizers anyone could have. As the piece de resistance, Hormigas was brought to the table by our host in the Hotel Cariongo. With great pride he explained they were only obtainable from one town about 100 kilometers distant. What are Hormigas? Ants; the flying kind, as our host explained it, from which the head had been removed. The full name being "Hormigas Colonas" which didn't make them taste any better though we did admit the crunchy samples were unique. He explained that they were delicious with beer. Our answer would be: They are not delicious with anything. As interesting as the ants were, more important was a comment the manager made while speaking of U.S. aid programs. He said that he liked Peace Corps people very much because they worked with their hands and not with their mouths. An opinion that was a startling indictment of some of our other efforts at helping Latin Americans.

The road to the next town was so ill-marked the manager sent one of his porters to ride along and show us the correct route. The boy did well and we were soon on our way to an overnight stop deeper into the fertile back country of Colombia. The topper of the day's drive appeared after we arrived in Bucaramanga and had checked into our Hotel Bucarica. Our first question was about a place to park the car. "Right in front of the hotel," said the clerk. Secondly, where can we buy gasoline? A porter gave us instructions and volunteered to ride along. It's just as well that he did, because we visited three service stations and from all were given the same answer "Sorry, we have no gasoline." It turned out that the entire town of Bucaramanga had, on the day we arrived, run out of gasoline. A railroad washout had blocked all resupply shipments. At one station we were told that if we waited about an hour they might be able to sell us some but all city buses and about 50 waiting cars would be served first. Then Pedro, our guide, mentioned a rumor that gasoline would be available about 9 o'clock that the evening. He suggested we go out later to see if we could buy sufficient fuel to keep the Mercury engine functioning under its 24-hour test regime. So after dinner Pedro and I drove around town again. This time we visited a different group of stations. Some were totally black. Others were illuminated but shut down while the owner guarded his pumps. The few that were open had block-long lines of trucks waiting to be replenished with fuel. The picture was clear: There was no gasoline for the Mercury that night. We returned to the hotel where I tipped Pedro for his help and shut off the engine: The first time it had ever been off for such an impossible reason. No gasoline!

Bucaramanga provided a number of additional surprises for us the following morning. At 6:30, almost to the dot, electricity in the hotel was turned off. As we learned later, the generating plant had such modest capacity that it could not serve both residents and industry. City fathers presumed everyone was up at 6:30 so unessential electricity was turned off in favor of more important industry. The second surprise was happier. While having breakfast in the hotel dining room, two Americans came over from an adjacent table and introduced themselves. Both were employees of Cities Service, a major United States oil company. While working in the Bucaramanga area, on a drilling and oil production project, they had received a warning of the impending gasoline shortage. Verifying what Pedro had told me, they said the shortage resulted from recent rains which had caused landslides to block both the railroad and the highway leading from a distant refinery. Anticipating the shortage, they had purchased 15 drums of gasoline and offered to fill our tank from one of them. As you can imagine, we accepted with appreciation. Leaving Bucaramanga after fueling proved to be quite simple. We followed instructions to go "About a mile that way, then keep making right turns all the way to Bogotá." However it wasn't far before a "Y" in the road caused understandable confusion because most traffic was turning left. By checking signs on buses which indicated Bogotá as the destination, we selected the correct road to travel through tall fields of sugar cane on a twisting highway that limited average speed to about 35 miles an hour. Most unusual were the number of religious statues perched high on pedestals so that each traveler could murmur a personal prayer for privilege.

One religious shrine, at a particularly dangerous corner, was decorated with several hundred motor vehicle headlamps: Perhaps in appreciation for their better illumination that kept local drivers from serious accidents.

The Mercury had its first problem when we passed over a section of pavement that had begun to crumble. After cleaning the debris, highway workers squared off edges of the damaged area so they had a rectangular shape to patch. Unfortunately patching materials must have been hard to come by. While waiting for asphalt, they filled the hole with large fist-sized jagged pieces of gravel. The theory being, I imagined, that trucks would beat the gravel into the hole and eventually smooth it off. This was fine but beating the same gravel with passenger car tires was punishment unbelievable. Our problem announced itself with an ominous clunking from the car's rear when the frame smacked the axle housing as though it too was striking a rock. The moment the road widened we stopped at a convenient site and I crawled underneath. Inspection disclosed that a bolt holding the left rear shock absorber to the body had fallen out and we'd lost the rubber attachment bushings. The shock absorber was inoperative and banging against the body on each bump. Tools were unpacked and in twelve minutes, by Renee's time, we were ready to roll again. The shock absorber was in the trunk for reinstallation in Bogotá. Though we bounced more than usual, at the slow speeds we were traveling it was obvious a shock absorber could be dispensed with. Adding to our fun was the next uncomfortable stretch of Inter-American Highway which was 30 kilometers of complete reconstruction. At one point a bulldozer operator hopped from his Cat and tossed small rocks out of the way so that our passing would be less a problem. Within a short distance we bumped through another stretch of wheel-tracks zigzagging along the center of a roadway that was mud, dirt and good-sized rocks. As we plowed through the mess, one of the larger rocks skillfully removed the muffler from the exhaust pipe. (16,313 miles.) Again, off to the side of the road and under the car I went. With the aid of a rock and a tire iron. I pried the muffler up into position, stuffed it onto the exhaust pipe, banged everything tight with the rock and prayed all would remain in place until we reached Bogotá where it could be properly reset.

At our lunch stop a "law enforcement" officer highlighted the day with an impressive nonperformance by accosting me in the center of the street before a gathering crowd. He flashed a wallet under my nose, with what appeared to be a badge, while I was busy with paperwork. I requested that he wait a moment until I completed what I was doing and then asked how I could be of help. He flipped the wallet under my nose again and had it back in his pocket before I could see the badge clearly. This "TV Detective" attitude bugged me to the point where I asked that he show his wallet a third time and allow me to inspect the badge. During this bit I read his identification card very, very, slowly and carefully compared the picture with his face. By now I was under his skin as much as he was under mine. First he wanted our passports. Instead I produced tourist cards for Colombia which were stamped and identified. These he looked at suspiciously and seemed to have great trouble realizing that Page Two was a carbon copy of Page One. His problem became Page Two (an exit permit) which bore no government stamp because we had not yet departed from Colombia. He asked to see papers for the car. Unfortunately our Carnet de Passage was printed in French which made everything incomprehensible to the Colombian gumshoe. He was curious as to how we entered the country. I pointed to the Cucuta stamp and he agreed that was a city of Colombia. But he was not sure whether such approval allowed us to circulate further into the nation. Our danger to regional tourism was obviously plagued by whether or not our car could properly circulate in areas other than Cucuta, that being his nation's legal port of entry on the Inter-American Highway. His worst problem of all was that by now we had collected a crowd of about 50 of Barbarosal's most prominent citizens, ranging from businessmen to shoe shine boys. To complicate matters further, I decided this would be the right time for me to stop trying to speak Spanish. The policeman was causing too much trouble for me to risk saying the wrong thing. I refused to understand anything more he said and insisted he speak English. Unfortunately he could not. I refused to say anything in Spanish and bystanders began laughing at his discomfort. One Secret Service man, detective, or whatever else he may have been, appeared to have lost every bit of respect his Colombian countrymen may have had for him. Men in the audience, who seemed to understand English, attempted to help by telling him that my tourist card and car papers were correct.

At first he had not appreciated their assistance and became wonderfully red in the face. Meanwhile, Renee's picture taking of the affair was adding additional discomfort. Finally he thought twice and asked people in our sizeable audience to help. Now, none would. He had only determined that we had arrived through Cucuta and that we were going to Bogotá; while behind his back there was laughter, grimaces and signs of encouragement to me to hold out. Our detective finally decided he wouldn't give back the tourist documents and I would have to go to his "Officina" which was in the police station. Off he wandered, papers in hand, to be met by two young men. During this affair I had noticed an officer of the Policia Nacionale sitting in his nearby jeep. Instead of following the papers I went to the officer and used my best Spanish to explain: The "detective" wasn't very bright. He couldn't read very well. And the papers were in order. The officer glanced over my shoulder to where my documents were being inspected by the detective and two young men. Then he told me to wait a minute and everything would be "Okay."

And it soon was. One of the young men approached, handed my papers back and said, in English, "Okay to go. Have a good trip."

Shortly afterward we came to more Pares (Stops). The first was only for logging our license number. The second Pare wanted tourist cards and Mercury papers for a ten minute inspection while we turned off lights in the car and curled up for a short nap. It was well deserved because we were somewhat beaten after more than 12 hours of continual bouncing over miserable roads. The guard at the third Pare merely waved his hand in salute and passed us on. Eventually we reached a fast highway for the last hundred miles to Bogotá's Autopista. A small fee paid the toll for 17 kilometers into the city. Streets were traffic-clogged and we had no city maps but somehow found a main boulevard which we followed across town vainly seeking some indication of our hotel. Suddenly an old blue Ford, which had been following since we arrived, pulled along side when we stopped for a traffic signal. The passenger commented in English on the charm of our Mercury. We asked him where the Continental Hotel was and he replied, "Follow us," and off they went. (More detectives?) We tailgated them back along the same boulevard, turned up side streets, inched down what appeared to be alleys, made a left turn and were in front of the Continental's entrance. The Ford driver waved as he drove away. Blessing of blessings, the hotel clerk had our reservations and a room was waiting. We crawled under the covers and died.

The following morning we automatically rolled out at six o'clock to begin another day. Thankfully it was a "no travel" day so we rolled back in for additional much-needed rest. As our first day in Bogotá, this Saturday was something of a dud for us. We could not reach our business contacts nor learn much about the city because the national tourist office was solidly closed. I wrote letters and business reports. Renee wandered around to visit a few open shops and learn something about emeralds for which Colombia was famous. At one jeweler she noticed that when the proprietor displayed a tray of cut stones, a clerk locked the door and stood guard; allowing entrance only to those who knocked. Among those who entered was a group of four German tourists with a sad question to ask. While walking along a boulevard they had been accosted by a street vender who allowed them to buy "emeralds" of great size and beauty at unbelievably low prices. After making their purchases they had "buyer's remorse" and decided to head for a jewelry store to find out what they had purchased. And what they had was not good. The stones were beautiful, gorgeous, pieces of green glass. The jeweler showed the Germans and Renee how true emeralds retain their color under ultraviolet light and glass changes to an awful outhouse brown. The tourists had been swindled and swindled to the hilt. Meanwhile, Renee had learned much about emeralds, including their size, clarity, perfection and cost. When she returned to the hotel room where I was slaving at a typewriter to make a dollar, she had already figured out a simple way to spend several hundreds of them.

Personal safety in Bogotá seemed to be questionable. On a subsequent business day, while Renee was cabbing from the tourist office to our hotel, the driver turned up a rather narrow street. Ahead she could see a large group of young men milling about in the center of the block. The taxi driver, without so much as an excuse, made a quick U-turn and used a totally different route to the hotel door. On another day the taxi driver requested that Renee roll up all windows in back and lock both doors before he slowly drove past fringes of another street crowd. The same door-locking procedure, as used by taxi drivers and the jeweler, accompanied us to lunch. We visited a recommended Spanish restaurant about a block from the hotel. To enter we had to knock at the door. After we left, the door was solidly locked behind us. Whether this was typical of Bogotá, or only of the days we visited, we'll never know. For sure it lent an air of somewhat hair-raising insecurity to be in a capital city with such uncommon civil unrest on the part of its citizens.

Our first night out on the town was also a welter of unusual experiences. We'd read somewhere that dinner didn't begin until ten o'clock. As we soon found out, that was quite true. Anyhow, about nine o'clock we sallied forth from the hotel and were met by a group of taxi drivers interested in carrying us to any desired destination. We asked them about the restaurant we wanted to visit and they told us it had been out of business for three years. We couldn't help but question this because we had just telephoned the Maitre d' about the his dinner hours. Nevertheless, realizing we may have telephoned the wrong restaurant and the drivers were right, we considered their information and asked where else we could go. With one voice they named a spot they all knew and recommended highly. Our next question involved fare negotiation. "How much?" The answer was 15 Pesos for the journey. Renee had been traveling around Bogotá for three and four Pesos a trip, so the evening fare didn't sound right. The deciding negotiation factor was a driver's comment that it was a "large" distance. We had no desire to dine on the outskirts of a strange city and find ourselves in difficulty obtaining late-night transportation. So back into the hotel we went. The first question to the clerk was, "Should we pay 15 Pesos to reach this restaurant?"

His answer was, "Of course not. You pay by the meter and it's only worth about six Pesos." This immediately destroyed all misplaced trust we had in Bogotá cabdrivers. We asked the clerk about another restaurant we had heard of. "Yes, it is very good" he replied and wrote down the address. Again we walked out into the arms of our small group of eager bandits. We told them no passengers unless they ran on the meter. They turned away and left us standing alone. We walked up the street toward a boulevard on which there was more traffic. An empty taxi pulled up and the driver agreed to run on the meter. Our destination charge was 6 Pesos including a tip. It was now a little after nine. We entered our destination restaurant, but it was still in the process of being made up for the night's trade. There were no tablecloths on the tables. We decided to walk the area and eventually wandered upstairs into a delightful little place with sweet music and no customers. The Maitre d' suggested that we return later because then there would be people. With further walking Renee noticed a couple entering "Don Quixote" and we decided to give it a whirl. The entry was locked but a youthful Indian face peered through a missing window pane, opened the gate and bowed us into a charming Latin foyer. We were in a "Spanish" restaurant with guitars, accordions and a wild pianist who played nothing but American jazz and musical comedy classics. Menu prices were modest and we could have ordered anything offered without disgracing our credit card. Musicians arrived at our table and asked if we wanted anything special. We have one piece we both consider very funny so they began sawing and swinging madly with an excellent rendition of "Never on Sunday." They played another piece of unidentifiable Latin origin before we decided that we'd had enough and tipped them. But, not knowing local customs, I had tipped far too much. The musicians presumed that we wanted more music. So for another 20 minutes Renee and I enjoyed our private orchestra, much to amazement and amusement of about 30 other diners. After our bill was paid I asked the waiter to send the gateman for a taxi. Within a few minutes Renee and I were bumping back to our hotel…on the meter.

Midway of the next day, after happily operating for the equivalent of over six and a half years of average driving, the water pump of the Mercury engine decided to give up the ghost. We drove to the Lincoln-Mercury service center and were there given the bad news. Due to Colombian government restrictions, which limited automobile dealerships to about ten percent of their orders for spare parts, no water pumps and no repair kits were available within the city. Not even for last year's car, let alone for ours which, as far as we could determine, was the only new car in the entire nation. Accordingly, the need for a water pump repair initiated a series of furious misadventures. Our Ford Motor representative checked other cities for availability of a spare part. A pump we hoped would fit was located in Medellin, a major Colombian city about 300 miles away. Instructions were sent by telegraph to put the pump on the next flight coming to Bogotá. About the time the airplane was ready to leave, the Medellin manager decided the pump wouldn't fit and didn't send it. More telegrams flew back and forth between Ford Bogotá and Ford Medellin before he was convinced to ship the pump on an afternoon flight. However, when he called their airport, it was explained that the plane had been grounded by fog. A few minutes later Bogotá learned that the fog had lifted and the plane was gone. A telephone call to Medellin disclosed that the pump had not been aboard the second flight.

Why?

Because the parts manager attempted to save time and money, so he said, by sending the pump with a crew member in personal baggage. But none of the crew would take the water pump. It remained 300 miles away. This was enough of a series of setbacks to again send us to revisit all local auto parts stores. Finally we found a water pump but it wouldn't fit. So we decided to let matters remain as they were, relax and see what could be done the next morning. While all this had been going on; we had a mechanic install the shock absorber, which I had removed several days before, and replace a clamp which had broken and allowed the muffler to fall free whenever we tangled with rocks or rubbish in the roadbed.

At breakfast the next day, the Ford service representative announced that he'd be willing to donate the water pump off his two-year old car. This would free us to depart for Quito, Ecuador, somewhat on schedule. He would wait for arrival of a water pump and install it on his car later. We hurried to the garage, removed his water pump and it fit the Mercury perfectly. I paid my car repair bill and drove to the hotel to pick up Renee. We packed and started for Ecuador. The first few miles out of Bogotá were rough, bumpy and clogged with buses and trucks. Soon traffic cleared and we began climbing through mountains toward what appeared to be a resort area for wealthy Bogotá residents. There was more gorgeous Colombian scenery crossing the Magdalena River and eventually a long drive along its valley; said to be the breadbasket of Bogotá. Soon we were again climbing through more mountains into a small town where a local train had stopped for water. While I was taking pictures the engineer shouted that if we waited for a few minutes he would be delighted to race us. But no dice. Our delayed departure from Bogotá forced us to hurry on in order to reach an overnight stop with adequate time to find a decent room. We didn't have much trouble finding a hotel. All we had to do was drive past the lobby door, then ask a policeman where it was. He pointed back up the street toward the sign we'd missed. Here, in Ibaque, we parked on the street where a crowd gathered such as we'd never seen before. They surrounded the Mercury three and four deep, including brave souls who partially blocked vehicle traffic. Eventually we rescued our car and parked it behind a barred gate. During our walk around town after dinner we visited a small but busy variety store. Our purchase was a huge bar of very crude locally made laundry soap which was mailed to our daughter as a reminder to wash behind both ears. Then it was into a tiny cafe for cold sodas.

A shoeshine boy came in, wandered around and agreed to polish my boots for a Peso. While shining he expressed surprise they were so terribly large, much larger than he'd expected, and really should be worth a Peso each. He also pointed out that if he shined the boot tops, this should also be an extra charge because he thought I was wearing only shoes. We neither agreed nor disagreed, but let him proceed at his own pace. He did a beautiful job and shined the tops on his own decision.

Accordingly, we paid him one Peso for each boot he shined. Meanwhile, a newspaper boy, pushing among patrons, became a little too friendly and knocked over my glass with one of his papers. Much to his surprise we merely called him a "Bad man" and let it go at that. As we left he accosted us on the street and, with a big smile, explained that he appreciated the fact we hadn't broken his neck for ruining my beverage.

Our next day was a dilly. It took five minutes more than ten hours to drive 194 miles of paved highway from Ibaque to Popayan. This was a route that many people in Colombia told us was the "bandito" area. We were advised several times never to travel this section at night, park in lonely sites nor stop for anyone or anything; even those in uniform who appeared in unusual places. What did we face? It was a wonderfully wide, twisting highway that was slow going because of heavy trucks and frequent buses cluttering the route. In this "touchy" area were dozens of fruit and vegetable stands lining the roadway, each one displaying mounds of huge carrots, beets, cabbages, and vegetables that shall forever remain nameless. At some we saw trucks parked while drivers haggled for fresh fruit. At one site a chauffeur-driven Buick, with its female passenger in the back seat, was parked by a large counter-top while the driver was buying fruits and vegetables. Just ahead, we could see a tired old kitchen chair on which were seated two fresh pineapples waiting for a purchaser.

Which brings up a logical question, "How did we feel about traveling through such an area?" Both of us were concerned to the point of making every effort to conduct ourselves with caution. Our only meal or gas stops were in large towns. We steered clear of all possible traffic confusion and did not pass too close to pedestrians who might toss something at or under the car. And much too often we peered at every bush to see if a bandit crew were lying in wait for us.

Then comes the question, "Was it necessary?" We don't know. We only know that we often saw pickup trucks with guards carrying shotguns. We noticed that truck drivers drove rapidly with their cab windows up. We saw a jeep in which the lone passenger wore a full bandolier of cartridges across his shoulder. And when a group of Army vehicles passed in a tight convoy, all the soldiers appeared to have their machine guns and side-arms ready

In paying for the water pump repairs I had depleted our supply of Colombian currency. Accordingly, we traveled part of the day short of funds though we tried three different banks in three different towns. In all it was the same reply: "Sorry, we do not cash Travelers Checks." Hunger took over as we drove into Cali about lunch time. Instead of searching for a bank we played it the other way. Our guide book suggested a major hotel as the place for lunch. After parking in front, I went in and asked the cashier to exchange my Travelers Checks for local currency. He did. We ate. And drove on with stomachs and wallet refreshed and fattened. Beyond Cali we saw more countryside of marvelous beauty, small ranches, valleys, rushing streams and high mountains which we soon crested. Needless to say, we were happy to reach our destination, Popayan; the most charming Colombian city we had the pleasure of visiting. One of the nicer things that happened there resulted from visiting the local tourist office. We had an introduction to its manager from the tourist office in Bogota, and what an introduction it must have been. After we talked a few minutes the Popayan manager offered to show us the city. This tour was to be in her official car, a ten-year-old Chevrolet sedan. The door was opened by the chauffeur and away we went. We visited a church, another church, a fabulous home full of delightful antiques and a somewhat quake-damaged building high on a hill overlooking the city. From there we photographed a magnificent sunset which crested surrounding mountains with scarlet clouds. While, at the same time, we could watch over the crowds of pedestrians hurrying home before dark and the street lights took over.

Information about the road from Popayan to the border with Ecuador had proved sparse and hard to come by. But, luckily, an English gentleman employed by the World Bank, who lived in Pasto, introduced himself while I was in our hotel lobby. After I answered questions about the Mercury, I queried him about our route ahead. He told me that it would take seven to nine hours of travel to reach Pasto because the road, most of which was all-weather dirt or gravel, was winding and twisting everywhere. He said it dipped to 900 feet above sea level, where the temperature was completely tropical and in other areas crested mountains high in the clouds. He insisted that an early start was advisable because afternoon cloud banks buried mountain sections of the route and made driving almost impossible. This sounded somewhat like the roads experienced before reaching the Venezuelan-Colombian border. From Pasto to the border and then to Quito, Ecuador, he said would be another two days driving for a distance our map listed as only 235 miles.

We could still see Popayan over our shoulders when we ran out of pavement early the following morning to begin what was to be the day-long journey to Pasto. In this area the Mercury's automatic transmission was priceless because I could easily shift to a lower gear when descending the many and continuing steep grades. There was one stretch I worked the shift lever continuously for almost three hours. This involved driving only 44 miles and making a short gasoline and coffee stop in the morning. The headache was that we were traveling along what seemed to be an endless section of the roadway that was barely one lane wide because the other lane was usually cluttered with piles of rock and gravel awaiting a road construction crew. When a car approached from the opposite direction one of us would dodge between two of the piles to wait until the other vehicle had passed. Our days "drive" from Popayan to Pasto, a total of 176 miles, took five minutes less than ten hours.

After registration in our hotel I fell asleep on the first bed that was convenient. On awakening Renee noticed that, for the first time, both my wrists and hands were swollen from the beating they had taken while keeping the Mercury under control over the rough dirt and gravel. At Pasto we inquired about condition of the roadway ahead and were told that construction could cause a complete shutdown from 7 o'clock in the morning until 7 o'clock in the evening. Accordingly, we made arrangements to be up and moving by 5 o'clock and, minus breakfast, left the hotel at exactly 5:30. It had been raining and city streets were a sea of mud. This was most discouraging because we knew from experience that the more rain, the more likely that landslides could close the roadway. Luckily the rain had been confined to Pasto. A few miles out of town the roadway had dried into its usual rough gravel surface and we trotted along at about 30 miles an hour. Twenty-five miles later we came to the construction area. A crew was widening a length of new roadbed where it had been cut into the side of a near-vertical sheer mountainside. Passage through the construction area was a one-way path because that was all the wider the bulldozer had made it. Renee's passenger-side door was only a few feet from the cliff which appeared to go up at least another thousand feet. On my side there was nothing but a nearly vertical drop through random clouds above a turbulent river far below. It is no exaggeration that, at times, the Mercury's left wheels were only a few feet away from the edge of this drop, with no guard rail or barrier to provide any sense of security. At the end of this lengthy construction zone a relaxed chain was draped across the path where the opposing way was closed to traffic. Here bus and car passengers napped, or snacked at one of numerous tiny restaurants scattered nearby, until the barrier was lowered. We passed around a chain post and continued along a two-lane bumpy gravel roadway through unique farming country. In this area we saw Indian boys using long forked sticks instead of pitch forks. Little girls leading pigs and cattle out to pasture. And dozens of women waiting by the side of the road for a bus to take them to Ipiales which was the frontier town. There we obtained entry visas from the Ecuadorian Consulate. Then it was five blocks further on to a Colombian government building to clear the car with Aduana and check ourselves out with the Migracion office. A short drive down one of the paved side streets, plus a mile on a dirt portion of the Inter-American Highway, brought us to the border. Here two nearly identical buildings faced each other across a tiny bridge. The nearer was Colombian the further Ecuadorian. We parked by the nearest building and chains were raised to block both front and back of the Mercury. While a vendor tried to sell me an absolutely beautiful parrot, Colombian officers checked our credentials and told us to walk across the bridge to Ecuador.

That nation's officers stamped our tourist card and said that we should report to government offices in the town of Tulcan. Only then was the chain in front of the Mercury dropped so *Aventura* could proceed over the bridge into Ecuador.

14

ECUADOR

Tulcan, ten minutes from the frontier, had only one paved street and we missed it on the way in. But we did find the central plaza. A taxi driver pointed out a building he thought was the tourist office. Instead it housed both Migracion and Adauna. On the ground floor we checked in and had tourist cards and passports stamped. Then we tramped upstairs where the Mercury was properly entered into the country. The Aduanero told us to go across the street to offices of the Transito Policia. Here the car's papers were re-stamped and the Mercury identified as being properly authorized for circulation within Ecuador. Before leaving town we visited one of several Cambios and exchanged Colombian money for Ecuadorian. Neither they nor the banks would cash Travelers Checks. After we left Tulcan we came to our first Ecuadorian Pare. This was staffed by a variety of officers who had to inspect our passports and documents covering the car. All was in order and we were told we could proceed. Then the officers began asking for money. This didn't really make any sense to me. They had performed no service and were paid by their own government, so why should we tip them? My Spanish completely vanished and the only thing I could think to say was, in English, "Why should I give you money?" This hopelessly confused the situation. They were faced with the problem of explaining in Spanish to a person who doesn't understand it, why they should be tipped. The result was they became frustrated and said "Good-bye" in English.

Somewhere earlier I should have mentioned that we carried a two-day supply of food. One day in each of two containers. Because there were so few places to eat in this area, we decided to pillage one of the food boxes. It wasn't a question of saving life, Only a matter of simple convenience to relax in the car and enjoy a meal at the time of hunger.

The highway beyond the Pare, and after lunch, was so pleasant we were looking forward to an easy run into Quito, Ecuador's capital city. Pleasure stopped within a mile, with suddenness that left us shaken. The highway became a muddy bog, cut up by tractors and filled with jagged rocks around which were deep ruts made by trucks squeegeeing their way through the muck. We tried our best but within a hundred yards the Mercury was completely hung up on the top of a ridge with the undercarriage dragging and both drive wheels spinning uselessly. I slogged back through mud to the trunk, extracted our tow cable and attached it to the front of the car. By this time a bulldozer thundered past in the opposite direction with a gasoline truck in tow. It appeared to have been stuck in the same mud and was being dragged through the mess to dry pavement behind us. On seeing our predicament, the "dozer" operator waved his hand and shouted, "Wait a few minutes and I'll be back." Soon we had a Caterpillar tractor the size of a house backed in front of the Mercury. Our tow cable was attached to the "cat hook" and away we bounced. It was a quarter-mile of clatter, thud, bump and splash as we were hauled out, like a toy sled, over the wet rubble of the construction section. After our arrival on solid ground we both shouted "Gracious", unhooked, and coiled the tow cable in the trunk. But to lurch forward on our merry way was not to last for long. About a half-mile ahead there was a similar construction area. It did not appear to be as bad so I drove ahead and promptly slammed onto a buried boulder. Whoops, there went the muffler/exhaust pipe connection. Again we sounded like an ancient truck. Ahead, on clear ground, I parked, found the proper size rock for a fulcrum and pried the muffler into place with our tire iron. By now I'd had enough practice to make this under-car operation quite easy. It was 264 more miles to Quito, which locals said would take seven hours. Now we believed it.

After driving this far south, where almost every previous road was burdened with large trucks and buses, we were surprised to discover that Ecuador had very little traffic on its primary route. So little in fact that for a while we were unsure as to whether we were traveling the right direction toward the capital city. After we stopped a truck driver to ask if we were on the correct route, he said, "Yes," and acknowledged that there were few signs to be found. Accordingly, at 25 to 30 miles an hour, we continued along this very long and bumpy cobblestone road.

A few miles south of Ibarra, as we climbed higher along the Andes, we passed a wedding celebration by the side of the roadway. The bride and groom were dancing together while each wore a backpack containing personal possessions. Their wedding clothes, which appeared to have been freshly laundered, glowed with bright colors in the sunlight. Music for the party was coming from a large drum, several brass horns and what appeared to be a group of string instruments. Surrounding the dancers were their friends, watching the performance and snacking. As we drove slowly past we could see into an adjacent yard area where other guests were preparing the wedding meal over an open fire. For what seemed years we continued on and on over this one-lane cobblestone paving as it lead us toward Quito. It was an unpleasant road; rough, choppy and most of all…noisy. The infrequent truck, and less frequent bus, needed the entire roadway and usually forced us onto the shoulder. We couldn't blame the other drivers. It was so difficult and dangerous in its own way that they needed every possible inch. The route was usually walled off within villages so that in such sections driving was somewhat like passing through a long, windowless, narrow alley. As darkness fell, travel became even more troublesome because we were so tired. Mountain passes were higher, steep curves sharper, and more difficult. "Steep" means it was first and second gear, mile after mile after mile. And curves being "sharp," means swinging the steering wheel as far as it would turn from right to left, and back again, to slowly round switchbacks as we climbed upward or cautiously braked downward toward a valley floor. In the darkness it was obvious that even truck and bus drivers considered the area difficult driving. They too were more cautious, slowed and pulled aside as they passed in the opposite direction. Suddenly our cobblestone ended. There were no more. We were bumping along on rutted dirt. This too gave up in about 100 yards when we rolled onto beautifully smooth well-engineered asphalt. It was the northern end of a paving project that would eventually give Ecuador a modern highway all the way to the Colombian border. Ahead we saw what appeared to be city lights, but they seemed to be receding instead of coming closer. Nevertheless we soon rounded a mountain and began rolling downhill into the city of Quito. No street map was in our file so we pulled into an open gas station, fueled and asked for instructions to reach our hotel. Though directions were clear, and I'm certain we could have followed them, a customer at the station offered to lead us. He hopped into his car and away we went, a tiny two-vehicle parade threading its way through the city toward the Hotel Colon. There, tired and beaten, after a full day of difficult roads at an average speed of less than 20 miles an hour, I flopped on the bed while Renee ordered dinner brought to our room. We ate and quietly collapsed.

The next morning I drove to Quito Motors, the major Ford-line dealer in the city, to restore the left rear shock absorber which had loosened again. While mechanics were under the car they noticed that our front sway-bar bushings were worn and one of the engine mounts was finger loose. The mount was tightened and sway bar bushings replaced. All of which was much a credit to the sharp-eyed Ecuadorian mechanics. The following day, we visited the central public market: San Rouque. Meat shops were almost American in appearance and the display of food stuffs was staggering. We saw heads of cabbage that were, without exaggeration, 12 to 16 inches in diameter. Our purchases? Six tiny handmade wooden spoons and three homemade dolls of the type local Indian children might play with.

That afternoon we went to bullfights that were held in celebration of the anniversary of the founding of the city. It was a colorful affair in the city's new bull ring. Europe's Spanish influence predominated with many attractive women wearing Spanish hats and shawls, accompanied by their men in traditional "Don" styles. Matadors were, for the most part, excellent. The bulls, unfortunately, not so. Only one could be said to have been a "good brave bull." Two were of modest quality and three were simply poor. One was so extremely bad that the crowd spent fifteen minutes telling the "President" of the celebration that he should obtain a new bull. But he could not. There were no spare bulls. This most unworthy bull's breeder was dishonored through the use of black streamers on banderillas that picudores stuck into the bull's back with great daring and skill. Nevertheless it was a stirring afternoon of relaxing in the sun, enjoying an enthusiastic crowd of colorful Latins while watching daring men who, at that critical moment of slaying the bull, must for overlong seconds take their eyes away from needle-sharp horns which could kill them.

Though we were up at four the following morning, to depart at five, our host had coffee, bread, jam and orange juice brought to our room to send us on our way. Our need to leave Quito early was to miss another bad driving situation high in the Andes near Gun. We were told that afternoon clouds often formed on the gorgeous Andean peaks and effectively reduced highway visibility to something approaching zero. Luckily we did pass through the mountain passes sufficiently ahead of the hazardous cloud banks to drive without trouble. Such preplanning also made it easy to wend our way through central Quito and eventually reach the major boulevard leading south to Peru. Lonely policemen swathed in ponchos, deserted wet streets and an infrequent car were the only sights as we departed. On the city's outskirts there were brilliant stars, occasional street lights and Ecuadorians on their way to work. Some wore Western clothes, sweaters, or coats. Other pedestrians were swathed in national costumes, with huge blankets wrapped around their body and across the face, to keep warm. Men wore large felt hats as did some of the women. It was rare, but there were even a few men on bicycles, with big ponchos flapping behind as they peddled along the highway. Amid the darkness of nearby fields we could see an occasional fire, around which were huddled three or four people cooking or warming. A solitary dog, alerted by noise of passing vehicles, was by the roadside, watching and waiting, hoping someone would feed him. Buses were already boarding groups of market-bound women and children from roadside stops, all with bundles of goods ready for the day's business. At our first Pare past the edge of the city, officers were wrapped in mufflers and heavy coats. They were examining a truck and waved us on by indicating that the road ahead was the proper direction for us. At another, the officer was asleep. We peeked into his guardhouse then drove on. Both Pares reminded us of the coming Christmas festival. Their wooden barriers, which were usually lowered across the road to stop traffic, were already gaily decorated with colored lights as a warning when lowered, and holiday decorative when angled high above the road. As we traveled through near total darkness toward the highlands, we could look back and see colorful blinking lights of Quito. Leaving a city early in the morning, as it comes to life, is somewhat like watching a child waking. It stirs, stretches, rolls over, and eventually begins to take coherent action. That was Quito. Reds, blues and greens of neons, mixed with blue-white pin points of street lights, defined the city amid surrounding mountain slopes. By the time we had driven 52 kilometers (33 miles) we were in the clouds. It was pleasant early morning travel as *Aventura* continued south toward Peru. We had 105 miles of excellent highway before pavement abruptly ended in wide dirt. This only continued for a short distance before we were back on fast pavement again into Riobamba where we purchased gasoline. Here we learned that in such small towns, the local gas station hid its pump inside a storeroom or garage fronting the street. We couldn't see pumps from the Mercury unless we looked directly through the front door. The best locating procedure for us was to slow down at every mechanic's sign or tire repair shop and then try to determine if there was a gas pump inside. In other areas we had noticed an extra-long gas hose exiting through the shop door and hanging over the sidewalk, with the nozzle laying on the curb for the next customer's use.

Not many miles further we ran out of useful roadway and entered another of Ecuador's construction projects. Rough and muddy, this one was no picnic. We thought we had cleared the worst of it, like two miles of continuous ruts and chuckholes, until we rounded a corner to stop behind a parked bus. Ahead of us a road crew was clearing a landslide which had effectively blocked traffic. It appeared that we were going to be here for quite a while. But passage was sooner than expected. Within 20 minutes the road clearing area was opened and we passed through. There were few rock and boulder strewn sections and only one in which we banged the chassis over a buried obstruction. At the end we reached pavement and cruised the last 22 miles into Cuenca at 45 and 50 miles an hour, our usual speed when a highway is cluttered with pedestrians and animals. Tired and well-beaten from the day's long drive we checked into the first service station for gas. The filling was almost completed when a small boy called my attention to a widening pool of fuel under the car. One look gave me the message. The drain plug, at the corner of the tank, had been smashed inward and the leakage of gasoline was something to break your heart.

We hurriedly found the Hotel Cuenca, unloaded bags and drove to a nearby garage where the car could be parked in their lot. Luckily enough, in this unpretentious small town, good fortune favored us as it had so many times in the past. I jacked up the car and fumbled with the leaking plug in hopes of tightening it to the point where it would no longer drip. Alas and alack, the plug was not the problem. It was the threaded ring, into which the plug was screwed, which had been torn loose from the gas tank skin. Stray children and the son of the garage owner were supervising my efforts. I suggested they find cans and I would be glad to give them all the gas draining from the tank. Soon a miscellaneous collection of battered pitchers, chipped wash basins, tin cans and a rusty barrel were at my disposal. Or, more properly, their's. It took about ten minutes for 15 gallons of gasoline to change ownership from the Mercury's tank to their containers and barrel. A sealing material that I had brought in anticipation of repairing such a break was put to use. Unfortunately in my hurry, or lack of reading the instructions, it did not harden properly and I began cursing mightily as the tank continued dripping. From my position under the car I saw shined shoes and suit pants approaching. It turned out to be the garage owner and father of one of the boys. He said that he was an excellent mechanic, all of his work was guaranteed and the best way to repair the leak would be to remove the tank and have the torn corner soldered. Discretion being the better part of valor, I agreed. Here was someone needing work and offering a more sensible repair suggestion than I was using. He changed clothes, we moved the car over a nearby mechanic's pit and both of us proceeded to unzip the gas tank. The worst part of the job being that we had to totally unload the trunk that had been so carefully packed to provide security and balance to the car. The tank was rinsed with water to prevent an explosion while mending. Then it was carried across the street to the soldadura who quickly did an excellent job of replacing and patching the damaged metal. The cost was five Sucres. We bolted the tank back in place and used five-gallons of spare fuel to start the Mercury and be sure the tank did not leak. Then it was back to the local service station where we refueled before parking for the night in the garage open-air lot.

The mechanic invited us into his home for a refreshment, an invitation which turned our smug "North-American tourist passing through" attitude upside own. Glasses were filled and we toasted everyone's health before I noticed that the mechanic's son, and a girl, who had been attending my attempts to fix the gas tank, were in the room. Others included the mechanic's wife and a very attractive young woman in her early 20s. The boy had been a watchful observer of the repair effort but the little girl, of six or eight, had been my most efficient helper. I had only to think of a needed tool and she would hand it to me…while the boy watched. Her constant smile had been comforting reassurance that whatever I was doing was perfection, even when the tank continued to leak. Now she was standing against the mechanic's chair, grasping his leg for security, while her huge brown eyes watched my every expression. She was wearing a freshly pressed dress. On the floor beside her were two large paper bags.

Then the mechanic began to tell us her story in elementary Spanish both Renee and I could understand. The young woman, who said nothing, was his daughter. As a teenager she had been involved with the son of a local banker. The little girl was the result of the affair. But the young man would not marry the child's mother because she was from a family far below his economic status. And, by custom, no one would marry the young woman because she was an unmarried parent. Suitors would happily accept the woman, but not another man's child.

Would we take the child with us? All her clothes were packed in the two paper bags. She was loving and gentle. An education in America would be everything the family had ever thought of. The mother could then marry and be happy knowing her daughter was with good people. They would pray for us many times. Please do this for us.

Renee and I looked toward each other. My mind, and I'm sure her mind as well, was in a turmoil. The little girl was a charmer. She could fit into our family and I was comfortable that Kim would take her to heart. What an opportunity to do something truly decent in a situation we were never likely to face again.

Then cold water covered my dreams. The child had no cedula, no passport, no permission to leave Ecuador and, most difficult of all, would be a legal hazard at every border crossing from there through Brasil and eventually into the United States. No matter our feelings, there was simply no possible means by which we could insert her into *Aventura.*

Today I'm not really certain how we explained the impossibility of honoring the mechanic's request. We left his home in silence. But the memory will be forever of a quiet dinner Renee and I shared at the hotel, time spent talking and re-talking the situation, and tears in my eyes as I sagged into bed with thoughts tumbling over each other about the smile and big brown eyes of a little girl who's name I never knew.

To leave Cuenca the clock was set for three in the morning. But about 4:30 we sat up in bed. We had overslept and neither of us heard the alarm go off. Quickly dressing, we sailed out of the hotel without breakfast, picked up the car and left town for what proved to be seven hours more of hard, wrist-straining, driving. Not only was the road narrow and twisting but it was almost totally devoid of villages or traffic. During the entire seven hour run, we encountered exactly two buses and one Jeep. That was it! Other traffic consisted of an occasional Indian aboard a mule or afoot and, even rarer, a tiny village with no services of any kind. Most unusual was one small town we entered in a most unique manner. The Inter-American Highway, which had been twisting and turning in the mountains high above a railroad in the valley, began to lead us downward. As we neared civilization we could see that railroad and roadway came together where both entered the main street over a single bridge. There were boards between and around the tracks but only room for one vehicle at a time. A truck facing us pulled aside while we crossed the bridge. Our question became: Who waits when a train appears?

We'd been told that after completing this rugged section of the Inter-American Highway, we would reach an Autopista prior to entering Machala near the border. "This," thought we, "must be a joke." But it proved not to be. About twenty miles outside of Machala, there was indeed a paved highway and a short distance down the highway a toll booth. We paid 2 Sucres for use of the broad asphalt ribbon on which we could roll at 55 and 60 miles an hour. Now all we had to do was find the Peruvian consulate. Because it was next to noon by the time we found the address, I had Renee hurry and run to the office before the Consul closed and left for lunch. My heart sank as she reached the door and found it locked. The Consul's wife was next door. After much discussion we understood her messages: Number One; the Consul was not there. Number Two; he was in Peru. Number Three; they didn't know when he was due back. Number Four, the nearest Consul was 250 miles away, back over the same terrible roads we just covered. Another Consul was in Guayaquil, some hundreds of miles distant, to which we could either drive or fly. Fortunately, in addition to the consul's wife there were several mature daughters hanging from a wall of windows while their mother discussed the problem with us. One of them asked if I was a "Norte Americano." On being told that I was, she said "There is now no problem. Go to the frontier. Present your passport and they will give you permission to enter the country." I found this difficult to believe and questioned her, and the others, closely. They all agreed that she was right. For a North American, it was possible to enter Peru by going directly to the frontier. In the car, I gave Renee the word. We could go ahead and perhaps be able to cross. We could drive 250 miles back. Or we could fly to Guayaquil for a visa. The border being nearest of all options, we decided to proceed to the frontier; exit ourselves from Ecuador and let the Peruvians decide what to do with us. But first, a soda and cheese sandwich to cheer us while waiting for controls to open after their lunchtime closure.

Afterward we found another autopista, paid the toll for 25 or 30 miles of pavement which led to broad gravel which caused no problems. A Pare for the military checked us into the border zone. Then we came to a tri-corner intersection where there was an Aduana and another military guard. We stopped and all our papers were inspected while I attempted to take a picture of the Pare. The officer said it was not permitted. So we put the cameras away in anticipation there would be no picture taking for the balance of the border crossing. Nor was there. This was the Ecuadorian border town of Huaquillas which was nothing to write home about. Its single dirt street down the center of town was also the Inter-American Highway. It could be called a "divided" thoroughfare with the center division being a group of tiny shacks from which storekeepers were vending clothing and household necessities. On our roadside were a number of frontier buildings for Ecuadorian government officials. On the far side it was a row of tacky restaurants where the best things to eat would come from branded bottles and cans. We arrived a little after one o'clock and attempted to cross into Peru. But our papers were not in order. We had failed to have Ecuadorian officers sign us out of the country. Their offices were back a block and a half from the frontier. On arrival we discovered that every office was closed for lunch and would remain so until two in the afternoon. We had additional lunch in a tiny Chinese cafe then charged into the Ecuadorian offices at 2 P.M.. to get checked out. Much to our disappointment, a large bus had set down 20 passengers who were waiting for the same service. We became the 21st, more or less, in line. At 2:30 the office opened with one little officer, behind one little window, at one little desk, taking care of our long line...one passport at a time. At five minutes of three his Jefe, apparently feeling sorry for me because I had only worked my way down to seventh in line, took me to his office and stamped our paperwork.

Now I hurried back to the car for a quick run across the border and entry into Peru.

15

PERU

In contrast to the Ecuadorian border town, the Peruvian side was a neatly laid out control area. There was practically no town. Nearly all structures were government buildings with only a few small stores selling plastic and glass novelties. Border-crossers were in well regulated lines, traffic was controlled, such as it was, and offices appeared neat and in good condition. We were directed to park with the Mercury's nose pointed toward a tiny building in which a Migracion officer was stationed. We presented passports and, after some discussion, he decided to issue tourist cards. They would cost of 160 Sols and be valid for 90 days. When he asked for Sols, I explained I had none because I had just come in from Ecuador. With this, other travelers in line gave me the "Why didn't you do it in Ecuador?" bit about changing money. I pointed Renee back across the bridge to get our money changed before a man in line said he'd be glad to make change for me. By now the Jefe of this Peruvian Immigration section wandered over to inspect our car and was talking with Renee. Though it was illegal to exchange money on the Peruvian side of the dry river bed he allowed us to do our thing by the open doorway of an unofficial cambio building. Midway in this financial transaction the Peruvian Migracion officer discovered that I had accidentally not given him enough money. While I had Peruvian money in one hand, and Renee was holding Ecuadorian money, I had to disappear into the immigration office, straighten matters out by completely undoing our fee payment and begin all over again. This completed, I then looked for the man who needed our Ecuadorian money and relieved his worried look by paying him. Eventually we had documents and change. We moved the car forward a few feet for a cursory Aduanero inspection. Once that was completed I walked across the street to where the National Security Police entered our names in their register of foreigners in the country. Then we drove about a block and stopped in front of another Aduana. Here the car was examined, the Carnet de Passage prepared and stamped, and luggage given a careful inspection. Now it was back across the street to another office where the National Transit Police checked the Mercury into their nation. Finally we were told that we were ready to go but within two blocks another officer stopped us to inspect everything done to date.

We departed the border on what proved to be the beginning of an excellent Peruvian highway from the north to the south of this long and unusual country. A half hour's drive over pleasantly smooth pavement brought us to Tumbes and our first overnight stop in one of the chain of government-owned tourist hotels. No rooms were available with bath, but we were so tired that the available room with a bed was more than satisfactory. A wash bowl on the wall promised to take care of face washing and doors down the hall aroma'd nature's necessities. Because the hotel was government owned we expected something along the line of a YMCA combined with a hash-house. Happily, food was excellent and service as good as any received to date. Perhaps our only disappointment in Tumbes was an inability to visit the local fair. The entire main street had been barricaded for two blocks to allow a city-wide celebration to take over. Unfortunately both of us were so tired we didn't have the energy to walk two blocks to enjoy the excitement of a country fair in Peru. (In retrospect we were darn fools not to have done so.)

The next morning proved a comedy of unsuspected proportions. While Renee was out of the room I decided to wash and shave. Holding a towel under the faucet, I turned it on. It pooped one small tablespoon of water and promptly expired into nothingness. There wasn't a drop of water to be had in the hotel. After breakfast, two somewhat dirty Americans prepared to check out. A Diners Club sign on the reservation desk indicated acceptance of this most useable American credit card. Unfortunately, like the hotel in Cuenca, this hotel had never made use of the charge facility before. At least not during our clerk's period of employment. He couldn't find the tickets, didn't know how to operate the printing machine, wasn't quite sure how to total the bill or present the proper information for payment. It became such a chore that I excused myself, leaving the clerk alone with his problems, to fill the Mercury's tank with gasoline. On return, everything was ready. Renee was downstairs with luggage, my Dincr's Card charge ticket been properly stamped, the amounts were in, and the clerk had even signed for me so it would be known that he was going to pay. I explained, as gently as possible, that it was nice of him to sign for my charge but the Diners' organization would not accept it unless I also signed, which I did. Our next stop in Tumbes was to cash a few Travelers Checks, which the hotel would not accept. We circled the tiny town twice before locating the single bank. Here we learned that only the manager could approve the cashing. After inspecting my passport, bank signature reference cards, and noting that the signatures on all were somewhat related to each other, he agreed to cash one twenty dollar check. I explained that this was not adequate funds to reach Lima. He explained that reaching Lima was only a day's drive and $20 (U.S.) would do it. After discussion, we upped the amount to $50 (U.S.), or 1900 Sols that were delivered to me in tattered 100 Sol notes. With local money in our pocket, stomachs padded with breakfast, and pavement ahead for the Mercury, we felt more like pleasure-seeking tourists. From a transportation standpoint, much of the day was delightfully easy. Our only unsuspected hazards turned out to be the police. A short distance out of Tumbres we were flagged to the side of the road and our passports and driver's license inspected by a patrol of the National Transit Police. Then came an endless sequence of Pares. It seemed that every time we would make the "mistake" of stopping we ran into a frustrating experience of additional passport and documents shuffling. Being typical foreigners, we had no idea which Pares we should miss (those inspecting trucks) or those at which we should stop (those inspecting people). Soon it became painfully obvious that many of the officers were totally unfamiliar with the documents we were presenting. In some instances they could not read them. Usually they had to search every office desk to find an appropriate book in which to enter the information.

Spice of the day was an unnecessary and irritating "interview" that took place in the Peruvian town of Piura, where we stopped for lunch. A Spanish omelet with chopped chicken for Renee, with chopped beef for me. Sodas for refreshment and a flock of the cutest little chickens you've ever seen wandering around underfoot; much to consternation of the pursuing restaurant owner and her son. Other patrons didn't think it was funny. The "interview" began as we walked toward our car to find a local policeman in attendance. We asked him if we were on the right road for the next town. He said that we were. As we opened the Mercury he asked for my driver's license. I gave it to him. He asked for registration of the car. I gave it to him. He asked for a passport. I gave him a tourist card and asked why he was giving us all the trouble. He didn't answer but, with papers in hand and my eagle eye on all documents, he began circling the car trying to find something. I was not sure what. Meanwhile I took a picture of him and included the group of boys who had gathered to watch the commotion. When the policeman and I were together again he began popping questions about where I'm from and where I'm going. While I'm answering, a loud, clear, American-style voice floats across the crowd, "You have trouble there."

I turned and spotted a young man of American appearance and asked him what the problem was. He replied in good English, "The police here are the big problem. They think they are very important. But they have no brains!"

I grinned to acknowledge appreciation of the message, said "Thanks," and returned to face my police protagonist. It seemed that he had many problems in addition to not knowing what he was looking for. But he had noticed a tourist sticker on a side window of the car. that proclaimed it was "Good for thirty days." He pointed to this and sputtered that it had expired and what was I doing in Peru. I sputtered a reply in a combination of Spanish and English, for by now I was completely unsettled, to explain that he was not very bright. The sticker was a tourist visa for Costa Rica, the Republic located in Central America, which had nothing to do with my being in Peru. Crestfallen that he had not found an obvious problem, he opened my passport and became unglued all over again. He could find no visa stamps in it. His problem now being that he was examining the first few pages which were devoted to printed instructions for the holder. I called his attention to other pages which contained our immigration permit for Peru and asked him in my best Spanish, "Why are you causing us so many problems?"

He told us that looking at things was his business. Eventually he deciphered the visa and gave the collection of paperwork back. As he angrily stomped off amid loud laughter of our youthful audience, I sincerely hoped I had ruined the man's day. We left town and continued on through a succession of small towns to our pleasantly uneventful overnight stop in another very nice government hotel in the town of Chiclayo.

Our next-day departure from there was another time-consuming haphazard affair, although we planned it otherwise. The first thing of the morning was to rush downstairs and find a porter who owned a bucket and rag to wash a hideous load of dirt off the Mercury. Next was a telephone call to Lima (about 570 miles away) to advise the Ford representative of our planned arrival schedule. I began making the telephone call at five minutes before eight and was talking to my party at five minutes after nine. Problems were availablity of the line to Lima, a lengthy discussion with an operator over whom I'd like to talk with and a busy connection at the other end. Then we had to wait at a highway crossing for a local freight train to pass. The tiny antiquated locomotive was towing a string of about 40 flatcars. All were connected by "link and pin" which railroad fans will recognize as a dangerous method of connection outlawed in the United States many years ago. For sure, I would not like to have been in the vicinity of that lengthy train when the engineer applied his brakes, for there was not a single brakeman on the string.

The first few miles outside of town limits were across a broad desert-like area in which the ribbon of asphalt was a smooth and pleasant companion. In was only then, on the comparative calm of Peruvian pavement, did I realize how dead tired my arms, shoulders and wrists were from the days of constant pounding since we'd left Bogata, Columbia. Be that as it may, we were rolling toward Lima through an area that is considered to be desert. Those of us from the United States, who think of a desert as either being a Sahara-like collection of vacant sand dunes, or vast wastelands such as are found in western portions of the U.S., would find the Peruvian desert truly unique. There were rolling sand dunes, rocky hills, flatland and small buttes. It was a never-ending collection of varied scenery whose only resemblance to a desert was that it displayed little or no vegetation. In the next government tourist hotel, in Trujillo, we were served chicken that was not really chicken. What the cook did was take a chicken leg and pound the meat so that it was almost paper thin while remaining attached to the bone. The resulting filet was dipped in batter and deep fried in cooking oil. On the plate it appeared to be an extremely thin veal cutlet with a chicken leg attached. But the Maitre d' assured us that it began with the pounding and ended with the unusual spicy flavor we thoroughly enjoyed.

The following Peruvian overnight in Huarmey was at a Hostalria. We counted ten sleeping rooms surrounding a small dining room, sitting room, tiny bar, and patio in which was a gasoline-powered electric light plant, by International Harvester, that provided the building's electricity. The final 200 miles into Lima was a relatively easy wander along the sea coast at the edge of a range of mountains, then a right turn over railroad tracks onto city streets with buses, taxis and pedestrians everywhere. Following a map in one of our books, Renee again located the proper street for our hotel. We checked into the El Alcazar a few minutes after noon, ordered lunch in our room and promptly went to bed for a long and well-deserved siesta after the arduous trip from Ecuador.

But peace was not to be our measure. Management telephoned to discuss the Mercury's engine operating in the basement. The first complaint was that it was against the law. A second complaint claimed it was making too much noise. Plus: it was dangerous. There is never any use fighting city hall or hotel management. We dressed, gassed the Mercury and drove to the Hotel Crillon, which had an open-air guarded parking lot behind it. During this move we ran into a difficult gasoline situation be- cause of a shortage of dollar exchange had limited the nation's importation of quality fuel. Some Lima stations sold what was called Populare for pennies a gallon. The price was so low, and quality so bad, that the Mercury engine would barely run on it. Later, we learned that some operators made a practice of diluting their Populare with less expensive kerosene to increase both profits and stretch their supply of fuel. The next best grade, Corriente, was seldom available. It cost a few cents more per gallon, but we could seldom find it. Another grade, found at upscale service stations dealing with private owners of late model cars, sold for twice the price of Populare. It had an octane rating in the low nineties. The best fuel of all, usually labeled Imported, had an octane rating of 95 to 98, and cost three times the price of Populare. With such a divergence of scarce product, the few service stations that had fuel were pumping fast and furious. As quickly as one car or truck was filled, the nozzle would be shoved into another tank and turned on full blast. But, our real problem was just finding one station a day that had any suitable gasoline to sell.

We collected a few maps to guide us while leaving Lima, plus plenty of instructions. But we didn't realize the importance of those specific instructions that ended with "Now be sure to ask someone when you get near the outskirts of town." It turned out that the beautiful main boulevard, with its central parkway dividing traffic, eventually deteriorated into a narrow residential street. This soon became rough dirt and finally terminated at a brick wall. Obviously we had come to the end of our way, though road maps and instructions claimed this was the Inter-American Highway Sur. We blundered about for 15 or 20 minutes while going back and forth, crossing and recrossing the southbound route out of town. One man said southbound was five miles from our current location. We backtracked in the direction he suggested in hopes of finding the highway that proved to be only three blocks away after a policeman pointed us in the proper direction. Soon we were on a Peruvian autopista leading from Lima. For a 10 Sol fee, we had 28 miles of excellent superhighway, with adequate signs everywhere. After we left the autopista the roadway wandered along beach areas near the Pacific Ocean. At one point we were traveling less than 100 feet from thundering breakers. Along this section, residents of tiny fishing villages between us and the ocean had an interesting manner of vending their catch. By the roadside, for a distance of about a mile, there were tables and chairs. In the chair, a woman. On the table, fish. As we passed, the women would quickly grab a single fish and hold it high for our inspection in hopes we would stop and buy. There must have been 25 or 30 of these venders at each end of the villages. When the Inter-American left the seacoast, and turned inland, the run from Lima to Nasca, our first overnight stop, could be best described as somewhat dull. The inland area was uninteresting, villages infrequent, and scenery conspicuous by its absence. Only an occasional green valley brightened the unending landscape of rocks.

Nasca turned out to be a tiny town similar to others we had seen; with few paved streets, mud or adobe buildings and dozens of people walking aimlessly in every direction. Our high spot was another government tourist motel. This one was a charming hacienda-type building constructed around a central patio with a swimming pool and hundreds of colorful, flowering plants. The kitchen was great and the Seviche (marinated raw fish) the best so far. Like previous rural hotels it had its own electricity plant and water pump to provide reasonable services most of the time. The next day's Peruvian run was much like the first: Barren countryside and an occasional village surrounded by greenery. Most of the villages were located in valleys through which a river was draining toward the sea. Our overnight stop at Camana was in another Peruvian government hotel which was, as usual, neat and clean. The bar served a fine variation of Pisco Punch and food was well prepared. Unfortunately the manager had several dogs. As did the family across the street in one direction, and across the street in every other direction. A car would drive along the dark city street and the dogs would begin to bark. This woke the chickens who would begin to crow. The chickens would wake cows, who would begin to bellow. To us, it seemed as though the hotel building would shudder to pieces from the barnyard ruckus.

As usual we left early in the morning, this time in hopes of reaching the Chilean border before it closed for the night. The first few miles were in dense fog which slowed us slightly, though later we cruised across Peruvian highlands at a casual 55 to 60 miles an hour on a broad paved highway. But smooth didn't last forever. Soon we were on rough gravel and tedious construction detours that not only slowed travel but deluged us with thick dust. In one place, the one-lane road climbed precariously along the edge of the mountain. Ahead of us, oncoming vehicles had stopped while waiting for a truck, one of the innumerable taxis and our *Aventura* Mercury to grind our way past in a cloud of fine powder dust. Otherwise the voyage from Camana to Arica was only a dull, exasperating journey. There were few places in which to eat and almost no supplies of fuel. Plus, on this last day out of Peru, we ran into an increasing number of Pares. At the first we had to display every document but nothing was noted except a record of our passage. The second Pare had a bar lowered across the road with a small boy in attendance. He lifted the bar at the toot of our horn. The third Pare housed a rather dyspeptic officer who requested everything in our portfolio: Papers for entering Peru with the car, for driving the car, owning the car, a passport for my being there and a passport for Renee. While the officer was working through our documents, I inspected the bulletin board. It appeared that in Peru there were rigid controls on bus and truck drivers. If a bus driver did not have a complete list of passengers, he was subject to a fine of 100 Sols. Should a truck driver not possess his operator's certificate he was subject to a fine of 50 Sols. Without his box of safety items; which should include flares, warning signals, tow cables and a first aid kit of 20 items (in total 65 pieces of equipment) the fine was 500 Sols. The fourth and fifth, our final "Pares," were for Migracion and Aduana officers who stamped our paperwork as we left their nation. We had been advised to exchange Sols back to dollars on the Peruvian side of the border before entering Chile. The basis of this was that we could obtain a better rate, like twice as much, for dollars exchanged in Chile. At Moquegua we scoured the town and eventually found a policeman who directed us toward the bank where we switched Sols for dollars. We didn't find a place to eat in town but outside, by a Pare, was a tiny restaurant. The best thing it offered was cold soda from an electric ice box next to the juke box. After lunch we paid our respects to officers at the Pare and signed out with Aduana, Migracion and the National Police. Soon we were on our way toward Arica in Chile.

But our planned border crossing from Peru into Chile almost didn't make it. The exit control officer, a member of the Guardia Civil was something less than civil. Our problem being that I did not have a passenger list or blank form for such a list. It seemed that Renee, though traveling on a separate passport and carrying Peruvian identification papers, had to be listed as a passenger of the vehicle as though she were in a public taxi. I jumped up and down, made terrible noises and eventually got nowhere. After gathering documents and passports I went to the office of the Chief of the Border Control Station. As I was explaining my problem to him, and he was explaining to me that this really was no problem, another member of his staff beckoned for me to return to the Control office. The control officer had regained his mind and found blank forms for me to complete with the required information. His previous opinion had been that without such blanks (and he said he had none) I never could leave Peru. The helpful Aduanero was more than polite, making up for Control's rudeness. He signed us out, wished us well, shook my hand and offered God's speed as we left for Chile. His wife was sitting on the office porch while knitting like Madame Lefarge, with every passerby apparently adding a stitch to the sweater.

16

CHILE

We drove toward the Chilean frontier station through a 17-mile "no-man's land" separating the two nations. If half of it belongs to Peru, the other half must belong to Chile. But why either would claim such an area is anyone's guess, for it was nothing but empty nothing. As we rolled into Chile's frontier station one of the guards was playing with his pistol. It seemed to be pointed in all directions at once so I sidestepped his gaze and ducked into the nearest office. Formalities were quick. Entrance papers were provided without the need for a Counsular Visa or identification other than our passports. We were officially in Chile and soon at Arica, our overnight stop. It was an isolated town of importance to the nation's economy because in it were, surprisingly enough, automobile assembly plants of American and European companies. Here we had one of the tires shifted, fuelled the Mercury and prepared for the 1500 mile four-day journey to the capital city of Santiago. All this before bedding down in a pleasantly modern motel with a plush restaurant and string trio for dancing. Two rows of carefully prepared dining tables circled the dance floor. Outside, on a veranda, there were additional chairs and tables for diners more interested in fresh air than hot food. The dinner was well-prepared, service inattentive and prices high. The hotel's 20 acres were well protected behind high fencing, a dense growth of shrubs and hundreds of trees. Inside this barrier were about 60 motel rooms, a huge swimming pool and the flowered central patio.

After leaving Arica the next morning we drove south for about an hour, into a magnificent grassy valley where, moments after crossing a bridge, we were stopped by a Pare barring the highway. Here, travel papers were inspected and rubber stamped by the Aduanero. Police officers checked both passports and listed us further forward into the nation. This time when I was asked for a list of passengers there was no surprise when I said I didn't have one. Instead, a blank sheet was pulled from a desk drawer, I filled in the data and everyone was fat and happy. There was no one to lift the highway barrier so, at Renee's suggestion, I did honors while she took pictures of my exercise for the day.

This first full day in Chile became so boring that we again became involved in evaluating roadside stone piling. This ancient art was practiced by Indians, road workers and truck drivers in most of Latin America. As mentioned earlier, we often found haphazard piles of stones almost directly in the road. Some were there to keep a vehicle from rolling either forward or backward while being repaired. On the other hand, road workers would place neat rows of rocks directly across the highway to stop you, divert your attention until you hit them, or indicate the direction in which you should leave the road to begin a detour. Other artistic stone pilings often indicated the entrance to dirt roads leaving the highway. These were undoubtedly the work of a truck driver or landowner, who wanted to mark his particular route in an unmistaken fashion. Flat rocks were sometimes piled in horizontal and/or vertical layers to create a pyramid effect. Other artists balanced round stones precariously until they had created a column 10, 12 or 15 stones high in which the uppermost stone appeared ready to roll off from the slightest breeze. In one area, for no reason that we could discover, there were interesting piles of rocks every few hundred yards to the right and left of the roadway. Each collection consisted of four to six round stones, again carefully balanced one on top of the other, ready to topple anytime.

Other stacked rocks, often used to support hazardous bridges or dirt fills in the mountains, always appeared as though they would give way at any moment and tumble us down into a river or valley far below. On the other hand, layers of stones placed along the side of the roadway, and usually painted white, served as a crash barrier. In one small town we rolled along a street with sharp stones placed in concrete, their points upward, along edges of the pavement. The hint here was not to drive off the roadway onto the grass or you would lose a few tires in the process.

Our maps showed that between Arica and Antofagasta there were a number of small towns. But we soon learned that there was no overnight place to stop between the two cities and only one or two stations from which to buy gasoline. Some of the mapped towns no longer existed or were ghostly relics of Chilean mining past. After our summation of the virtues of stone-piling, the continual boredom and desolation of this area created a second informal and long-running discussion. This one was about the most important aspects of making a comfort stop.

For the male sex we decided that an initial consideration would be to face in the proper direction to be polite and to avoid snickering laughter of one's female companions. The second requirement would be to face away from the wind so clothes were not going to be spattered by airborne moisture. The third need was to be certain of standing uphill so that your shoes do not become wet. The female member of the *Aventura* crew reported that the most hazardous situation, from her point of view, was inches high prickly grass or bushes. Availability of a downhill slope to prevent a widening puddle from ruining shoes or boots was a consideration of importance equal to a generous supply of tissues from the car's container. Perhaps the greatest hazard of all for the female of the species, said Renee, is a complete inability to look nonchalant when a trespasser crests a nearby hill or stumbles around a bush onto moments of privacy.

The Chilean government tourist hotel at Antofagasta was easy to find by the waterfront. After unloading our baggage I drove to a nearby service station to fuel the Mercury for its continuing engine operation. On return to the hotel a taxi driver tapped at a window and told me a tire was soft, and indeed it was. The right rear tire was about half down. I hurried back to the service station where a skilled Chilean mechanic quickly repaired the tire after extracting a tiny nail which had caused the loss of air. The next morning we ran into something new in hotel experiences. Breakfast, at a fixed price, was part of hotel services. But orange juice was a concession of the Maitre d' who managed the breakfast room. His price was 50 cents (U.S.) per glass for fresh juice which he prepared in a corner of the dining room. The charge was paid separately from our modest hotel bill.

Between Antofagasta and Chanaral, our third night's stop, we had been warned to purchase gasoline at the midpoint as there were no other gasoline stations between the two towns. We never did find any midway stations and relied upon our spare ten gallons for courage to drive straight through. Despite the continuing desolation, during these first few days in Chile we met many friendly people who spoke English and were most helpful in assisting us on our journey. A man we met in the office of a desert Pare provided us with maps and hotel information. In one of our hotels the sales manager for a General Motors dealership introduced himself and offered to be of assistance because he spoke English. An oasis along this area's barren mining towns was the Hotel Touristico in Chanaral. This being a small seaport town with no industry, no commerce and no nothing. A railroad and trucks brought ore to the coast and residents of the town made their living from its transshipment to seagoing vessels. Amid a collection of tired shacks, clean streets and an infrequent new building: the hotel's excellent dining room and white-coated waiters were a welcome treat for these weary travelers. And there was little question but what the hotel was also the center of social life for town. It jumped all evening until far after our usual bedtime. Which was not important because it was the only place for us to overnight.

In the morning we left Chanaral, after coffee and cake, to continue south with instructions to be certain to stop at a marine restaurant about 30 miles further on. "It looks like someone's idea of a ship," a Chilean told us the night before. We finally found the Posada Obispito hidden behind a high stone wall built in the shape of a seagoing vessel, with salvaged concrete pipe for portholes and oil drums for smokestacks. From a distance it might appear to be something like a ship passing in the night. In the daytime it was an interesting piece of scenery. We stopped and, true to its reputation, found a clean patio with pleasant shaded tables and a courteous host who spoke a bit of English. His fame: "The best seafood in all Chile." His imagination: Evident by a homemade children's playground featuring satellite rockets made from old oil drums.

Though we had a large and complete city map of Santiago, our usual luck at finding our hotel failed this time. We arrived in the city at five in the afternoon when heavy traffic was on the way home from work. After fueling and obtaining better destination instructions we started off for our overnight. An hour later the Mercury was parked in their nearby garage and we were safely tucked into our room for deep hot baths to relax tired bones. Renee decided to order dinner, a simple decision which toward the end became a comedy of complete frustration. Because it was too early for dining room service, the telephone operator took the order. "Coffee and steaks." Much later, nothing had happened.

We called the operator again. She said that the order would be arriving shortly. Finally the maid in charge of our floor, who handled early evening room service, arrived with a tray of coffee, tea and bread. We sent her back for a more complete order which by now included beer, the same steak request and strawberries as dessert for both of us. But it seemed that the word for strawberries we'd used successfully north of Chile was not used in Santiago. This time she returned with beer and two dishes of fresh fruit: including bananas, apricots, peaches and cherries. No steak! Eventually a waiter arrived and managed to explain that Monday was a meatless day in Santiago and no steak was available. Would we please order something else. We did. We ordered the national fish dish, the name of which I made no record. Our waiter disappeared, then returned 15 minutes later to explain that the kitchen had no such fish. Would we please order something else. We finally made a sensible decision and asked what they had. It turned out to be Corbina. Two and a half hours after initiating this gastronomic pilgrimage, we enjoyed a fine dinner.

The handling of money in Chile was a multifaceted problem. Value of the currency, Escuda, was established by the government. On the free market the rate of exchange was extremely flexible. When we decided that we would like to buy Argentine money for our next nation, we were told that it was not available at the bank and we would have to go to the money changers. At the money changer's we were told that we could not convert dollars into Argentine money in Chile but it would be possible to convert the Escuda into Argentine Pesos.

Beyond such minor problems, Santiago was a delightful colonial city of narrow one-way streets. There was a high standard of cleanliness in the country and restaurants we visited were equal to what we had enjoyed in the United States. One was operated by a Monsieur Jac whose small lunchroom featured French cuisine. Though our luncheon host ordered from the French menu, Monsieur Jac prepared pepper steaks for Renee and I. They were thick-cut filets into which had been pounded freshly ground pepper, the edges wrapped with bacon and the steaks broiled. Our appreciation of this meal stemmed from being in Santiago and expecting beef, to discover that official meat "holidays" had turned most menus into a replica from a Fisherman's Wharf chowder house. We were told that Chilean cattle raising had not kept pace with an increasing public appetite for beef. In recent years slaughtering had increased at a rate faster than the growth of herds. Accordingly, breeding stock had diminished to the point where the nation suffered a severe meat shortage. No beef was arriving from England but some illegal beef was smuggled in from Argentina. Available stocks were only sufficient to provide three meat days a week (Friday, Saturday and Sunday) in the capitol city. The rest of the time residents ate fish, pork or fowl. One of our best afternoons in Santiago was a visit to a showing of local Arts & Crafts in the central park of a residential district. We also found craftsmen from rural areas of Chile with beautiful handmade bedspreads and blankets, interesting wood carvings, fantastic pottery, and a wild and wonderful collection of woven straw. As you can imagine, prices were extremely low and like all good tourists, we found much that was typical to bring home with us. Surrounding this cluster of national crafts was a large exhibit of paintings and sculptures by students in the area. Some were extremely good and we also brought samples of their work.

What we did over the Christmas holidays boiled down to not very much. We found a theater that had an American film and learned that a movie with English dialogue and Spanish subtitles could be enjoyed even though it was a rather dull presentation. After the film we proceeded to a restaurant that a business associate had recommended for the evening. It turned out to be a below-ground night club and cabaret advertising "Genuine Chilean food and entertainment". It offered neither. The special Christmas dinner for the evening was menu'd as baked chicken preceded by fruit salad and followed by ice cream. We were so early we were the first couple to arrive. This being about 8:30 P.M.. The owner was finishing his dinner in a far distant corner of the dining room but, for some reason or other, became interested in our conversation. We explained that we didn't particularly want chicken and could he whip us up a steak? This he agreed to do. Accordingly, our night before Christmas dinner consisted of fresh-caught lobster as the appetizer followed by thick friendly steaks, and big desert dishes of home-style ice cream. Surrounding all this were two bottles of white Chilean wine and considerate service by a waiter who apparently understood our lonely distance from home. The restaurant began to fill and by 10 o'clock troubadours were playing Mexican songs, American songs, Latin songs and a few Chilean songs. About half the clients were obviously Americans, the other half were, for the most part, from outside the country. We easily spotted Argentines and Brasilians amid very few Peruvians, because each table with foreigners bore a flag from the guest's homeland. Ours carried both a Chilean and United States flag. Shortly before midnight the waiter brought paper hats and tiny horns as though for a New Year party. We had been treated royally but this was about the right time to leave so at 12:10 we upped and wandered back to our hotel. Here, slightly tipsy from a pleasant evening, we had a spot of rum (left over from that purchased in Colombia) and toasted a brilliant green artificial Christmas tree Renee had bought on the streets of Santiago. It had been made in a broom factory and that hotel employees had decorated it for us, with tinsel and paper streamers for our pleasure, made an enourmous difference. We were delighted to have a tree of our own. But, if you want to know how we really felt on Christmas...we were homesick and a little lonely.

The day after Christmas we left Santiago bright and early. Nor did we get lost thanks to the previous day's scouting about for the correct route. Within twelve minutes from the heart of the city we were in rural countryside. The highway from Santiago to Los Andes, our first stop, was two lane pavement with very few trucks and buses to keep us company or force us toward the shoulders. In Los Andes we circled the town several times to find its only service station and fuel the Mercury. The next stretch was a minor matter of 50 miles to Portillo, our overnight stop only three miles from the Argentine border. The road to Portillo, after leaving Los Andes, climbed and climbed most abruptly. It changed from concrete pavement to narrow asphalt, to narrow concrete and finally to a rough road through a construction zone. In some areas we could see "the old road" where its route wandered back and forth up a mountainside. In one short length we counted a dozen old switchbacks leading up the face of an impressive Andean mountain.

Portillo, at 9300 feet, was a Chilean government ski resort which in 1966 was the site of World Championship ski runs. During the summer the hotel and its facilities were open for tourist and itinerant travelers such as *Aventura.* It was a delightful place with magnificent snow-covered Andean scenery surrounding the hotel. Beside it was the tiny valley-bound Laguna del Inca reflecting the brilliant sky and scurried gray clouds responding to vagrant winds. The Gran Hotel Portillo, during this off-season period, was so delightfully informal we only saw the manager when we checked in. Checking out was done with the solitary waiter. There were ten Argentine tourists who dined together at one long table. We, the only other guests, ate at another. The waiter took care of all of us. In addition; the same dining room was used by cooks, bus boys, yard workers and a few stray truck drivers from nearby roadway construction crews. They would arrive, load trays at the cafeteria-like counter, and enjoy the same comfortable surroundings we were enjoying. The only difference between guests and help was that the waiter brought meals to the guest tables. After leaving Portillo, the rugged dirt and gravel road continued to climb for the entire three miles to the Chilean border. Our crossing was easy. I waited in line while a National Police officer stamped both passports for our departure. At the Aduana documents for the Mercury were duly processed and a 10 Escuda fee collected. In the courtyard, which was primarily a welter of railroad tracks, the Mercury was mixed with buses and other private cars. Here a policeman checked our license plates to be certain that we were the car which had been inspected. Then we drove forward and parked near a wooden gate closing off a railway tunnel through the Andes.

This was the point where vehicular traffic merged with train traffic. Both stop, pass through the same customs inspections at the same place, because electric trains and road vehicles use the same tunnel. Gatemen at each end of the tunnel are in contact by telephone to allow a specified number of vehicles through from one direction, then allow another group to pass from the other end. All traffic from Chile was parked alongside the track, by the tunnel entrance, while trains rumbled our of this interesting international hole in the ground. Because there was an over-the-Andes gravel road, usable only during summer months, the narrow tunnel had been originally built to handle only railroad traffic To eliminate the difficulty of driving up and down the Andes the two governments had dirt poured along one side of the tracks. As a result, while driving from Chile into Argentina, our left side wheels bumped along on ties between the rails and the right wheels thudded over rough dirt between a rail and the drainage ditch. For sure, passage through the unlit Trans-Andean Railway tunnel was not conducive to relaxed driving. Because water often sprayed from wheels dropping into tremendous puddles fed by drips from the ceiling, this was the first time in my life I have ever had to use windshield wipers while hundreds of feet beneath solid rock. Midway through the tunnel our eyes caught a border marker with the national symbols of both nations painted on the tunnel wall. Nothing would do but I had to back up, while keeping a wary eye to the rear to make sure a train was not following us through; so that Renee could view the border between Chile and Argentina, far below the Andes.

Aventura Alaska Brasil

17

ARGENTINA

By the time we again saw daylight at the far end of the Trans-Andean tunnel we agreed it was one of *Aventura*'s more memorable experiences. At the tunnel's Argentine exit/entrance a young guard took our receipt for passage, raised the barrier and let us out. A dozen cars, which had been waiting for us to complete passage, were then released to race west through this dark hole joining the two interesting nations.

We traveled only a short distance further on this portion of the Inter-American Highway before turning right to drive up to a mountain peak 12,800 feet above sea level. There, the statue "Cristo Redempter" was sited on the borderline between the two nations. The road upward was listed as 5 miles long, which fooled us with visions of a quick trip. For the most part the one-lane dirt had so many sharp switchbacks that it was even difficult for the Mercury's short wheel base. I don't believe we averaged more than 10 miles an hour up this hazardous mountain roadway. On arrival at the top we were able to look toward both countries, stand on the exact borderline between them and, in a single photograph, include statue and a plaque marking the boundary It read "Sooner shall these mountains crumple to dust than Argentina and Chile shall break the peace sworn at the feet of Cristo Redempter."

Moments after we had parked an excursion bus arrived. It was loaded with school girls from the Argentine city of Rosario. This was their first trip to visit the statue but unfortunately the objective of the trip became a little mixed up. They sighted the beautiful Mercury and surrounded it instead of the statue, while swamping Renee with questions in Spanish and English. After I returned from photographing the border plaque the girls and their bus driver decided to take pictures of us. To turn the tables I asked the girls to cluster with me while Renee grumpily photographed my good fortune at being surrounded by so much Latin charm. Eventually we inched back down the narrow dirt road into the valley, toward Mendoza, where we were processed through Aduana and Migracion into Argentina. This was uncomplicated because we arrived when the border was closed. By paying a fee for "Extraordinary Services" in the amount of $2.00 (U.S.) for Aduana and $2.00 (U.S.) for Migracion we were passed quickly through. Such fees are legal and make it possible for travellers in a hurry to pass at odd hours. It may be worth pointing out that neither Chile nor Argentina inspected our car or luggage. Both were accepted at face value, as was our tourist status. A few feet further along the highway we stopped for several minutes to check in with Transito officers registering vehicles entering the country. Then we were free to proceed. But it was slow going.

The roadway was dirt and gravel for what seemed endless miles. It was a steep downgrade into a valley and steeper back up. In some areas we crawled through narrow one-lane tunnels cut through walls of rock. Some tunnels were awash with water, others were dry. Each was potentially hazardous because there was no place to pass another vehicle within hundreds of feet in either direction. Frequent signs warned drivers to sound the horn on corners and we found ourselves eagerly obeying these admonitions. Somewhere along the line I made the mistake of suggesting to Renee that it would be nice if it were to rain. Minutes later it did. Like a deluge. Between hail and water the storm was a real buster. At one place we parked to examine, through binoculars, a sleek streamline passenger train which had derailed itself on rain-weakened tracks across the valley. Even as we watched, the wreck and its rescue train disappeared in the obscurity of even heavier rain. As I was restarting, a passenger bus sailed by. We decided to follow and could see just enough roadway to drive, though both windshield wipers were doing their best. Soon the pavement became a river of rushing water that was a foot or so deep. So suddenly, and so severely, had the rain fallen that in some areas enough dirt washed from the hills to make it almost impassible for normal traffic. We were lucky because the bus, being heavier, broke trail through these muddy areas and we religiously followed in its tracks. This was not half so disturbing as when we rounded a mountain curve and found, just ahead of us, that fist-size rocks were dribbling from the rocky hillside. As every mountain person knows, this could be the beginning of a landslide or activity that precedes falling boulders. I murmured a silent prayer, stepped on the gas and kept going. Luckily nothing fell while we were there. About the time we ran out of rain, we rolled onto good pavement and the world became more peaceful. A traffic control policeman was helpful to the point of directing our attention to a new map on the wall which detailed a shortcut towards nearby Mendoza.

This was to be our first overnight in Argentina. We circled the city several times in search of our hotel before finding a policeman who pointed us in the proper direction: “Three blocks to the right, a half block to the left, three more blocks to the right, six or seven blocks to the left and about a half block to the left and across the street from the gray building.” How we found the Sussex we’ll never know. Eventually we registered for a room with an air-conditioner in the window to take the bite off afternoon heat. The Sussex clerk explained that they had no hotel parking garage but there was a public garage about three blocks away. I’d sighted both a service station and garage about two blocks away which was a block less to walk back so I headed there. After fueling I asked about parking and the manager said, “Certainly, inside.”

I drove inside where the place to park was to be in a wash rack. Instantly we were surrounded by eager mechanics who insisted they wanted to wash the car, grease the car, look at the engine and drive the Mercury. All were discouraged by my moving it into an open stall and firmly explaining that I desired nothing but parking for the night. There were disappointed faces on the young enthusiasts, who wanted nothing more than to get hands on a beautiful car unlike any they had ever seen before.

After we left Mendoza the following morning we drove for miles through tiny villages with clean streets, good-looking houses and mile after mile of vineyards. This was the heart of the Argentine wine industry with such wonderful contrasts as a blacksmith’s shop by the side of the highway where they were shoeing horses and building wagons with wooden wheels. In one area a huge highway freighter, similar to those used in the western United States, was tailgating us. There was no question as to who drove because the truck owner’s name was painted on the radiator backward, so we could read it in our rearview mirror. Here we revised our interpretation of light signals that truck drivers gave us. In some nations we learned that intermittent flashing of brake lights meant "Slow down, don't pass me." In other nations, the same intermittent flashing meant "OK, I'm slowing down, you may pass." We often found drivers who used their left turn signals while we were following to indicate that it was not safe for us to pass them. Other would use the left turn signal, when we were following, to tell us that it was safe to pass. Some approaching drivers had the left turn signals on, indicating a turn toward us, or telling us that our headlights were on. But when their turn signals indicated a turn away from us, or to their right, they were indicating that they are pulling over so we could pass safely, on a one-way road without slowing. On the other hand, in a different nation the same signal could mean "You pull over, I'm going to stay right in the center of the road," which they frequently did.

Throughout the world only a Willys Jeep is a "Jeep" except in Argentina where every four-wheel drive vehicle was licensed as a Jeep. I am not sure how the factory managed to pull it off, but if you own a four-wheel drive vehicle in the Argentine you wear a license plate which proclaims it to be a Jeep; though it may be a Land Rover, Toyota, Bronco or other popular make of go-anywhere transportation. In Argentina, between the Provinces of Mendoza and San Luis, we came to our largest and most elaborate traffic control. It included an arch over the highway which narrowed passage to a single lane in each direction. Surrounding the arch were numerous officers and about 25 or 30 huge highway haulers. Apparently, when passing from one province to another, trucks must stop and present cargo certifications. For us, it was merely a matter of driving through slowly while an officer wrote down the Mercury's license number and waved us on. Somewhere earlier I hope I have mentioned the disadvantages of accepting route or lodging advice from locals. If I haven't...this is it. Don't do it!

We stopped along the road during our first full day in Argentina while I napped. Within minutes a family car parked behind us. Father and four children piled out while mother remained in the car. Father went to work on Renee with questions about the Mercury which eventually woke me up. While walking back and forth to exercise my legs, he asked where we were going. I explained our ultimate destination which prompted our visitor to claim there was a good hotel at Vanado Tuerto. "On the right side of the road, just past the crossing."

Well, we tried it. Though rates were low, so were the small crawlers on the floor as compared with the level of noise from other guests. Apparently, there wasn't a door in the hotel that could be closed without slamming, or a piece of furniture that could be moved without scraping it along the floor. And for some reason or other, every table and chair had to be moved several times that night! We even left the bathroom light on all night so that we could see the bugs before squashing them with bare feet. It was here that another guest in the hotel decided (at 11:30 in the evening) that I must turn the Mercury's engine off. His decision was apparently made with the help of too much local wine. Not only was he knocking but he was also trying to kick our room door open. I couldn't manage to explain to him, though I'm using Spanish words that had been understood before, that it was perfectly proper for the automobile engine to function all night. His persistence began to worry me a bit with visions of fire or other damaging event. I asked him to wait a moment while I dressed. As I'm fumbling with shoes he began to kick our door again and in the doing had other guests awake. He also made me mad. I slammed the door with my fist, so hard that it rattled the building, and told him to shut up and wait a moment. By the time I was in the hallway not a single person was to be seen. On my way toward the lobby door I passed one of the house maids and glared at her. Further on another guest stuck his head out of a doorway and said in broken English: "He's trying to tell you that your car is operating." After explaining that my car was being tested, was supposed to operate and I was really not worried, I continued on. Outside our Mercury was happily chugging no hotter than usual, which is cool enough to allow your hand to be placed anywhere on the hood.

Argentina was almost unique in its people's aggressive interest in things automotive. This was astounding after experiencing the apathetic attitude toward the Mercury in some other nations. Here, we were followed by trucks, waved at by drivers, and when stopped on city streets the *Aventura* coupe was almost immediately surrounded by men: Old men, young men and businessmen. Everyone seemed to be keenly aware of the Mercury's smart lines, which in their eyes related it to successful racing cars. While driving toward Buenos Aires through thickening traffic, we noticed the increasing frequency of service stations marked "Auto Club." In hopes of finding a map we stopped at one and found them to be delightful little places with friendliness of American standards.

But no maps. One attendant recommended we drive another 60 miles to the next station who would have maps. We did, but they didn't. However the manager of the station came to our rescue. Using blank paper and a map glued to the wall, he drew an excellent representation of a route into Buenos Aires which we used to drive directly to the Claridge Hotel located on Tocuman Street. It was an older Buenos Aires facility with character and quality that we considered superior for this trip. Among the more interesting touches: We could not lunch in a dining room unless I wore a coat. Our room contained a small refrigerator with soft drinks, courtesy of the management, and liquor which could be purchased by the miniature bottle. And personnel so delightful to be with, it was our genuine regret to leave. Everyone from the chambermaid to the doorman appeared to be thoroughly concerned with our welfare.

Some of the best advice received during *Aventura* came from Jorge, the Concierge of the Claridge. It surfaced one afternoon when Jorge inquired about the purpose of our run. I replied that we were writing a book and he offered the following suggestions: "If more Americans would speak good English using simple words while talking slowly, they would have less trouble being understood in Latin America than if they hastily learn a few words of Spanish. It is also better to have a book of simple phrases than it is to try to use a dictionary to decide how to ask for something you need. I believe that many Americans bring along too many clothes. They bring things they couldn't possibly ever wear or will carry items which can be purchased in all major South American cities.

"Don't display too much money as most people are rather poor," Jorge continued. "It is easier to be swindled or overcharged in a small town where they never see tourists than it is in a large town or city where an element of commercial morality exists. Don't trust mechanics. As a matter of ego, they all say that they are completely familiar with your car, though it may be as complicated as a 12-cylinder Ferrari. Fords and Chevrolets, with a manual transmission, will give them little problem. Anything more complicated, such as an automatic transmission, power steering or power brakes, is often beyond their ability.

"Accordingly", he added, "American drivers should have with them a modest number of spare parts and either the knowledge or a shop manual to insure that the vehicle is being properly repaired under their complete supervision. In other words, don't leave a car to be serviced and walk away hoping that when you return it will have been done properly. If the Latin mechanic breaks something he will be most apologetic and you will likely wish to kill him. Then you will have to wait anything from a day to a month for the replacement spare part to arrive."

When we told Jorge about being charged 800 Pesos for a simple lunch in a tiny, roadside restaurant he laughed and said, "So, why didn't you ask the price of the meal before you ordered it? After all, when you ask someone how much a thing is, is there not a tendency to quote the lowest possible price?" Jorge also pointed out that many Americans wear "funny clothes" such as tropical helmets and white suits in anticipation of penetrating the deepest jungle while driving to Buenos Aires. He suggested that tourists can be too friendly and invite trouble by drinking in small alley bars or walking in remote areas with people they do not know. "Yet, on the other hand, it is easy to be too suspicious when in fact, you could relax and allow people to be of help," he concluded.

Buenos Aires was one metropolitan city that could appeal to every visitor. There were subways, a fabulous interurban railroad service radiating in all directions from the capitol city and a beautiful downtown mishmash of the old and new. Historic architecture obviously stemmed from English foundations of the Argentine economy while newer structures were more modern in the Latin style. Traffic was fast and frantic. Service stations were everywhere. Most streets were cobblestoned and it was rare to face a traffic light because traffic control was by uniformed policemen. Flashing of headlamps at an uncontrolled intersections requested the right of way, the occasional tooting of a horn broke thc law as an unnecessary noise, while the frequent prayer of a passenger car driver, when a huge bus arrived without any appearance to stopping, was part and parcel of the scene.

New Year's Eve was a delightful mixture of the believable, the unbelievable, the impossible and "How did it ever happen to us." Our initial objective was to find a somewhat public party that could be attended through purchase of tickets. Jorge, our most important guide to finding our way about the city, suggested we visit the Hotel Avarrio for their New Year's party. We hopped a taxi and rode over to buy two tickets. Total cost: $20.00 (U.S.) for dinners, dancing and a bottle of champagne. Through some manner of good fortune, while accepting tickets and passing over money, we inquired about proper clothing. We were told it was "black tie" which of course left us out in the cold. Though Renee had an evening gown with her, I had no black tie and would not have been permitted to enter in my business suit. Back with tickets and over came our money, much to the amazement and amusement of the hotel clerk handling our transaction. Another taxi back to our hotel where Jorge was told of our predicament. By carefully reading Buenos Aires newspapers he found a restaurant that was having a New Year's party. Reservations were accordingly made. We were told a car would pick us up at 8:30 and take us to the restaurant in time for advertised activities. Elated by his success, we retired for an afternoon siesta then prepared to leave that evening. Promptly at 8:30 the telephone rang with news that "our" car was there. We went downstairs and found a relatively new vehicle, but it was not a taxi. We asked the doorman how much it would cost and he talked to the driver in Spanish and we were told it would be 450 pesos. Says the doorman, "This is normal for the trip." So away we went. We toured the city, rode across the city and back through the city. Fairly soon, we meandered along a narrow side street and stopped before Wa Tu, a large and noticeably new Chinese restaurant. Inside was a table reserved for "Senor Carrol, Dos Personas." The music was from a Latin combo, the food somewhat Argentine, but mostly Chinese, served by a tiny Chinese waitress. We had a wonderful evening of dancing amid this frantic combination. Meanwhile Wa Tu filled with loving couples, elderly tourists and families (complete with 5 or 6 year old noisemakers) bent on observing passage of the year. Shortly after the New Year arrived Renee and I decided that we'd had enough of good things, paid our modest tab and left. Outside there were taxis going in all directions at once but none would stop for us. We walked a block and waited. No taxi. We walked another block and waited again. One came close enough for me to hail the driver. On being informed that we wanted to go the Claridge he indicated that he could not take us there, put his sedan in gear and zipped off. Though it was 3 o'clock in the morning, the street continued thronged with pedestrians and traffic almost as thick as during the day. Finally, good fortune favored us and a taxi stopped sufficiently close by for us to hop in and ride back to our hotel.

Though we entered Argentina through a railroad tunnel we departed on a ferryboat; the most unusual combination of entrances and exits during the *Aventura* run. From Buenos Aires we were scheduled to go to Uruguay and enjoy a few days in the capitol city, Montevideo. One of two ways to travel there was to drive somewhat northwest along the Argentine bank of the Rio de la Plata, cross a bridge, then drive back on the opposite bank to Montevideo. This would be a journey of many hundreds of miles. On the other hand, crossing the Rio de la Plata, one of the world's wider rivers, was more quickly done on Uruguayan and Argentine ferryboats which carried passengers, trucks and automobiles. We had been told that one ferry left at 4 o'clock the next afternoon and decided it would be good to sleep in for a change and take that afternoon departure. However, when we went to buy tickets we were told that our desired afternoon ferry had been cancelled. Perhaps the disappointment on our faces was a deciding factor for the ticket salesman suddenly remembered an early morning ferry which left about 7:30. Unfortunately, he couldn't sell us any tickets. It was sold out. But he would give us a dock entrance coupon which would allow us to park in line to make use of any space available as the result of someone not appearing.

At 4 o'clock the following morning, Renee and I tumbled out of bed. This was much a credit to the Claridge night clerk who not only provided a persistent nonstop telephone call to wake us but concurrently forwarded a porter with steaming coffee, orange juice and rolls: A combination designed to get sleepy gringos out of bed. I dressed, fueled the car and returned to load Renee. At a quarter of seven we were in a line of about 200 cars and trucks on a cobblestone street in Buenos Aires' harbor. Ahead of us the ferry, around us vacationing Argentine travelers on their way to Uruguay where their Peso would go about twice as far as at home. We had no ticket, had not been cleared through Aduana, had not been passed out of Migracion, had no visas for Uruguay, in fact had nothing but faith, hope and confidence in our "standby" coupon. Nevertheless, with the help of an Argentine friend, we managed to convince two teenage ticket-takers that we should be allowed to board the ferry first and buy tickets later. On we went, but the Mercury remained on the cobblestones, mixed with other cars seeking passage. On board we found the purser who agreed to sell us tickets. We left our passports and passage money with him. Then back to the dock to explain to the ticket-takers that we had bought tickets. A representative of the Argentine Aduana signed the Mercury's Carnet to indicate that our car was leaving the country. An Aduanero was told of our progress and marked the windshield with crayon as the Carnet disappeared into his bundle of papers. We now had neither passports, passage money nor Carnet. On the windshield we had a mystic mark. Soon traffic began to move toward the ferry. While I drove forward Renee took pictures. But I didn't get very far. An Argentine policeman, in civilian clothes, stopped me. To his left, an Aduanero also in civilian clothes, waved his arms and said, "This one is OK" so we continued on. In the car and truck deck of the ferry the Mercury was parked solidly against the hull and locked in place. Now it was Renee's turn to come aboard. When she reached the gangplank a sailor stopped her and said she couldn't pass. Renee explained that her car, husband and documents were on the ferry. The sailor began questioning the two Uruguayan ticket-takers who, for some blessed reason or other, remembered Renee. They told the sailor it was alright for her to board the Uruguayan Ferry *Atlantic* and join her husband.

A half hour later two tugs backed us into the river to begin a three-hour crossing to Colonia, the terminal point in Uruguay. Meanwhile the ferry's purser became our savior. He prepared documents and arranged for Uruguayan Migracion officers on the ferry to stamp our passports and provide entrance and exit permits. The Uruguayan Aduanero had our Carnet (heaven only knows how it arrived on the ship) and prepared it for entrance into his nation. Soon all were returned to us, except the Carnet. For it, we were given a small numbered claim check for use on arrival in Uruguay. Then we had breakfast on the *Atlantic.*

Though our conversations had been in Spanish, it was a welcome delight, once we arrived in Uruguay, that several officials wished us a good trip...in well-spoken English.

18

URUGUAY

On arrival in Uruguay the ferry's cargo of cars and trucks were owner-driven down the unloading ramp to be parked in a fenced yard adjacent to the Aduana office. Here all was simple for the officers seemed well-practiced in handling the arrival of vehicles. The only thing necessary was for passengers to line up, ten at a time, with their car owner holding the numbered claim check. Beginning with the lowest ten, owners were ushered into a space where a representative of the Uruguayan Automobile Club returned the Carnet de Passage. Once stamped and signed we were legally on wheels in the country. In the parking lot an Aduanero affixed a huge sticker to our windshield which indicated we'd passed through all formalities. Free to leave we were. Nearby we found the Cambio in a small sheet metal shed on the sidewalk in front of the passenger terminal. There was some confusion as I had the ratio of exchange backward and expected twice instead of half. This was explained and proved to be completely correct. In line with this I'd suggest obtaining change where there are a great number of other clients. It is unlikely that you would be cheated in the face of many observers. With money in hand we left the parking area for a concrete two-laner and the 100 mile run into Montevideo. With only the most rudimentary map, and by following a large bus, we eventually reached the central city area. We stopped at a Shell station to fuel the Mercury where the station manager drew a simple map directing us toward our hotel. This led us to the front door of the

Columbia Palace on the waterfront of Montevideo where we were given a delightful room on the third floor overlooking the Rio de la Plata. Because we had only two hours sleep the night before, as the result of our late-evening New Year party, and four o'clock up-and-at-it time, we immediately siesta'd into bed. In the next block a small parking lot contained the *Aventura* Mercury, securely locked and protected from harassment by small boys or eager fingers.

That evening, while returning from dinner, we stumbled (in fact, not fiction.) into a totally new situation. The result was a warning for each other about walking at night in Latin America. A situation that concerned feet not pocketbooks and was recorded as "The case of the open Montevideo manhole." While charging down a lightless sidewalk from the direction of the restaurant, my right foot dropped about a foot and a half into a hole in the pavement. Every tooth vibrated as I hit bottom. It was one of many such holes we noticed later in which the sidewalk cover over a water meter was missing. This first night's episode could have been a leg-breaker had I dropped in the wrong direction or lost my balance. From then on I walked much more carefully.

The next day involved three very unhappy men, one of whom was Carroll, making terribly loud noises at each other in the Brasilian Consul's Montevideo office. The occasion was my attempt to arrange visas and frontier passage from Uruguay into Brasil with the Mercury. The problem being that Brasil demanded a cash deposit be made, into a Brasilian bank, in a dollar amount equal to twice the value of our Mercury. This "value" was said to be approximately equal to Custom's Duty and excise tax charges were the car to be illegally sold in Brasil. Secondly, the nation's laws would not allow any car to enter the country if it were valued at more than $3500, which the Mercury was not. Our method of preparing (so we thought) to solve this problem had been to arrange for a letter of credit to be established which had the effect of depositing $6,500 (U.S.), into the Brasilian branch of a New York bank. On the basis of this deposit, guaranteeing exportation of our car, the Argentine Auto Club had issued a Carnet de Passage good only for Brasil and nowhere else. Armed with our special Carnet, passports and pictures, we had arrived at their Consulate in Montevideo. There was no hitch in filling out the forms. Problems (plural) began when a minor official implied that our Carnet from the Argentine Club was no good. In effect he was claiming that we had not really deposited that much money into the Brasilian bank and by some devious means had obtained a document that stated that we had. Besides, he said, there is a three-day wait in Montevideo to obtain approval to enter Brasil. A very pleasant young Consular official was advised of our trouble, inspected our documents and questioned the negative-minded official. Nothing would do: We could not pass into their country. There was no chance our documents were valid. In fact, they were not much better than my Spanish.

Eventually Renee and I were seated in the Vice-Consul's office where, for the tenth time, he was telling me "No". But his Spanish was much too rapid for me and my Spanish much too poor for him. Between the two of us we managed to clarify only two points. He was unhappy with me and I was unhappy with him. The headache being that we really could not go into Brasil and, if we did, what was going to happen to the car? I never was able to make the point clear that the car was already scheduled to be exported back to the United States on a Grace Lines freighter, due to leave a few days after we planned to arrive in Rio. Then he told us the frontier would be closed on both Saturday and Sunday. Previously another Brasilian had said it was closed on Saturday, for a holiday, and open on Sunday. By now we reached the finger-shaking stage and I was ready to take off both shoes and settle down for a sit-in, pending approval of our valid papers. We must have reached a fever-pitch when the Consul walked in. He proved to be a very pleasant gentleman who was kind enough to speak English. To him I re-explained the problem. He turned to the young man who had originally inspected our documents and asked if he would approve our entrance into Brasil. He said yes, indicating that he had already stamped my wife's passport but could not stamp mine because there was insufficient space. A few moments later he telephoned the United States Embassy and made it possible for me to have additional pages immediately added to my passport for insertion of the proper Brasilian stamps. While I was gone, the Consul and the Vice-Consul telephoned their frontier, an outstanding courtesy to two most bewildered tourists, and made inquiry as to exact status of the holiday closing schedule. They reported that the frontier would be closed on Saturday for a national holiday. Though it would be open on Sunday, we would not be able to pass because Aduana officials could not properly handle our Carnet on a Sunday. Monday would be our time for passage. By now, Brasilian courtesy came to our rescue and the Consul, Vice-Consul and helpful young man were most interested in our situation. Eventually we were supplied with the name and address of the Brasilian Consul on the Uruguayan frontier through which we must cross. We were told to contact that Consul should any problem whatsoever arise and he would take whatever steps necessary to ease the situation. (To eliminate skipping pages to read ahead: he didn't.) Adding to our relief, the Vice-Consul gave Renee names and addresses of two of the finest restaurants in Montevideo.

Then all of us enjoyed an excellent Espresso.

How it was all worked out we'll never know. Originally the Brasilian passport office said that it would take three days for our passports to be approved. For some reason or other, all the commotion about our car bypassed this regulation. Both passports were returned to us within minutes, at the same time the Carnet was approved for border crossing. From bewilderment to disappointment, to unhappiness, to friendly termination of our visit took two and a half hours. It was our regret that we had so disturbed peaceful operations of the Consul's office. He acknowledged that it was a bad situation to attempt to take an American car, registered in the United States, into their nation. Said the Consul, "We have not had one of these before." [Now we knew what the commotion was all about and why our initial efforts had caused so much trouble.]

On a happier note, in the touristing area, Montevideo provided us with an eating experience on the fun side of visiting Latin America. Previously I had walked by the open door of a restaurant, Los Posas, and was charmed by their method of cooking meat and chicken on a large merry-go-round barbecue surrounding a central fire of hardwood. The place had been extremely busy so we decided to find it again. And well worth the trouble it was. The waiter who seated us, and later gave us a business card indicating his name was Raul, was most helpful. We asked for cold beer. It was at the table before we could turn around. When there was indecision on our part as to which appetizer to order, he emerged from the kitchen with tiny plate bearing samples of three: Spaghetti, ravioli and a specialty of the house , a three-cornered ravioli containing chicken. This we tried covered with a non-meat Italian sauce. Then we made our "mistake", or should I say we made the right move in the wrong direction. We ordered steak barbecued on the charcoal fired merry-go-round. It proved to be a T-bone of elephantine size which hung over every edge of our extremely large plates. No potatoes. No salad. No vegetables. None necessary. The steak was all we could eat and still manage to wiggle. We also added a new definition to our modest Spanish vocabulary. Previously, to request steaks prepared medium-rare, we were told to order as "mediano rojo" or half-red. In Montevideo Raul introduced us to another way. He explained they should be ordered with or without blood (con-sangre or sin-sangre). Somewhere along the end of this fascinating lunch we enjoyed lemon ice cream pie fresh from the kitchen. Needless to say, we left Los Posas absolutely charmed with this tiny restaurant which was thoroughly and completely jammed with families, couples and individuals stuffing themselves to the ears.

Occasionally we went to the trouble of checking exchanges of one currency for another, with paper and pencil, either before or during the transaction. Each time we've agreed within pennies which speaks well of Latin honesty or our lack of mathematical talent. However, when checking out of our Montevideo hotel, we penciled the exchange to discover that the clerk had made a mistake of about $10 (U.S.) in his favor. It was my opinion that this was an honest error rather than any desire to cheat. He accepted my correcting figures without question and proceeded to count out 600 Pesos too much in our favor. We returned the excess change while he gestured toward a passing bevy of high school girls as cause for his mishandling of dollars and pesos in the same transaction.

The highway out of Montevideo was not too difficult. An excellent city map and our Sunday morning departure eliminated much of the normally confusing traffic. Once outside the city we were on two-lane concrete some of which was good .... and some of which was well broken. As was my heart when we passed a beautiful 1926 Model T Ford touring car shoved under a tree to rot. Less interesting fenced fields contained a full quota of cattle or sheep, or a pond with swans and ducklings. The few cattle we saw walking on the side of the road were well herded by vaqueros on horseback. Our overnight destination, Melo near the Brasilian frontier, was a simple colonial town laid out in perfectly square blocks of one-way streets. We eventually found our small hotel in which most of the rooms opened off the central patio. Our Mercury was parked by the kitchen door behind high wrought iron gates. At this overnight stop we bought gasoline where the price was exactly double that on the pump. The attendant explained that the pump was so old it could not register Pesos in Uruguay's inflated large numbers. So the pump had been set to register half the amount due which was then doubled. We didn't question his honesty because the doubled gasoline price approximated what we had been paying in Montevideo. After leaving Melo in the morning we drove only a few miles on well graded dirt to the Uruguay-Brasil frontier. We managed to not become lost and found our way into the frontier town of Rio Branco with little trouble. Only one inquiry was necessary to find the border's "Friendship" bridge and we were soon on it. On the Uruguayan side, an Auduanero checked our Carnet for the Mercury; stamped, signed and initialed it, tore off his piece of paper and returned the rest. We had officially left Uruguay.

Thus began one of our more adventurous and the least pleasant portion of all *Aventura.*

19

BRASIL

Our drive of some 200 yards across the Rio Branco river bridge was without incident. On the far side was the Brasilian Customs house where an officer told us to bring our papers to his office. On taking a quick look at them he realized they called for more attention than he was prepared to handle at the moment. Besides, we were now blocking traffic on his bridge. So would we please proceed forward into Brasil and park the car at the foot of the bridge. This we did. Lucky for us!

Back in the Custom's house, we stood in line behind another group waiting to have vehicles approved for passage into Brasil. When our turn came, the officer inspecting our documents came to the conclusion they were not correct. He called for his superior. The superior looked at them and began speaking to us in Portuguese, the official language of Brasil. We barely understood Spanish which made Portuguese totally out of the question. Communication was nonexistent. After listening to him for a few minutes, and not making sense out of what he was explaining, we showed him the name of the Brasilian Consulate in Montevideo who had discussed our entrance with the Brasilian Consul in Rio Branco, where we had been. This brought forth our typed note which broadly translated into requesting the officer talking with us to provide every possible assistance. Apparently they were not friends. This seemed to be the point at which his tone toward us hardened into a firm "No, you shall not pass. These papers are no good."

We were never able to understand why except that he would not accept them as they were. We must wait until 1:30 in the afternoon when his superior, the Inspector, would arrive. When we asked permission to go to a bank and also make a telephone call, on the Brasilian side, he made sure we understood that all banks were closed and there was no telephone or telegraph office in Jaguarao, his Brasilian town of entry. "Your must return to Uruguay," says he.

"Okay," I replied, in my most fluent Spanish. "That's fine. We'll leave the car downstairs and walk to Uruguay across the bridge."

"No," he said in his best Portuguese, using the one word we both understood clearly, and waved his arms to indicate that we should take the car with us. Thinking better of his proposal, we decided "No" was equally good for us and insisted the car remain in Brasil. He then decided, "You will not go to Uruguay, you will have to wait here."

Recognizing that his problem was with the Mercury, and not with Renee or me, I gave our paperwork to Renee and told her, "Hurry back into Uruguay and telephone for help." She headed across the bridge while I sat in the Customs office, grinning broadly at presenting myself as a hostage. The officer with the strong "No" was aghast. Now he had a hostage on his hands and a car he didn't want. Two problems not bargained for in dealing with American tourists. While waiting I couldn't help but reflect on the byplay of misrepresentation we faced. When we asked the first officer to please make a telephone call to clarify the matter, he told us there was no telephone in the Custom's office on the bridge. Whether it was true or not was a matter clarified later: There was a telephone. Our hostage taker slipped a bit more and told me there were no telephones in town and all banks were closed. When we learned that the town banks were open, it was obvious he had been prevaricating. Fellow officers, whom I believe were inferior to his position, began to needle him unmercifully at his childishness in making me sit there. Finally, he relented and said I too could go to Uruguay. In a moment I was chasing Renee across the bridge to try and untangle the mess. At the foot of the bridge entrance we found a horse-drawn taxi, climbed aboard and asked the driver to hurry us to the telephone office of which there was usually at least one in every town. We clopped along at a leisurely pace, stirring more dust than speed. By the time we arrived at the telephone office we were tapped for a fare twice what a Uruguayan woman had paid for a trip of exactly one block less. When I called the driver a robber he grinned and tipped his hat. We both knew what he was doing but there was little that could be done about it because of my inability to adequately "Bless" or argue with him in Spanish.

At the telephone office, we found an inexperienced girl running the switchboard and presented her with three requests: One: A telephone call to Rio de Janeiro. This she said was not possible, there was no line to Rio. We then presented her with Two: Ring the Brasilian Consul in Rio Branco. She made the call and discovered the Consul was not there. We then presented her with request Three: Please connect with our contact in Montevideo. This she added to her list of Montevideo calls. It took us about an hour and a half before the call was completed over the single line. But all we could gather from the other end was, "I cannot hear you...I cannot hear you...I cannot hear you…" Discouraged, we started walking back toward the bridge. A tired Ford taxi, parked at the plaza, appeared ready to take off. We hailed him for a trip to the Brasilian Consulate and stuck a business card, with a plea for help, in the door grill, hoping the Consul would come to our rescue. A few blocks of walking put us back on the "Friendship" bridge As we passed the Brasilian Custom's office, while on our way to check on operation of the Mercury parked below the bridge, I was hailed by one of the officers and introduced to a young man speaking Spanish we could somewhat understand. He explained slowly and in detail that the problem was dual in nature. Less than a year ago, the Brasilian government had issued an order to all border control offices that no passenger cars, other than from Uruguay or Paraguay, should enter the country on a Carnet de Passage unless The Touring Club do Brasil had sent a special telegram to the Customs office, through a local branch of the Touring Club, indicating that the proper deposits had in fact been made. We had the Carnet but as far as we knew, no one had sent a "proper" telegram. A second question in their minds, he said, was that because there was no free entry of dollars into Brazil, how in the world had we ever managed to make such a sizable deposit, as the $6,500 (U.S.) dollars we claimed was there, into a Brazilian bank? The last question was easily cleared up. I displayed a letter of credit established by the New York City Bank in their branch in Sao Paulo.

Nevertheless, they did not have the "proper" telegram and pass we could not until such a message had been received..

On reflection it became obvious that neither the Touring Club of Argentina who issued our Carnet, nor the Brasilian Consul in Montevideo who visa'd our passports, were aware of this special order. A dilly of a hang-up, plus of course, the fact that we claimed to have deposited so much money ($6,500) that poorly-paid Custom's officials could hardly believe anyone would allow a Brasilian bank to hold that many dollars for permission to drive a car in their country. Our Spanish-speaking official gave us our first break He evidenced a small amount of English and said that he would take us to his "Maestro", the teacher of English in Jaguarao. Within minutes we were bumping along in a Volkswagen truck, over three or four blocks of city cobblestones, to reach a charming little pink plaster house where we met the Maestro who turned out to be our friend in need. At first the Maestro read all our documentation and listened to his pupil's explanation, in Portuguese, of our problem. Then, in high school English he explained to us that there really was no problem that could not be cleared up soon. He put on his shirt and away we Volkswagened townward for offices of the Touring Club do Brazil.

At their tiny office we again displayed all the documentation. But the Touring Club manager said they had received no telegram and accordingly could not approve our papers. The Maestro was not to be daunted. Back to the Volkswagen and away we went to the bridge to meet with the Inspector of the Customs office. Again there was much conversation, much displaying of documents and questioning of their meaning. But basically it boiled down to : "No telegram, no passage." The Carnet had not been recertified by the Touring Club and accordingly, we could not proceed. Renee and I were in good shape. We could enter or leave Brasil as we wished. The car, "No". But the *Aventura* Mercury was far more important than we were. It was suggested we telegraph for help. I agreed. Then someone suggested that first we radiotelephone. This was a simple proposal that turned out to involve a long wait. It was about 2:30 in the afternoon when we reached the office of Coral, a major transportation and trucking firm in Brasil. Luckily for us, in Jaguarao they had a radio communications facility. With the aid of their local superintendent, Coral people began trying to contact the Touring Club. We were in their office from 2:30 until 5:30, during which time we had effectively absorbed three hours time of at least one staff member to accomplish a simple radiotelephone call to Rio de Janeiro. In addition we were unable to complete a second call to the Ford Motor Company, in Sao Paulo, whom we hoped could help.

In desperation over so much lost time, I insisted that we be directed toward the telegraph office. At 6:00 we finally reached the National Telegraph Office and sent cables in two directions to Ford, ahead to Rio and behind to Montevideo, seeking immediate assistance. Next was our need for a hotel. The Maestro took us to one that was full. At the second we obtained a pleasantly small and clean room after the entrepreneur owner decided he had two wealthy American tourists on his hands and should charge the limit. Our rate, for twin beds and private bath overnight, was 15,000 Brazilian Cruzados. Because she was completely worn out by now, I sidetracked Renee at the hotel for a quick rest.

The Maestro and I walked back to the bridge to rescue our car from hands of the Custom's office. Along the way it was soon obvious that our friend knew everyone in town. There were constant salutations right and left. Younger people knew him best, while older folks undoubtedly knew him as the teacher of their children. There was little shyness on the Maestro's part. When we were in the telegraph office he had gone behind the window to act as the clerk for us. At the Customs Office, he pounded on the Inspector's desk and spoke with great sweeps of the arms to make sure he represented us to the best of his ability. And while riding back to the hotel in the Mercury he evidenced all the pride a man could show in the pleasure of traveling in a modern motor car. The Maestro owned no car but said he looked forward to it "some day."

The Customs' staff were not particularly unhappy to see me because they no longer wanted the responsibility of our vehicle on their hands. Accordingly when I agreed to leave the Carnet with them, they approved use our car to drive within Jaguarao and most particularly to the hotel. With handshakes and sour smiles, we departed: First for gasoline and secondly for security behind an iron gate of the hotel parking lot. Here our Mercury was the object of a thousand eyes. If there was a single person in town that did not look at the lovely coupe that first night, we can't imagine who they were. The owner of the hotel, proud as a peacock, strutted back and forth while basking in the attention given his establishment. So appealing was our car to the Brasilians that, while the Maestro, Renee and I were enjoying cool beverages, a tiny barefoot boy appeared and uncorked a mouthful of Portuguese at me. Not really knowing what he was saying but realizing that the intense expression on his face indicated some form of question, I very slowly waved my finger under his nose and said, "No", on which he departed in a burst of speed.

The Maestro burst out laughing, turned to friends sitting behind us and told them a long and involved story in Portuguese. Then he returned to us and explained in English that the boy, and his friends playing in the street, had seen the car. After careful examination they began to argue. One group claimed it would fly. The other group claimed it would not. The small boy had asked me, "Would it fly?"

Unknowingly I had answered, truthfully, that it would not.

The bet was settled.

While this was going on, the Maestro had been explaining that he came to Jaguarao about nine years previously. On arrival, he liked the town very much and had since attempted to instruct his students in English. As he explained it, "In all the town, I am the only one that understands the language." He told us that at first, he tried diligently to improve local standards of language instruction, even going to the point of paying for an expensive English-edition of Webster's Unabridged Dictionary. As far as he knows, it was the only one in town. Eventually he married, fathered three children but was now somewhat discouraged with local school authorities. Though his school had an allotment of four English teachers, he remained the only one. He instructs four classes, occasionally teaches science and reads the American edition of Life Magazine because "It is the important edition...full of much good material…for my science students."

Then he added, "I have about three hundred students to whom I am teaching English. It is too bad they do not have someone to talk with as I have with you today. In a year I talk with only a few English speaking people. In a year the students talk with none. That is bad because they never really learn to think in English. They only repeat what is in books." Thoughtfully he continued, "And not all of them have books."

It is no understatement that without his help we would have never reached the people in Coral who had the best communications in Jaguarao. We could never have found the telegraph office. And I doubted very much if we could have retrieved our car from Customs or found a comfortable hotel with such ease. When we apologized for taking so much of his time, he said, "This is my vacation. (School vacations in Brasil were in November, December, January and February) and I am glad to do it. With you is one of my few opportunities to speak English and it is important for me to practice." And practice he did. I'm sure the Maestro exercised all his vocabulary for in time his English improved.

The robber baron who owned the hotel, a pleasantly quiet gentleman of about 280 pounds, had previously agreed to our residence at a price of 15,000 Cruzados per day, which was about double his usual rate for such accommodations. However, when we were ready to make payment the following morning, he presented me with a written bill for 20,000 Cruzados. I reminded him of the previously quoted rate and paid its agreed upon 15,000. He indicated that he had only tried and if I wasn't mad at him, he wasn't mad at me.

That important matters moved slowly in Brasil is an understatement. During the following day it took from 8:00 in the morning until nearly noon for the radio operator at Coral Transport to reach Sao Paulo and transmit an urgent message to the Ford Motor Company explaining our situation. Around 1:30, while we were at lunch, the operator zipped into the dining room. He had heard from Sao Paulo and a telegram would be dispatched to free us from our problem with the border control office. Later we circulated around town before visiting the Touring Club. Again we were reminded that our Spanish was not good, our English was not understood and it was very difficult to explain that all we wanted to know was: "Have you received a telegram about our car?" After twenty minutes of conversation, we all finally reached agreement. They had not.

At the telegraph office, we checked but no such messages had been received. On my return later there were no messages but I noticed an operator banging away at an ancient teletype machine. This I found was also available for possible communication. Quickly I had a message put on the teletype to Ford. I wanted them to know we had not received a "release" telegram, we had sent "help" telegrams the previous day and again expressing a strong request that they communicate with us. The telegraph operator told me the message would be in Sao Paulo within fifteen minutes after being relayed through three small towns along the wire. I questioned him closely and was soon convinced there was no two ways about it. From Jaguarao to the outside world, there existed no long distance telephone; only a telegraph line and the radio of Coral Transport. While at lunch a boy of 12 to 14 asked the Maestro, who was dining with us on cognac, if our car was the car that could fly. He too was told that "No, it could not." On the street a local reporter stopped the Maestro and interviewed him on the purpose of our vehicle and what it was doing in Brasil.

As usual, policeman followed our walks as did an occasional soldier. Whether out of curiosity, or as part of an official "Watching the *Aventura* car," we knew not. But we frequently noticed the same face, above a uniform, wherever we parked and occasionally when we lunched. On the other hand, the curiosity of the town's citizens was a pleasant and refreshing experience. They were invariably noisy about their interest in the car and courteously remote from hammering or beating on sheet metal, doors, or windows. The Maestro assured us we'd have no trouble with the car here. We had no reason to disbelieve him as to its safety, though at night we made sure it was behind locked yard gates of the hotel.

The next day, after lunch, we all trooped back to the telegraph office but were told no messages had arrived. The reason? Electricity had failed and the teletype machine was not operating. Obviously, executives of a corporations such as Ford were not going to send communications by anything so modest as normal telegraph. The logical thing would be to send it by Telex which is much more direct. But there was no way they would know that our Telex machine, at this far end of the world, did not function. We checked at three, four, and at six in the afternoon but still no functioning machine. A final visit, at seven, disclosed that no word for us had been received by either Telex or telegraph. As things stood, we had been stuck in town for another day of visiting with officers on the bridge, wandering about the business district and taking the Mercury out for its daily drive; much to consternation and amazement of town residents who were endlessly marveling at its ever-running engine.

There was no question but what inability to communicate with the outside world is a complete and frustrating experience. But, as I explained to a bridge officer with whom I was having a lengthy conversation while he practiced English, there is no use in fighting the problem. We must seek only a solution or an answer to the question. He agreed that if we did not receive a reply shortly, some other action must be taken to free the car for circulation within the Brasilian nation. He suggested that it was too bad that we could not have become stranded in a more sociable place, such as at one of the beach resorts of Montevideo or Buenos Aires. We could not have agreed more.

As usual we bumped our noses while trying to cash Travelers Checks. We had been told that conversion of dollars into local currency could be difficult. Not surprisingly, it was. We drove around all four blocks of town after breakfast while seeking the banks. Though we passed both, we failed to recognize either until the second drive-by. The larger was closed. Pedestrians told us that it would not open until 1:00 P.M.. in the afternoon. As I walked past an open window, one of the officers was visible inside. We managed to communicate that I needed information. He indicated that within a few minutes they would open the door and let me in. I waited the appropriate few minutes and returned. The door was still locked. I went to the window where the officer saw me and, with a wave of his hand, said to wait a bit. Back to the front door I went. Within a few minutes they opened it, let me in, relocked the door and in Spanish we tried to discuss money exchange problems. The manager of the bank explained, in halting English, that his bank could not cash Travelers Checks as it was not authorized to handle foreign money. But there was a town three hours away where "Maybe" I could exchange checks. I explained that this was not at all reasonable because I had to pay our hotel bill, we needed money for gasoline, and I would like to be able to buy lunch for my wife. He and his teller conversed in Portuguese for a few moments before they told me that a Cambio up the street could "possibly" do this for us. But the bank was sorry, they could not and "Thank you, the door we are opening."

We found the side street and the Cambio where an exchange of money was successfully achieved at the legal Cruzado rate for American dollars. The young man behind the counter inquired about the cost of our Mercury then offered to double my money if I would sell it to him right there. This offer was in addition to previous offers by townspeople to trade it for sheep skins, a hat on the head of a passerby or for a new Volkswagen the owner was backing from a street-side garage.

That night, after another frustrating day of hoping for telegrams that did not arrive, the police arrived in force. While we were eating, an officer from the Radio Patrol walked into the hotel. His battle fatigues were in good condition and boots were as brilliantly polished as the steel helmet crouched in the corner of one elbow. They somewhat matched the bright smile on his face. On sighting our table he approached the Maestro and shot off a volley of questions in Portuguese. The Maestro, perhaps to make sure we didn't hear what he was saying, as though we could have understood it anyway, turned his back to us. He proceeded to respond to the officer's questions in a quiet voice. At least we hoped this is what he was doing. After additional questions and answers the military policeman left. About twenty minutes later an older officer, in unmarked fatigues without a rank symbol of any type, arrived, caught the Maestro's attention and beckoned him to the rear of the dining room. The professor excused himself before he and the officer, who appeared to be of importance, went to where our car was parked in the hotel courtyard. This time it took the professor thirty minutes to return. He explained that he had been acting like a reporter in telling the military about our situation while answering the officer's questions.

Though the military presence seemed comfortable with us, about now the local police department became noticeably concerned. Their problem apparently was: Were we in the country legally and what were we doing there? Accordingly, we more frequently noticed that the same policemen, also dressed in fatigues, appeared at every corner we were near. When we parked for breakfast they were in the street. When we went to the telegraph office, one wandered in. When we parked by the bridge we'd see one at the end of the driveway. At other times uniformed patrolmen, wearing military clothing, battle helmets and carrying side arms, were constantly around wherever we were. Once we drove three or four blocks into the rural area surrounding Jaguarao to put an STP solution through the carburetor to clean the fouling spark plugs. We had no sooner stopped than two men arrived in a little car, parked and approached us. By now we were so irritated by this constant official attention that we slammed the hood and drove around the corner. From there we could watch them discuss the matter with nearby householders. Soon the two drove around the same corner and passed without even a courtesy wave. It was obvious that these men were not particularly interested in the Mercury but were more concerned with our actions. Such attention was completely unpleasant, though somewhat understandable. The frontier sector of any nation is a sensitive area and we can appreciate why both military and civilian police would be concerned about us. However the surveillance was unwarranted in view of the fact that we carried valid passports, appropriately stamped and endorsed by their border officers. In critique of this situation it is worth pointing out that a simple solution to our entering Brasil, with an American-registry car would have been to arrange for issuance of the carnet by the Touring Club do Brasil.

This organization's semiofficial status was of great importance to custom house officials and accordingly we could have expected that documentation would be accepted without question. But we did not know this, nor did anyone outside the nation's borders. None of this was as unpleasant as the total inability of Brasilian officialdom to consider that there must be another legal way to move our car forward into Sao Paulo to arrange for and obtain whatever documents were required.

Morning sun in Jaguarao brought another day of complete frustration. We went to the telegraph office bright and early, found that machinery was operating but there were no telegrams for us. Then it was to a quiet corner, to escape the crowds and pour more STP cleaning fluid through the carburetor. We had to do this often because the Mercury engine's spark plugs were fouling badly from inferior Brasilian gasoline which had an extremely high sulfur content. The extended period of engine idling, without any highway-speed operation, was loading the plugs with debris. We now prepared a collection of brand new letters and telegrams to all concerned. When nothing arrived for us at ten, although messages had been promised for that time, we sent a new selection of telegrams to the Rio de Janeiro American Consulate, the American Consulate in Sao Paulo and to Ford and Firestone of Brasil advising them of our unhappy situation, unscheduled delay and asking for assistance..

Shortly thereafter, Renee walked across the bridge into Uruguay while my heart sank to my boots, hoping she'd have no trouble returning. In Rio Branco it took an hour and a half for her to make a long distance telephone call to Montevideo. She finally reached offices of the Ford Motor Company, explained our plight and requested their immediate assistance. There was no question at Ford, they would take every possible action to free us. On her return, much to my relief, we had lunch with a Brazilian businessman who shared stories of life and times in his vast nation which is so much like the United States. Afterward we began our frustrating rounds again: To the Touring Club and to the telegraph office. Though promised information by 6 o'clock, and believe me we were there at six, no information was available.

Another radio telephone call over private equipment of Transportes Coral produced only the discouraging: "It is too late. All offices in Rio were long since closed."

That evening we were so bored that we decided to take in a movie. There were two theatres in Jaguarao: One on the south side of town and one on the north. That on the north charged us 15 cents (U.S.) each for good seats on the main floor to watch an elderly German motion picture in which subtitles, printed across the bottom, were in Portuguese. Our personal entertainment was watching the action, listening to German of which we had heard a bit, and trying to interpret printed Portuguese which we knew not at all. It was a completely relaxing evening, if for no other reason than we understood only a little of was going on but were thoroughly entertained by juggling interpretation problems we could not solve.

The next morning, true to form, we showed up at the telegraph office at 8 o'clock to see if any messages had arrived. The teletypewriter sputtered into action and indicated that there was a message for us. It then sputtered a bit more and expired. The operator turned to rattling the Morse code key and took down two messages which she typed on an elderly Underwood typewriter. One told us that our business contacts in Sao Paulo had been in touch with the Touring Club in Rio. The second reported that two telegrams had been dispatched to us two days previously. Both telegrams were to have the effect of passing our car northward to Rio de Janeiro.

But personnel at the Jaguarao telegraph office said that neither had been received and none such were on their list of messages. The young man who appeared to manage the office suggested that I go with him to visit the Inspector of Custom's, the gentleman who only showed up for work at 1:30 in the afternoon. At his home we were told that he had not received any telegrams and accordingly we could not pass. However, he indicated that if we came to his office that afternoon he would try to find some other way to allow us to enter the country with the Mercury.

Thanking him for his courtesy, the telegraph office manager and I went to the Touring Club. We showed them the telegram which indicated the two previous messages had been sent. The Touring Club manager said they'd received nothing. Back we went to the telegraph office where the Telex machine had come to life and hammered out about 20 messages, according to Renee who was waiting there. When they were completed at long last, the Telex was then used to transmit what seemed to have been our dozenth telegram toward Sao Paulo seeking assistance. Needless to say the matter of missing telegrams and lack of communication between Sao Paulo and Jaguarao was completely bewildering. Other telegrams seemed to come and go with great rapidity. But the two necessary for our freedom had, for some mysterious reason or other, been "lost" in a mass of correspondence. What disturbed us most was that no one in the telegraph office would actually review the record of received messages to determine if ours had ever passed through their hands. "We've not seen them" was only a reflection of their memory. We could not help but wonder if somewhere along the line there was a bureaucratic fumble or a form of "official" interference in our affairs.

At 8 o'clock the following morning we visited the telegraph office and were told that everyone had arrived late and accordingly there were no telegrams available. We waited. Shortly afterward the teletype machine became operative for a few minutes. It indicated to the operator that there were messages for us. The teletype machine then failed. The operator shifted to the Morse key and took down two Western Telex messages, by means of code, from the previous transfer point. The first message had left Sao Paulo at two o'clock the previous afternoon. It read as follows: "Press conference cancelled Stop Since yesterday we were in close contact with Touring Club Stop Any further information ready to provide Stop Regards, Ramirez, Ford Motor".

The second message received immediately thereafter was dated from Sao Paulo, at three o'clock that same afternoon. It read: "We inform that we went to Touring Club and two Telex's were sent to Jaguarao yesterday. One for the Custom's Inspector the other for Touring representative, Mr. Francisco Victoreo. Stop we are at your disposal if further information is requested. Stop Regards, Ramirez, Ford Motor."

Following receipt of these telegrams, the telegraph operator and I again walked to the home of the Inspector of Customs. He repeated that there was no means of passing the car without the "proper" telegram he had originally requested. We asked for his consideration of another way of sending the Mercury to Sao Paulo with a special permission or perhaps with a member of the Customs staff riding in the car with us and returning via airplane. The Inspector replied that he had thought of that possibility and this same afternoon would arrange to pass us through in some special manner. After we left the Inspector's home, the telegraph operator cautioned me to say nothing about this possible arrangement while in the telegraph office. This confirmed my belief that a Brazilian security office in the telegraph building was monitoring incoming and outgoing messages. That the security office had abstracted the two telegrams, which would provide us with travel to Rio de Janeiro, became a logical second thought. This opinion was somewhat confirmed by bridge officers who always seemed to know details of our correspondence. And further supported by reluctance of the telegraph office staff to inspect their writtten record of incoming messages to determine if and when our missing telegrams had in fact passed through the office.

When we visited the telegraph office about noon there was no word for us. However, both clerks agreed that perhaps there was checking that could be done. On their own initiative, they activated the teletype line and checked the previous relay point. Their question: "Were there any messages for Carroll? The Touring Club? Or the Inspector of Customs?" In each instance the answer was a firm "No". For sure, at this stage of the game we found it hard to believe anyone. Was this a performance for our benefit, or was the information truly accurate?

We drove around town for a while to air out the Mercury's engine, poured more carbon remover through the carburetor in hopes of cleaning spark plugs and stopped at a local gas station to refill the tank. While I was overseeing the gas pump, and Renee was across the street taking pictures, a young man drove up in a DKW sedan. He walked around our car and began asking questions about it because he had read of the *Aventura* run in a Spanish-language motoring magazine and was delighted to see the Mercury in town. His English was fluent and what was more important he soon proved to be an important ally.

His name: Jenancio Ayres de Mesquita Filho. His job, Public Prosecutor (Attorney General) for the District of Rio Grande de Sole in which Jaguarao was located. He was in town to prosecute criminal offences, a special trip for him and a blessing for us. We all lunched together and discussed automobiles and mutual objectives. Near the conclusion of lunch, he volunteered his efforts to provide what help he could to clarify the situation. I left and went to the bridge Customs office to visit the Inspector of the section, who had previously told me he would arrange a method of passing us through without the telegram. His greeting was "Nix" as he indicated that it would not be possible for him to issue a piece of paper allowing us to proceed further. I asked if there could be another way? He had considered my suggestion of carrying a Funcionario from his office and now thought that might be acceptable. If I would return later that afternoon, he would determine what could be arranged. I showed him the business card of our newly found friend, the Public Prosecutor, and explained in Spanish that this man would be willing to translate for us from Portuguese to English. The Chief immediately became a totally worried man and explained in extremely good English, which I had suspected he spoke all the time, "It is not necessary", and attempted to keep the business card. I retrieved the card and said we'd be back at 3 o'clock to see what could be worked out.

Two blocks down the street, in the restaurant where Renee and our newly-found friend were completing their lunch, I walked in with a sad look on my face. Renee instantly guessed that I had been unsuccessful. I explained what had taken place. The Public Prosecutor suggested that it would be helpful for him to go with me to find out exactly what was happening and to make sure I understood properly what I had been told. Lunch finished, the three of us trouped over to the Customs house and found the Inspector in his office. He explained to the Public Prosecutor what the problem was and displayed a mimeographed bulletin, which I had not seen before, detailing the temporary importation of an automobile. At the same time saying "A ley, is a ley, is a ley, is a ley." All of which supported his decision that there was nothing to be done because the law was explicit and there was no other way.

Our new friend tried to reason with the man but was unsuccessful in getting him to understand that while a law is the law, there are usually other methods to accomplish an objective when hardship is being worked. The Inspector remained adamant and said that my suggestion of a Funcionario traveling with us was really the only answer he would accept as a means of moving us toward our destination.

The Public Prosecutor who knew the Superintendent at the Coral Transportation Company, suggested that we go there. At their office a long conversation in Portuguese ensued between the Superintendent and the District Attorney. We did not participate nor were we asked any questions. Soon we left for the telegraph office where the District Attorney wanted to find out what had been happening to our telegrams. All he could learn was that we had been sending telegrams and none had been received that were directed toward us. This obviously inaccuraate information did not include the "Press Conference" cancellation notice that Ford had sent us earlier, or the follow up report on Ford's contacts with the Touring Club. However, the clerk said, telegrams were expected momentarily: To us, the Touring Club and Customs, advising one and all that our Carnet was acceptable. How the clerk knew what would be in telegrams yet to arrive was not explained nor did we bother to ask.

Besides, we had been hearing this story for three days. The Public Prosecutor commented on this point and was not particularly impressed either. The result was that we parted at the telegraph office: He for the Forum (Court House) and we for a siesta. We agreed to pick him up at the Forum about 5:30 P.M.. to start the process all over again.

About 4:30 there was a knock at our hotel door. In came Senor Francisco Silva, the man with whom all our trouble began. He reintroduced himself and said (In English) that he and the Inspector of Customs had been talking the matter over and decided that he, Francisco Silva, could ride with us to Rio de Janeiro and straighten the matter out with the Customs office there. He also made sure that we understood he had a doctorate and was a licensed attorney. To "prove" the matter, Francisco displayed a finger ring with a brilliant red stone. According to Francisco, we were to visit the Inspector at his house and discuss the matter at 6:30 that evening where arrangements would be completed. We were not to go to the bridge Customs office and discuss it. This was a private matter!

Francisco's "private matter" reminded me that when we had been talking, during our initial entry onto Brazilian soil, he had indicated a need for money while rubbing his fingers together. This was done in a room with other people standing behind his back. He was facing me and I had interpreted his actions as meaning additional money for deposit with Customs to certify the security and reexport of the car. Now that he was in our hotel room, willing (or shall we say desiring) to ride to Rio with us, my suspicious mind finally realized the obvious: He had been asking for "Mordita" (the small bribe) to sign our papers. My misunderstanding the request had him withholding permission to proceed. The result of Francisco Silva's visit was that we said "Fine", accepted an address with directions, and agreed to pick him up at 9:00 the following morning after visiting his superior that evening at 6:30.

About 5:00 we went to the telegraph office. There was no action. The clerks were kind enough to work the teletype machine to the next station up the line (there were said to be three relay stations between Jaguarao and Sao Paulo) to see if messages existed. According to reports, there were none and had been none. We then drove to the Forum to meet our attorney friend. Though busy, he allowed us to wait in his office while he conducted legal matters of the state. Suddenly the superintendent of Coral came in with a big smile on his face and a fat notebook clutched under his arm.

He had our permission. What happened, we were told, was that he had managed to reach the Automobile Club in Rio on his radio using a telephone "patch" at the Rio end. They read the exact telegram dispatched, so they said, several days before. He had copied it down in longhand and there it was for the Public Prosecutor's advice. After a bit of consultation, they agreed that Coral's superintendent would go to the Customs office and explain the circumstances by which the telegram had been transmitted. He left and a few minutes later returned with an even bigger grin on his face. The Inspector had decided that he would accept the release; if the local secretary of the Touring Club would sign it, as though it had arrived by means of the regular Telex network. The Forum's portable typewriter was unleashed and Coral's handwritten message re-typed in a more formal manner. Now we all headed out to find the secretary of the Touring Club. Our parade of cars was lead by the tiny blue VW belonging to the superintendent of Coral. The second car, a DKW, belonged to the Public Prosecutor. Last was our big Mercury coupe. We trailed through city streets and pulled up in front of the Touring Club office. To our disappointment, it was closed. While discussing the matter at the curb, the superintendent of Coral saw a friend walking about a half block away and shouted to him for the address of the secretary. This was provided and away we went to raise more dust from between every cobblestone. But we missed. For some reason, the address given was not correct. Though we banged on every door on the block, we couldn't find anyone. The Public Prosecutor went to a service station across the street and telephoned. He reached the Touring Club secretary and was given directions on how to find the secretary's home. It was exactly one block away on a tiny side street. Back to our cars we ran and dusted up the unpaved roadway to where the secretary of the Touring Club lived on a 20-acre farm only these few blocks from the center of town.

He was in the back yard repairing his car. On hearing more about misdirected telegrams, our detention in the town, and arrival of the confirmation message through the Coral radio network, he agreed that while this was somewhat irregular, it was certainly proper. He would be delighted to sign on. Back to our cars, along more dusty streets and now to the Customs office before it closed.

The appearance of Francisco Silva's face when he was presented with our document, typed on official Forum stationary, was almost (but not really) worth the days of delay. The presence of the Public Prosecutor and the Secretary of the Touring Club, both of whom agreed that it was perfectly legal, was just too much. We were now approved to travel and Silva would not have his free trip to Rio. I had never before seen a man appear so crestfallen, so unhappy or so bewildered. It was almost as though someone had told him his wife had just given birth to four green children, he'd lost his job, his pants had fallen off and his name was really John Smith. When Silva recovered his poise he disappeared to contact the Inspector with a telephone he had previously told me did not exist.

The Secretary of the Touring Club signed the forms and Francisco Silva had to sit himself down and prepare our documents under supervision. I was given a form to sign and finally realize that we were free to travel again. Handshakes were something less than cordial on the part of the border officials. One had lost a free trip to Rio.His chief had suffered a setback in attempts to operate in a "do nothing, see nothing" atmosphere. And the State's Public Prosecutor knew all about it.

Too soon we parted from our Public Prosecutor friend, who had done so much for total strangers, and the Coral superintendent who, for days, worked so diligently on our behalf. Both men were far more representative of the many delightful Brasilian citizens we met later. After one Jaguarao businessman heard of our release, he came to the hotel and told us, in extremely good English, "Now I can tell you that sometimes we are so ashamed of many people in government offices. They do not represent the spirit of the peoples of Brasil."

We made our hotel in time to have dinner. Afterward I fueled the Mercury and parked on the street outside our room for a quick getaway. Inside the hotel I found Renee, surrounded by about 20 children. We had completely forgotten that this was the night of our English class. Several days previously, while in the bridge customs house trying to obtain help or information, I met a pair of school girls who were learning English. They were speaking English with me for practice while I was trying to learn some elements of Portuguese from them. They had come to invite us to visit their home across from the hotel so they could practice English with two North Americans. In traffic-free Jaguarao it was a quick street crossing followed by a small parade of local citizens and children interested in what we were doing. For about two hours, we enjoyed a pleasant evening with the two young women and their family. While I worked with them, in clarifying their English speech, Renee talked with the mother and a brother of the girls. He loaded Renee with information about things to do in Rio while breaking her heart with stories of places we had missed in Buenos Aires and Montevideo. Of our many experiences enjoyed during *Aventura*, the two hours "at home" with this family was a highlight we long remember. About 10:00 we returned to the hotel, hopefully for peaceful rest.

But this was not to be. The Mercury in front of the hotel (with the engine operating, as it always did) had attracted another crowd. The newspaper of a nearby town had published a picture and story about both car and trip. This edition had reached Jaguarao that day. Everyone subscribing now knew what the lovely Coral-colored car was doing in town. Those who had seen the Mercury before now had to return again to inspect the car with an engine that never stopped. A conservative estimate would be that from the time we had parked at 8:30 P.M., until well after midnight, there always were from 20 to 50 people in the street and on the sidewalk looking at the *Aventura* car. Vehicular traffic was blocked by those who were double-parked. Horse-drawn farm carts pulled up while their owners leaned over to inspect the beautiful coupe. And we couldn't sleep while all this commotion was under our window. The Mercury's audience was laughing, talking, and discussing with, in some instances, the same voices continuing for over an hour. Finally, in desperation, occupants of the adjoining room became so unhappy that they began banging on their window. At the same time they screamed for sidewalk bystanders to go home and/or be quiet so that sleep could take over.

We were out of bed at 5:00 A.M. and by 6:00 had everything in the car, doors shut and the travel log organized. Both of us were sorry to leave the many people who had been courteous to us. But we were not at all sorry to leave behind the days of frustration and nerve-wracking delusion from troublesome border officials. The streets were totally deserted. Not even a stray dog barked as we began our run toward Sao Paulo. Street lights were out and only occasionally could we see illuminated shutters where a householder was sleepily rolling out of bed. The slap of our tires against the cobblestones was the loudest sound. Then it was 109 miles of dirt to the first pavement of the main highway along the coast toward Rio. Plus 206 miles more before we found a service station which had anything more than the "ping happy" regular grade which was the only fuel previously available. Soon we enjoyed a complete and major surprise because we wanted to stop at Porto Alegre and visit the American Consulate to whom we had appealed for assistance.

Our surprise came on crossing the bridge into the city. We had thought of Porto Alegre as being a tiny seaport servicing an occasional vessel. Instead we found a fabulous metropolis of over a million people with dozens of buildings 10, 15 and 20 stories high. There were streetcars and buses, three railroad systems, blocks of wharves and docks, ship repair facilities, canals and suspension bridges. By finding a city map in a Brasilian guide book we managed to locate the nation's tourist office and the American consulate. The reason for the tourist office visit was that Francisco Silva had insisted that we must stop in Porto Alegre to have our passports inspected by tourist officials. Unfortunately the tourist office didn't appcar to have been open for any portion of recent decades. The interior was totally dark and the floor, behind the front doors, was littered with dusty mail that had been tossed through the slot. We inspected the lobby directory and discovered that the American Consulate was in the same building. On the 11th floor its office door was open. We walked in and saw no one except a cleaning woman. We explained to her that it was very important that we talk to someone and gave her our card. She disappeared around the corner and soon came back and invited us to the office of Cooper Hewitt, American Consul for Porto Alegre.

Hewitt's father, an engineer, lived in Pasadena which immediately gave us grounds for conversation as our home was not far from there. He was relieved to discover that we were free, particularly because they had only received our telegram that morning, two days after it was sent from Jaguarao. Hewitt invited us to lunch with him though we were dirty and unkempt. The finest hotel in Porto Alegre soon had two tired Americans enjoying cold roast beef, potato salad and local wine. During our luncheon conversation Consul Hewitt emphasized manners of conduct we wished we had known earlier. He said "It is important that at no time should an American traveling in a foreign country ever give up his passport. You must display it upon request but you must not give it to any other person. The reason for this is that they may lose it, they may put it to an illegal use and, in any event, you will be effectively blockaded from travel because you have no means of identification."

The second thing Hewitt said was, "The moment you have trouble advise us by all possible communications methods. In many countries, communications are somewhat primitive and you cannot always be sure that we will promptly receive what you are sending us". In light of our difficulty, he suggested we should have used telephone, telegraph and mail services on the first day. Then, on the following day, have used all three again. In addition, as in our situation, when stuck at a border crossing we should have arranged for temporary permission to return into the previous nation and repeat the multiple message performance to the American Consul in the capital city we had left. He emphasized, that we should have used every method possible to contact an American Consul. "Then," he said, "rest assured someone will soon come to your assistance. If there is a delay, it will ordinarily be a delay in our receiving knowledge of your predicament, not in our staff's response time."

On our way back to Hewitt's office we were approached by a young man carrying a motion picture camera. He was from a local television station, had seen the car and wanted to photograph us with it. This was fine and dandy with us. The cameraman and his assistant agreed to wait while we went upstairs to be introduced to other members of the Consulate staff. There we learned that one of them had already been assigned the rather unpleasant job of driving to Jaguarao the following day to find us. Additionally they had already contacted the Chief of Brasil's immigration services and asked him to do what he could to help. As far as the television people downstairs were concerned, we were not quite sure whether they were more interested in our trip from Alaska or had heard about our problems and wanted to show that two Americans could really bring an American car past Brasil's border. There was no interview. Only a matter of their shooting film with Carroll proudly demonstrating the Mercury product. We gave them a copy of the press release we had prepared in Spanish. One of the boys indicated that it could be read with little or no difficulty by the station's editorial people.

Soon we left Porto Alegre and started for our hotel stop in Bacarone. The Alvarado, a modest, middle class Latin American establishment would, by United States standards, be considered pretty punk. But we were totally delighted because there was a hot shower and a big bed onto which we could collapse after dinner. However business came first and we needed the local telephone and telegraph office. But our attempts to contact Sao Paulo, only a few hundred miles away, were fruitless. The girl operator advised us "The line is in bad condition" by writing across the bottom of our request for the Sao Paulo number. Fortunately the words she wrote were so close to Spanish that we had little trouble deciding that there was no chance of making a phone call that evening. So we trooped over to the telegraph office which was also the Post Office. It was closed. We were too late.

The next project was dinner and there we almost foundered We ordered a Brasilian "Churasco" and explained to the waiter that we also wanted local white wine with mineral water. Within minutes he returned with our wine/water order and a tray of appetizers. There was a plate of spaghetti under meat sauce, sliced cucumbers in vinegarette, sliced tomatoes, rice and fat black beans swimming in their own broth; plus bread and butter. By the time we had heaped our plates with these samples another waiter appeared bearing a three-foot sword on which were impaled beef filets which had been barbecued over a wood fire. By resting the tip of the sword in the middle of our plate he used a fork to plump off several fillets for each of us. We thought this was a pretty nice way to complete our dinner. But it didn't! Two mouthfuls later our first waiter returned with another sword on which was a huge sirloin steak. It too had been broiled over a wood fire. This sword was jammed into a holder attached to the table. The steak was ours to eat, or not eat, as we wished. By watching other patrons, we discovered that the proper technique was to stick a fork into the steak and cut off what one could handle. Several minutes later he reappeared with a second steak impaled on another sword. The second sword and steak were not a table decoration. Like every other table in the restaurant, we now had a two-sword centerpiece of skewered meat and a table full of food. Our waiter had previously asked if we wanted any chicken. Luckily we said no, or we would have had a third sword on which would have been impaled a half chicken or so. Needless to say we were soon stuffed.

We left Bacarone on our morning drive toward Curityba, another major city of Brasil. Along the way we were as high as 3,000 feet through wine country mixed with lumber industry sites and cattle raising on both sides of the two-lane pavement. In Curityba we finally made telephone contact with Sao Paulo, now about 250 miles north, to notify our business contacts that we were free. Fortunately they had previously been in touch with our Consulate in Sao Paulo who had received a radio communication from Porto Alegre that we were on the way. Accordingly, our business friends had already made arrangements for our comfort in their metropolitan city, the eight largest in the world. As we left Curityba on the first stage of our run into Sao Paulo, all traffic was halted by the sound of sirens. We too stopped, fortunately in the row of cars fronting the intersection. Ahead we could see three motorcycle patrolmen clearing the street for what appeared to be a truck or two. It turned out that the local Mercedes Benz dealer had received a shipment of ten huge tank trucks and arranged with the police department to parade his new fleet throughout the town. On the side of each truck were posters and banners attesting to the success of his business enterprise.

Midway between Curityba and Sao Paulo, we stopped at a roadside lunch stand for a snack. You would have thought you were in the United States, except for the corner bar where hard liquor was available. As an experiment we ordered the "Sandwich Americana", for no other reason than to find out what Brasilians think an American sandwich should be. It arrived and we were surprised. Slightly toasted white bread, one leaf of lettuce, a slice of tomato, one fried egg and a slice of hot cheese. This: "The Sandwich Americana."

This contrast between ridiculous and sublime added much to the pleasure of our first evening in Sao Paulo. Our decision was to visit the city's most exclusive restaurant, a roof top dining salon 43 stories above the street on the Edifico Italia. At the rooftop lobby we left the elevator to be greeted by the Maitre d', were relayed to a captain who in turn passed us to the senior waiter for a station of six tables. We were seated overlooking the city's spectacular view of a community of nearly six million people. Waiters were immaculately dressed, careful to handle silverware only by the handle and, to keep from rattling plates together, managed to use a napkin to separate china while delivering it from service center to table. In fact, they were so well trained that they handled our napkins with tongs instead of their fingers. After we ordered, bread and butter were promptly placed on the table. A unique touch was that each French roll was packed in its own tiny little paper bag. We decided we'd like to nibble a half a roll but there were no butter plates. Feeling a little silly after a tiring day, we very carefully removed one roll from its paper bag, tore the bag into two equal pieces and spread each to the left of our plates. On each portion of paper bag we placed half a roll and proceeded to use the paper as though it were a butter plate. Our question became, how long would it take before this conglomeration were removed and a proper butter plate supplied? Water was brought to the table. Then wine. Fully a dozen waiters passed, inspected our table and continued on. An inspection of other tables disclosed that only we two Americans were sufficiently dainty as to use a paper bag to keep bread off the immaculate linen tablecloth. All other diners had littered the cloth with broken pieces of bread and crumbs. Eventually we'd had our fun to the limit. We called the Maitre d' over and told him that while we enjoyed his classy service we thought it was quite funny that no one had ever gotten around to giving us a plate for the roll. He thought this was a tremendous joke and hurried immediately to the kitchen. Eventually our waiter showed up with two plates delicately wrapped in napkins and placed them next to the improvised paper platters which he did not remove. We completed the transfer job and eventually all the torn paper disappeared kitchenward.

When our Brasilian guests arrived a few minutes later, they could only gasp at our tomfoolery, "You were doing such a thing here?" they gasped. In retrospect it appears we were more tired than sensible.

Too early for breakfast, we left Sao Paulo while I was lighthearted and light-footed. By following a bus driver's suggestion we threaded several back streets and arrived onto a dual highway cutting through the city center. His guidance was greatly appreciated because it began to rain cats and dogs. People were going to work, some dressed for the rain, others not. Those on bicycles were almost drowned as cars squished past while spraying water in all directions. Nevertheless, we found our way through the damp and hazy weather to eventually reach open country and cruise at a steady 60 miles an hour. It wasn't long before our "no breakfast" departure, and the imminence of starvation, began to take their toll in hunger pains. We drove for what seemed a thousand miles, but what was in reality about 20, before finding a small roadside lunch counter for the last rural lunch of *Aventura*. The proprietor came from behind his counter, decided that what we were asking for was sandwiches and eventually produced a couple of fresh buns in which he placed thick slabs of local cheese. This, plus cups of equally thick black coffee, put us in a more amiable frame of mind. The highway from Sao Paulo ended outside Rio in a large cloverleaf. Luckily we turned in the right direction and soon found ourselves amid traffic signals, more traffic, and eventually downtown Rio. A city map given to us in Montevideo was a great help. It lead us to a broad boulevard which gracefully curved along the edge of the justly famous Copacabana Beach. We slowly threaded our way through throngs of bathers, millions of children, and an occasional vendor loaded with sodas or umbrellas.

One disadvantage of not knowing where your hotel is that, like all things not quickly found along a two and a half mile oceanfront, it will always be the furthest or least easily seen. We did arrive and after registering telephoned a business associate, told him that we were in Rio, and inquired about a place to park the car. The hotel, surprisingly enough, had no garage and did not know where any automobile could be parked, except on the street. Eventually, our business contact suggested where we could park behind gates in a well-ventilated space.

That night we visited our hotel's second-floor restaurant for dinner. While there we received our first taste of Rio's personality, described later as "The most beautiful and most charming city in the world .... where nothing works." For this evening, the "nothing works" was electricity. We had no sooner been seated than half the lights on Copacabana Beach were suddenly extinguished. From our view window we could look back a mile to where the distant area was illuminated like a fabulous horizontal Christmas tree. In contrast, our nearby beach blocks were as dark as dark could be. It didn't amount to more than a minute before a waiter placed a freshly burning candle on our table and soon the entire restaurant was charmingly aglow with light most flattering to our tired faces. It must have been about midnight when the telephone rang in our room. Our business contact was on the line. "Bill, you've got to come down and get the car. The people in my apartment building are complaining. They say it smells too bad and exhaust from the continually running engine is going to kill them."

"Okay" says Bill, "I'll be right there."

"I'll meet you in the lobby," he replied and there he was when I stepped off the elevator. We drove to his apartment, backed the Mercury onto the street and tried to decide what to do; this at 12:30 in the morning. My friend remembered that a watchman on the street was guarding open carports of an apartment across the way. He talked with the watchman who, for a small fee, agreed to watch the Mercury if we parked it on the sidewalk in front of his building. The result was that our *Aventura* coupe spent its first night in Rio with one pair of wheels in the gutter, the other two on the sidewalk. Here the ever-running engine hummed merrily with about 3000 hours of use, the equivalent of over eleven years of average driving, under its sturdy belt. The following morning my business contact sent his private secretary to guide me to the Simoniz plant where we were to take pictures. The girl was beautiful, busty and thoroughly Brasilian. Her English was excellent and she talked up a storm while explaining everything we were seeing and where we were going. As we drove along Copacabana Beach she identified each sidewalk cafe along the way, explained the food they served and type of clientele that were usually there. After leaving the beach area we cruised through an area of narrow side streets and eventually past a shopping district which she identified as the shortcut to her boss's plant. Here, on Aventura's final days, one of the older city busses almost nailed one of our car's fenders.

We were stuck in a traffic jam and the city bus was on our left in one of the two rows of vehicles. As we inched forward the bus driver decided that he could go faster in my lane than in his. Without determining whether anyone was in the way he began to pull into the side of our car. I sounded the horn and tapped on the side of the bus. The driver either didn't hear me or chose to ignore it. I then hit the side of his bus much harder in hopes that he would stop. He did. But not for long. Apparently he assumed that in two seconds I could drive completely out of the way, though there was neither room forward nor backward. At this moment, traffic in my lane began to move and the bus driver decided to cut in. Unfortunately, the more he cut the closer he came. About the time my right wheels were over the curb and approaching the sidewalk I was swinging a fat tire iron to batter a number of deep new dents along the side of his bus. Now he got the idea and waited for me to pull ahead so he could move in behind the Mercury.

In Rio's Simoniz plant we turned off the engine at noon to conclude the endurance test it had been undergoing since leaving Alaska The Mercury's odometer recorded 24,876 miles of travel. There were 2924.4 hours of nearly continuous engine operation which, on the basis of 260 hours average use each year, equaled eleven years and three months of relatively troublefree service for the average American driver. Or, on the basis of miles traveled, our use was the equivalent of 108,202 miles of engine operation. We'd bought an estimated 2,500 gallons of gas driving from Detroit to Alaska and then to Rio de Janeiro. Total driving time was 76 days of travel plus 49 days for business or touristing around cities in which we had stopped for business or pleasure.

After pictures were taken of the brilliantly polished Mercury a second, and equally charming, secretary guided my return trip to make certain I didn't become lost. This time we went to the Copacabana Palace Hotel where arrangements had been made to display the Mercury on a front patio. This was in anticipation of our final press conference scheduled for that evening. While I'd been driving around town with charming Brasilians, Renee had been working. Following Consul Hewitt's suggestions she had visited the American Embassy to organize final arrangements to get our car out of Brasil and be sure our peculiar entrance into the nation was legal. At our Embassy she was told that they would call Brasilian Immigration and Customs offices to find out what, if anything, should be done. "Come back tomorrow and we'll tell you what to do."

She also contacted the offices of Fink and Company to confirm shipping our car home. They had been recommended by the Grace Line agent who said that we must employ a freight forwarder to send our car out of the country. Renee told Fink that we wanted to ship the car on the *Santa Regina* which was due to arrive in six days and we would deliver the car to them two days hence. "It is impossible to do it that way. The law of Brasil says that you cannot ship personal goods out of the nation before you leave. Besides," the Fink manager said, "paper work takes time and an export license from the Bank of Brazil takes a very long time. "But," he concluded, "Come on over and we'll see what we can do." When I returned to the hotel, and Renee told me of her discussions, I also telephoned the Fink office and was given the same information. Apparently, as far as Fink was concerned, there was no way to hurry this up. On the other hand, Ford people had told me that something could be shipped out in two days if enough urgency was generated in shifting papers to, from, and through, the various government offices. With more confidence than knowledge, I made an appointment to meet the Fink people on the second morning and organize the shipment of our car as scheduled.

Our press conference that night, at the Hotel Copacabana, included ten reporters, an equal number of photographers and heavy rain. The Brasilian media were intensely interested in the point that we had undertaken this trip in a standard car and several reporters were openly doubtful. One was quoted as saying, "Look at that car.... they sent it here on a truck and expect us to believe they drove it over the road." Eventually we convinced them that we'd actually driven the car everywhere we said we had. The clincher was showing them the original equipment tires which, though they had considerable tread depth, displayed evidence of having endured a considerable number of miserable miles over gravel roads. The conference and picture-taking session lasted about two hours during which innumerable canapés, hors d'oeuvres and dishes of peanuts were consumed by our hungry guests.

This over, the director of the Firestone Tire Company in Brasil invited Renee and I to accompany him to dinner. The place? A hotel building that had not been completed but on the top of which was a fine restaurant. He drove for miles through a maze of narrow twisting one-way streets before arriving at a cluttered construction site where the bare steel skeleton of a hotel decorated the side of a sheer cliff. The Firestone man's description was accurate. "We'll take the elevator and follow the carpet." It was a strange feeling to walk into a deserted building where illumination was from hanging bare light bulbs and wait for an elevator by the side of an unfinished concrete wall. At the top we left the cage onto a bare concrete floor around which were no windows or walls. Only flimsy wooden railings protected the unwary from walking off the edge and falling 20 stories straight down. Leading from the elevator was a red carpet which wandered across the vast expanse of rough concrete and disappeared into the distance. About halfway along this pathway, a tilted sign nailed onto a plywood wall indicated that we should turn to the right. We did. Ahead were more dangling light bulbs. Eventually, the three of us were cautiously wending our way along a concrete walk on the cliff-facing side of the structure. Wind, rolling in off the sea, buffeted us from side to side and occasionally blasted water off damp trees above us on the mountain side. After a hundred feet or so of navigating this peculiar entrance route we rounded a corner and stopped, open mouthed, on a side of this unfinished building. We were overlooking all of Rio de Janeiro and the Bay of Guanbara from the roughest and crudest place imaginable. And we had only reached the viewpoint after stumbling our way around construction materials and half-completed concrete frameworks while seeking a restaurant we were not really sure existed. There was no going back. We continued down a flight of stairs to suddenly exit by a huge open-air swimming pool hanging far out over the side of the structure. To the left was the restaurant. Behind its glass doors there were patrons and empty tables. To the right, more of Rio with the open sea sparkling like a jewel in the moonlight. No entertainment was necessary because the wind was blowing so strongly that it was lifting huge chunks of water out of the pool and throwing them against the glass doors. Our suspense was "Would the doors hold?" As time passed several couples attempted to dine on the veranda but eventually abandoned their tables and moved inside to escape the new rain that was beginning to ruin both food and clothing.

The next morning was an up and early for me at something like 5 o'clock. My project of the day was to put a last group of miles onto the *Aventura* Mercury chassis and complete observations necessary to finalize judgments accepted during the trip. I left the hotel without breakfast and taxi'd to the Copacabana Palace where I hoped our car had remained untouched while parked in the patio. It was, with the overnight porter keeping his eye on it from his nearby desk. I paid the taxi driver what was on the meter and gave him a modest tip. My reward was a fabulous performance that almost broke my heart and led me to tears. His story was: Brazilian money had no value. It would not buy anything. Though I paid him what was on the meter he was starving to death. He could not afford to operate a cab for such little money. And he was hopelessly and totally underpaid because no matter how much he made the money was not worth anything. For some reason I was tremendously hard-hearted about this tear-jerking tale and merely thanked him for his courtesy and left the cab. As I walked toward the coral Mercury he asked if it was my car. "Yes," I replied. At that moment his sad, sad story was completely forgotten. He was out of the cab, I was his big friend and would I please tell him all about the *Alaska Brasil* car. I did.

Minutes later I was on the boulevard out of Rio. Early in the morning, with little traffic to impede progress, it was a delight to drive. Within a half-hour I was on the route for Sao Paulo, a super-highway that I knew, and one that could be driven rapidly while I made notes regarding the Mercury's operation. I had planned to dictate this final report but unfortunately the Stenorette unit I selected had exhausted its batteries. They were totally dead. And might well they be. They had powered the dictation of 20 tapes and traveled from Alaska to Brasil. There was no questions but what they deserved to expire with grace. Accordingly, my drive part way to Sao Paulo and back could could be called a busman's holiday. I relaxed, toured easily, made a few pencil notes and enjoyed the day without struggle. But comfort was not to last forever.

When I completed the run I parked in front of our Rio hotel in the only parking space available. As I was leaving the car somcone came over and said that I was in the "Taxi Zone." But there were no taxis to be seen nor 'Taxis Only" on any street signs. I told the man I would be back in a little while to move the car. Upstairs the telephone rang and I was hearing things in Portuguese I couldn't understand. Finally the porter called to tell me, in English, that I was in the taxi zone. I explained to him that I would be glad to move the car in a short while but please let me sleep for a short while. For some reason or other the telephone operator was never clued in for she kept ringing the 'phone. Eventually I snatched it off the hook and angrily threw it under the bed. There was a knock at the door which I declined to answer. Eventually the door opened and our floor maid came to tell me something in Portuguese. I threw a pillow in her direction and told her to get out and leave me alone.

The moment they left me alone I dropped off and didn't wake until Renee came in. She had been completing the shipping paperwork and getting us organized. The American Embassy had given her a letter, signed by a Vice-Consul, which listed our passport numbers, explained that we were citizens of the United States, that we had recently entered Brasil and requested the Brasilian government to arrange for legal "Dis-embarkation." Renee's next stop had been in a dingy downtown office building to visit the Chief of Maritime Police. She was directed toward a private office, no questions were asked and in moments we were both checked into the country for a 90 day visit. Both personnel in the Chief's office, and the American Vice-Consul, said it was not necessary to get an "SRE' number as long as we had the disembarkation stamp on our pass-port. However, clerks at Pan-American Airways, where she checked to find out about buying tickets home, said that we must have the "SRE" number. Accordingly, wisdom being her forte, she went to the Immigra-tion office of the Brazilian government where there were ten windows to handle "Temporary people." Through good fortune she was directed to the exact window to handle this particular problem. A young woman inspected the disembarkation stamp carefully, typed an "SRE" card for each passport, made a ledger entry, noted that we were touring for 90 days, went through the passport page by page and discharged us with no question or answers as to our visit to her nation. We now had "SRE" numbers which allowed us to leave the country. Without them "You are not going to get past the Airport gate" we had been told. After her run about town Renee and the wife of the Simoniz factory manager decided to have lunch. They found a restaurant that was reported to have excel-lent food and ordered a cooling drink before reading the menu. When they finally decided to select their lunch the waiter said, "I'm sorry, but the cook has just walked off the job."

The two women explained that they would like something to eat and asked about what could be done. After the waiter visited the kitchen he returned and said, "I'll be glad to cook you a steak, if that's what you would like. Or you can come back about five o'clock because we should have a cook by then." They finished their refreshments and left for another restaurant with more stable help.

By now it was near dinner time and Renee and I decided not to go anywhere. Dinner in the hotel, with early sack time, sounded awfully good. We had just ordered when one of the porters arrived to tell me that it would be good if I would move my car because the taxi drivers were very unhappy. This I agreed to do if they would help me find a parking place. Out to the Mercury I went and put my key into the driver's door lock. It wouldn't enter nor would it work in the passenger's door. What happened was that taxi drivers, seeking to impress me with parking in the wrong place, had plugged both door locks with matchsticks. I went back into the hotel, explained to Renee what had happened, then went downstairs and asked the porter if he could find a locksmith for me so we could get the car open and moving. By the time I reached the car a second time one of the bellboys was there with a couple of bent pins. With light from matches and a flashlight borrowed from a neighbor, he worked at the lock trying to get the wooden sticks out. Unfortunately he failed. We left, thoroughly discouraged. Upstairs, I sat with Renee and explained what had been done. While I was doing this the hotel manager introduced himself and said, "Please don't judge us by what happened. Not all Brasilians are like that." After dinner I went back to the car for a few more minutes with bent pins. Residents of the area were watching and I could hear them speaking sympathetically of our plight while saying unhappy things about ill-bred cab drivers who would molest such a lovely vehicle. Eventually a young man, who turned out to be the porter for a small apartment across the way, said that if I could get the car moved he had a garage in which it could be parked. This was the clue to the whole thing. With a straightened coat hanger I popped one of the windows, pulled up the lock button and opened the door. Within minutes *Aventura* was safely in its garage for the night.

Fink and Company was my first stop the next morning. Their downtown office, over a complex of airline agencies, was ready to handle my special needs for freight forwarding. I gave them a list of 'exceptions' on the Mercury which included not applying wax to the paint finish or oil preservatives to the chrome. Nor did I want them to drain the oil or water, or in any way attempt to start the engine. After a small discussion they accepted everything. We bought insurance to the tune of $3,000 U.S.) on the car and $900 (U.S.) on souvenirs and clothes we were stuffing in the trunk. The last thing the Fink clerk did was to give me a map of the city, to show me the route to their warehouse and say: "Look for a church high on a hill on the left, and a World War II airplane in a children's playground on the right. Take the first left turn and our warehouse is on the corner. Here is the address."

Little did I know I would need all these instructions, and more, to find the building where we eventually left the Mercury later that day.

My next job was to find the Pan American Airways ticket office. We had made flight reservations by telephone and the clerk had to complete only a few modest moves to finalize our ticketing. First, he inspected both passports and was delighted to find we had the "SRE" numbers which he previously told Renee was necessary. Then he wrote two tickets. These I wished to pay for with my Diner's Card, as I do for most major purchases, but Pan American only accepted $750 worth of Diner's charges. The rest had to be paid in local currency.

Later I met Renee at the hotel and we walked along Copacabana Beach to a delightful little sidewalk cafe where we had a pleasant Italian-type lunch. The sea breeze was cool, with bikinis better than a floor show in Las Vegas and much faster moving. Back at the hotel we packed or wrapped everything that could fit into the Mercury's trunk. I went to the apartment house garage, found my porter and overpaid him valiantly, for storing the car for one night, and as appreciation of the trouble he faced in making space to place our car under cover. To load the Mercury for shipping I double-parked in front of the hotel, much to disgust of a traffic policeman. While Renee ran up and down the hotel stairs with loads of goodies, I took the lighter out of the car and locked it in the glove-box. Wheel discs were removed and placed in the trunk. On top of our cargo went things that we had bought on our trip, and clothing we did not wish to carry with us on the plane. The interior of the car was stripped bare and the trunk loaded to the point where we just barely packed our Chilean Christmas tree without ruining it. With the aid of a friend, and his chauffeur, we then toured around Rio seeking interesting places at which to take last-minute pictures. We didn't take many.

But a heartwarming thing happened while I was stopped at a traffic signal as was a truck diagonally across the street. When the signal changed we both inched across the street toward each other. As we passed, the truck driver leaned down, said "Hi Bill' and waved his hand. He obviously had seen our picture in the newspaper that morning and was greeting us in English, knowing full well we would not have understood a word he could have said in Portuguese.

To find the Fink warehouse both the chauffeur and I were using the same instructions: "Look for the church on the hill on the left, and World War II airplane on the right in a children's playground."

The first church I saw was high on a hill to the left, and close to the road, but there wasn't a left turn for a mile and a half further on. Eventually we came to another church that was far-distant on a hill to the left and. On the right, there was an old Douglas torpedo bomber propped on concrete blocks in a playground for children of people working for the Brasilian Navy. Unfortunately, the road in this area was under construction. The next left turn was wrong and was I lost.

Meanwhile Renee, thanks to her chauffeur's skill in navigating Rio's suburban areas, arrived at the warehouse. As she explained it later, inside she found a Senor Daniels and asked him; "Did a car just drive in here? A Mr. Carroll, with a red car?"

Daniels replied, "No, we don't have any shipments for you."

"Oh yes, you do," Renee said. Then she and her chauffeur charged off in hopes of finding then leading me to the proper address.

I arrived a few minutes after Renee left. I too found Senor Daniels and said, "My name is Carroll. I have car here that you want."

"Oh yes," replied Daniels, "your wife was here and asked if we had any papers for you."

"No," I don't need papers. All I have is a car for you."

"What!" replied Daniels, "You have no papers! We don't know anything about your car. What are we supposed to do with it?" All of which initiated a lengthy discussion with Daniels, the only person there who spoke English. He was told we had arranged for shipment of the car with Fink's downtown office that morning and would he please call. His reply was, "Well, we don't know anything about the car, how can we call?" This problem was simply remedied by giving him details of color and serial number; after which he contacted the downtown office to learn that he was really permitted to accept our car for shipment. This much settled we took pictures of the body from all four corners which was our way of proving that the Mercury was delivered in excellent condition. On the Fink Company's part, Daniels gave us a receipt for our vehicle which listed the ship that it was supposed to travel on.

Meanwhile Renee arrived. Now the chauffeur-driven car, loaned to us by the Firestone people, could return us to our hotel. We telephoned our friends a fond adieu and said good-by to business for the rest of our visit to Rio. We decided that because we had a few days left for sight-seeing that we would cash our Travelers Checks for local money, and exchange any excess for U.S. funds the day we would leave. As we were riding down in the elevator, a tall and impressive gentleman wearing dark trousers and a gorgeous white military-type jacket, with gold braid on the sleeves and decorated shoulder-boards, shared the cage with us. He left the elevator at the second floor to enter the hotel dining room.

The moment the elevator door closed I asked if this man was an important officer in the Brazilian Navy. The operator laughed aloud. "No, Senor, he is from the Pan American Airways."

We walked out to find a Cambio. There, as I changed 200 U.S. dollars into local currency, memory bugged me about a regulation that I had heard of. Something about only 30% of Brasilian currency could be converted back to U.S. dollars when a visitor left the country. By now the clerk had counted out a two-inch thick bundle of Brasilian bills. When I asked if the exchange regulation was enforced, she replied, "Yes, it is Sir. You can only exchange back 30% of the money that you are exchanging today." Enough of this I thought and, without further ado, reduced our dollar exchange by half which saved us a great deal of trouble later on.

Somewhere along the line we had collected a list of "in" places in Rio, where one could quietly enjoy dinner and not be bothered by too many tourists or nightclub affairs. One name suggested was El Chalet, at Rua da Matriz 54, in Botafoga. El Chalet, so we were told, was one of the finest small restaurants anywhere. It was owned and operated by a Negro singer, Black Joe, who was the best host the city could boast of. After a nap, Renee and I found a taxi and rode to the Chalet for an evening of sheer and complete pleasure.

On this trip I was reminded that while in Brasil we had to watch commas and decimal points of taxi meters, gas pumps and restaurant bills. The nation's inflated currency had been steadily losing value to the point where a 10,000 Cruzado bank note was worth very little. Eventually, the impact of public and institutional complaints made an impression on government officials and all money was devalued. A 10,000 Cruzado note became worth 10 Cruzados. The resulting headache was that most taxi meters, gasoline pumps and other charge indicating units remained calibrated in the old monetary system. This was brought to light with great force after Renee and I taxied to this restaurant. I could read the meter all right. It was well lit. But for some reason or other my mind bogged down while determining the proper amount of money to give the driver. Inasmuch as we couldn't communicate, there was no use asking him. So I paid what I thought was proper. It turned out that I gave him 15,000 to pay for a 1,500 taxi ride. The driver inspected the bundle of money I handed him but said nothing until after Renee and I left the cab. Then he leaned out the window, said "Good Bye," and drove away as rapidly as his little Volkswagen would go. It was my later opinion that I now owned a tiny portion of one taxi. Or as a Brasilian friend said,, "You are responsible for putting a smile on a happy driver".

El Chalet was a lovely private house in the modest Botafoga commercial district of Rio. There were three tables in the front room, several in the next room, and a few more further back. That, plus a kitchen, was it. Black Joe seated us and presented a lengthy menu printed in Portuguese. We asked if he would do nothing more than provide us with a bottle of Brazilian champagne and a typical dinner. This he agreed to do. The champagne was to celebrate completion of *Aventura Alaska Brasil*: The testing and evaluation of a Ford engine, Simoniz Master Wax, Firestone Tires and STP oil treatment. Plus dictating this book about driving a standard Mercury coupe from one end of the Inter-American Highway to the other, and shipping it home undamaged. The "typical' Brazilian meal request was obvious in that we did not know what was typical and could not read Portuguese to tell what we were ordering anyhow. During our superior meal Black Joe came to our table, with his guitar, and sang soft love songs for Renee's benefit. He later returned with an album of his music which we had the wisdom to buy. When played at home, it proved to be a most unique musical remembrance of a delightful evening, in addition to being excellent music in its own right.

For our last full day in Rio we made up our minds to do nothing but genuine honest-to-goodness touristing. We upped early and took a taxi in the general direction of a cogwheel tram which carried passengers hundreds of feet above Rio to the rock peak bearing Rio's Cristo Redentor, a large statue of Christ overlooking the city. After purchasing tickets, and passing a turnstile, we found a small patio-type postcard shop where Renee proceeded to make her purchase of the day. Not only was she buying postcards for us to mail to mutual friends, but she had a standing order to buy 30 cards in each major city for one of her close friends. Between our purchases, and the 30 cards, the postcard stand did well that day. The cogwheel tram was an interesting contrivance. The first unit was the power car, a small electric donkey engine with a huge cogwheel hanging down between the rails. It engaged the rack and controlled the attached one-unit passenger car with hard wooden bench seats mounted from side to side. The passenger unit had no power and was pushed uphill or held back on down grades by the mule ahead of it. As we clattered up hill the two-piece tram would stop to pick up or let off passengers for small residential settlements along the way. Apparently, said settlements had no other connection with Rio than through the cog-wheel system. At last we arrived at the top, far above the city from where we could look over Rio and its environs. As we exited the car everyone was herded behind a rope barrier. A photographer took our picture and told us all to ask for picture No. 6 while riding back down. On the peak there were tourists everywhere, including a few Americans, wandering around the base of the Cristo. Surrounding it was a small restaurant, numerous souvenir stands and pushcarts selling ice cream and other edibles. Our purchases were two. First, something to eat because we had no breakfast. Second, a necklace of huge horse teeth for our daughter who was intensely interested in things Indian. In our mind horses' teeth were somewhat Indian. Perhaps she could use them. (At least our intentions were good.) And like every other tourist we took a set of pictures in which Renee is standing in front of the Cristo, I am standing in front of the Cristo, Renee is looking over the city and I am looking over the city. The return cogwheel trip included inspecting group pictures that were passed from hand to hand. We asked for No. 6 and bought a copy. The rattling ride down was punctuated by the click of my camera as I tried for scenes depicting this interesting ride. At the bottom station we found a Volkswagen taxi and directed its driver to the base of the funicular which carries cars from downtown Rio to Sugarloaf peak in the harbor.

On arrival we wandered over to the ticket office where, surprisingly enough, there was no line in front of the clerk. I proceeded to attempt to buy tickets. "No," said the ticket man, "you must get in line."

I could see no line so I asked, "But where is the line?"

He pointed with an "Over there." Only then did we understand that a group of about 200 people, sitting on benches rimming the patio, were indeed the line. In the center of the patio a refreshment stand was busy doing a land-office business with waiters serving the waiters. We joined the end of the line and waited. Waited. And waited. Every now and again a group of twenty or thirty people would leave the far end of the line, buy tickets and disappear up narrow stairs toward the loading platform for the passenger cabins.

About halfway around the loop we became involved with a magnificent multi-toned blue Brasilian beetle about the size of my fat thumb. A small boy discovered the beetle wandering across the patio and covered it with leaves to see what would happen. Invariably the beautiful bug struggled from under the leaves and continued its disturbed journey. It wandered in my direction and I moved my foot enough to let it pass. Standing next to me was a young woman teetering back and forth, first on one foot, then the other, as she talked with her mother. The beetle passed my shoe and neared her's. Almost as if on signal, when the beetle touched her shoe the young lady tilted up that side of her foot. The beetle, not knowing what was ahead, went forward while my heart dropped. He was underneath her shoe and had been stopped by the upward slanting sole. The woman at this time didn't have any idea what was happening though about twenty of us were watching the performance and anticipating demise of the beetle. At this moment she shifted her foot again. Instead of setting it down flat, which would have squashed the beetle, she titled backward on her heel which raised the entire shoe. The way was now clear. The beetle proceeded forward to safety as all of us broke up in the nervous laughter of relief. The woman looked to see what was happening and then too moved aside to allow the beautiful bug to continue its journey toward nearby bushes.

Eventually we bought tickets and went upstairs for a short wait before entering the suspension cabin. What a trip it was. We zoomed up, way up over the cable station and in seconds were swinging high above city strects toward the middle way-station at the topof a mid-sized hill. The ride was quick, something like five minutes. Therc we stepped out of the cabin almost a thousand feet above Rio. Recognizing that many people would be waiting here, Renee and I proceeded rapidly to the next station of the line. Here, there were almost a hundred people waiting to ride further up to Sugar Loaf, the terminus. Eventually it was our turn to enter a cabin with another 25 passengers. In moments we were suspended between the two peaks and high above airliners departing from a nearby airport. Eventually we reached Sugar Loaf and left the car to enjoy one of the most beautiful sights of the entire trip.

The view of Rio de Janeiro from 1280 feet in the sky.

From one side to the other of the platform, Renee and I snapped pictures and eagerly pointed to landmarks we recognized. The topmost platform was ostensibly closed to the public but mischievous persons had pushed aside the barrier. We didn't have to dislodge anything to step over a couple of boards to be on the highest viewpoint of the peak from which we could watch the cable cabin swing back and forth on its trips. It was becoming late and, knowing we wanted to go out for dinner that evening, we joined a departing group to enjoy a short ride down to wait again at the midway station before reaching city streets below us. Total time for Sugar Loaf: Five hours, most of which was spent sitting or standing in line. But well worthwhile.

The next morning, our last in Rio, we woke but didn't get out of bed. The windows were open, and we lay quietly listening to sounds of the city, sounds of automobile horns, people laughing as they walked to the beach, muted roar of the ocean and more hum and buzz of humanity enjoying itself in this delightful spot. If there ever before had been such music, it was similar to sounds that we had enjoyed in Berlin and in Rome, and the non-sound of a brilliant sunrise over the Swiss Alps. Shortly after we dressed Renee and I were hanging out of a window enjoying our last look at Copacabana Beach. A brass band was outside. Four musicians had a small boy carrying a placard while they paraded along the beach front in some form of advertising campaign. Their brassy music was a spicy coda to the murmur of pedestrian sounds that mellowed our day.

The telephone rang to announce that transportation had arrived. Downstairs we went for the last pictures. I braced myself against a convenient lamppost while Renee caught me with the Sunday crowd at the beach, plus pictures of the hotel and a record shot of our 20-year-old Chevrolet taxi. Our trip through Rio on Sunday morning was a delight. Traffic was light, there were few people on city streets and beaches were crowded, more crowded and really crowded. For sure, everyone in Rio must have gone to the beach that Sunday. Small waterways, used by launches between lagoons, were clogged with boats. And beach sand was completely covered by sun worshippers, bathers and small children. Eventually we arrived at Rio's tiny airport, a facility so small as to belie it's city's importance. There was little traffic, very few people and inside only two stores were open to sell souvenirs. However, there was something we had never seen before and that was civilians carrying machine guns.

Fortunately, for our piece of mind, they turned out to be actors in a film that depicted the arrival of American gangsters. As best we could figure it out, the scenario included armed guards to protect "the boss". Actors were being directed to hurry through the airport toward a new black Chevrolet sedan which would pull up, collect the boss, and storm away behind a private motorcycle guard. We watched the performance and fun as the film was made. In it, with the actors, were genuine airport patrons wandering back and forth through the action scene as the cameraman seemed to be shooting in all directions at once. Eventually the take was completed, machine guns disappeared into a locking suitcase and Rio's airport relaxed back to being a sleepy little operation totally unlike the jumping town it served. At the Pan American Airways check-in counter departure was simple. Our bags were taken, passports disappeared through a slot in the wall and we were told we would get them back when we passed through the boarding gate.

No fees were involved. This left a bit of local currency so we headed for a souvenir shop to find something that would absorb money. Plastic dolls and ceramic ashtrays were not for us, but high up on a case, dirty and dusty, we found a delightful silver table bell. The handle was carved in the typical Brazilian symbol of good luck, the Figa, in which the thumb is placed between the first and second fingers. By now a small amount of thirst set in so we climbed stairs to the restaurant and ordered sodas. Once downed and paid for, together we had something like 85 Cruzados. At the airport Cambio, which was pleasantly air-conditioned in comparison to the high humidity and heat of outside air, we placed our bundle of local bills on the counter. The clerk looked at them and asked, "Is this all the money you have?"

"Of course. We would like to exchange it for American money."

He ran a total on his magic machinery, to figure out what our hoard was worth, and grinned. "Senor," he said, "this is equal to 20 cents. I am sorry we do not have such small change,"

We stood there laughing at our inability to comprehend the hopelessly inflated money. Into our pockets it went as souvenirs of the trip The clerk wished us a happy journey home. A few minutes later Pan-Am called our flight and we retrieved our passports while passing through the exit gate. Boarding was like anywhere: Up the ramp and find your seat. Soon our jet lumbered along the runway to become airborne with the smooth suddenness that is always such a pleasant shock.

As it clawed for altitude both of us could see warehouses and docks on our right, the city spread beneath us, the Cristo and finally Sugar Loaf, the highest point in the area...just outside the cabin windows.

Suddenly the plane banked left and there was nothing to watch but jungle, a vast wilderness of undeveloped land amid one of the world's largest nations. In seconds my reverie of *Aventura* memories was broken when a stewardess appeared and asked, in good Texas-style English, "Would ya'll like a martini, Sir?"

It was delicious.

Printed in the United Kingdom
by Lightning Source UK Ltd.
99724UKS00001B/216

9 780910 390101